MINISTRY WITH PERSONS
WITH MENTAL ILLNESS AND THEIR FAMILIES

MINISTRY WITH PERSONS WITH
MENTAL ILLNESS AND THEIR FAMILIES

Robert H. Albers, William H. Meller,
Steven D. Thurber, Editors

Fortress Press
Minneapolis

MINISTRY WITH PERSONS WITH MENTAL ILLNESS AND THEIR
FAMILIES

Unless otherwise noted, scripture quotations are the author's own translation or from
the New Revised Standard Version Bible, copyright © 1989 by the Division of Christian Education of the National Council of Churches of Christ in the USA, and are
used with permission.

Cover image: Van Gogh Museum, Amsterdam, Netherlands/SuperStock
Cover design: Laurie Ingram
Book design: PerfecType, Nashville, TN

Library of Congress Cataloging-in-Publication Data
Ministry with persons with mental illness and their families / Robert H. Albers,
William H. Meller, Steven D. Thurber, editors.
    p. cm.
  Includes bibliographical references and index.
  ISBN 978-0-8006-9874-4 (alk. paper)
    1. Church work with the mentally ill. 2. Mentally ill—Pastoral counseling of.
3. Pastoral psychology. I. Albers, Robert H. II. Meller, William. III. Thurber, Steven D.
  BV4461.M56 2012
  259'.42—dc23

                                                                          2011042713

The paper used in this publication meets the minimum requirements of American
National Standard for Information Sciences—Permanence of Paper for Printed
Library Materials, ANSI Z329.48-1984.

Manufactured in the U.S.A.
16 15 14 13 12   2 3 4 5 6 7 8 9 10

CONTENTS

1740

126787

EDITORS AND CONTRIBUTORS

Editors

Robert H. Albers received his MDiv from Wartburg Theological Seminary and PhD from the Southern California School of Theology in Claremont. The initial part of his career was as a parish pastor, and for the past three decades he has taught pastoral theology. His current position is as Distinguished Visiting Professor of Pastoral Theology at United Theological Seminary of the Twin Cities. He has published numerous books and articles; his book *Shame: A Faith Perspective* (1995) received an award from the Academy of Pastoral Clergy as one of the top ten books for pastors published that year. He was also editor of *The Journal of Ministry in Addiction and Recovery* from 1993 to 2000.

William H. Meller, MD, is an associate professor of psychiatry at the University of Minnesota and has served as co–course director of Ministry to the Mentally Ill at Luther Seminary. He has published extensively in the areas of affective disorder and consultation psychiatry. He is president of the Itasca Psychosomatic Research Society. His daughter, *Sarah J. Meller*, who assisted in writing the afterword on psychopharmacology, does neuroscience research at Rockefeller University and has served as a Howard Hughes Medical Institute scholar at Stony Brook University.

Steven D. Thurber received his PhD from the University of Texas at Austin with additional postdoctoral training in child development and early interventions from the University of Minnesota. He graduated from the postdoctoral training program in pediatric psychology from the University of Oklahoma College of Medicine. He has been an academician (Boise State University and University of California, San Francisco), clinical director of two psychiatric hospitals, and is currently child psychologist in a youth partial hospitalization program at Woodland Centers in Willmar, Minnesota. His published research has been in the areas of autism, developmental psychopathology, and measurement. He is associate editor of *Archives of Assessment Psychology*.

Contributors

Donald W. Black is professor of psychiatry at the University of Iowa. He is a board-certified psychiatrist and is listed in *Best Doctors in America*. He has authored more than three hundred publications, including, *Bad Boys, Bad Men—Confronting Antisocial Personality Disorder* (1999).

Hollie Holt-Woehl is an ordained minister in the Evangelical Lutheran Church in America (ELCA), specializing in ministry to people with mental illnesses and developmental disabilities. She is an "intentional interim pastor" in the Minneapolis Area Synod of the ELCA and an adjunct professor at Luther Seminary, St. Paul.

Elayne Lipp is a retired pastor of the Evangelical Lutheran Church of America (ELCA). She served an inner-city parish in Minneapolis for seventeen years. She has both professional and personal experience with Alzheimer's disease. She is a guest lecturer at Luther Seminary, St. Paul, in pastoral care.

Thomas Mackenzie, MD, is currently the Distinguished Teaching Professor of Psychiatry at the University of Minnesota. He is also the vice chair for education and the program director of psychiatry residency and a professor of psychiatry at the University of Minnesota Medical School.

Joretta L. Marshall is an ordained United Methodist clergywoman from the Rocky Mountain Conference. She teaches at Brite Divinity School in Fort Worth, Texas, where she shares a home with her family. She is author of *Counseling Lesbian Partners* and *How Can I Forgive?* as well as of numerous other articles and publications.

Sarah J. Meller graduated magna cum laude from Carleton College and has several awards for academic excellence. She is currently a research assistant in the Molecular and Cellular Neuroscience Laboratory at Rockefeller University, directed by Nobel laureate Paul Greengard.

Christie Cozad Neuger has served as professor of pastoral care at Princeton Theological Seminary, United Theological Seminary of the Twin Cities, and Brite Divinity School. She is currently a senior scholar and founding director of the Institute for the Support of Pastoral Ministries at United Theological Seminary. Besides numerous articles and chapters, she has published four books.

Stephen Olson, MD, is associate professor of psychiatry at the University of Minnesota, where he is director of the Schizophrenia Specialty Clinic, specializing in schizophrenia and related disorders, including psychopharmacology, phenomenology, treatment-resistant psychosis, and mood disorders. He received his MD from the University of Minnesota and did his residency in psychiatry at the University of Iowa.

Lawrence M. Pray is the senior pastoral scholar at Methodist Healthcare, in Memphis, Tennessee. He is coauthor of *Leading Causes of Life* (2004) and author of *Journey of a Diabetic* (1982). His writing addresses the issues of healing and living with chronic disease. He is ordained in the United Church of Christ and lives in Minneapolis.

Janet Ramsey is professor emeritus of congregational care and ministry at Luther Seminary in St. Paul. A pastor in the Evangelical Lutheran Church in America (ELCA), a licensed marriage and family therapist, and a diplomat in the American Association of Pastoral Counselors, her most recent book, *Spiritual Resiliency and Aging: Hope, Relationality, and the Creative Self*, was published in 2011.

William Sheehan, MD, is a psychiatrist currently leading a neurodevelopmental disorders program in Willmar, Minnesota. His special interests are evolutionary psychiatry, neurodevelopment (especially autism), applied neuroscience, nutritional and metabolic disorders in mental illnesses, traumatic brain injury, and functional neuroimaging.

Sheila Specker, MD, is an addiction psychiatrist and associate professor of psychiatry in the department of psychiatry at the University of Minnesota, where she also serves as the medical director of the combined mental illness/substance abuse treatment program. She has authored more than thirty publications in her area of expertise.

Diana Thierry is the married mother of three college-aged children. She is in recovery from an eating disorder from her time as a teen ballet dancer. She studied at both Harvard and Yale School of Divinity and was a chaplain at the New York Foundling Hospital for abused and neglected children. She has also served as a local director of religious education.

Ruth Marie Thomson is a senior neurology resident at the University of Minnesota. She plans to complete a vascular neurology fellowship and will practice in northern Minnesota once she finishes her training. Ruth has two children and loves to spend time with them and her extended family.

William Yates is a psychiatrist as well as a professor of research at the University of Oklahoma College of Medicine in Tulsa. He has conducted research related to eating disorders for more than twenty-five years. He authors a blog providing analysis and commentary on clinical neuroscience research at http://brainposts.blogspot.com.

INTRODUCTION

Robert H. Albers

On a dark and dreary night, there was a knock at the door of the pastor's study from a thinly clad man seeking refuge from the bitter cold. He was hungry and weary with exhaustion. Before the pastor could call the local homeless shelter to secure food, clothing, and lodging, the man launched into a bizarre story of having heard the voice of God speaking to him through the small transistor radio that he had managed to protect from others on the street.

The man related in graphic detail how the voice of God had convicted him of his sin and that his eternal fate was sealed in everlasting damnation. He was overwhelmed by the immensity of God's indictment, and at times the auditory messages were accompanied by frightening visions of torment in the pit of hell. The intensity of his voice rose in a crescendo of laments as he poured out his abject fear of God and of "other people" who he was convinced were intent on harming him.

The pastor was both frightened and flabbergasted by the experience and attempted to calm the man down and assure him that his fears were unfounded. But the man became more agitated as he sensed the pastor did not believe his story. After some time had passed, the man nearly collapsed because of hunger and exhaustion and was persuaded to accompany the pastor to the homeless shelter where he would receive food, clothing, and a place to sleep for the night.

⚭ The homeless man in the above vignette undoubtedly was suffering from a mental illness that resulted in his being homeless, pushed to the margins of society, having no advocate for his well-being, and no treatment available for his malady. Irrespective of the ultimate diagnosis, there are literally millions of people on the streets, but also in our synagogues, churches, and mosques, who are suffering from a variety of mental illnesses, as well as family members and significant others who are often clueless as to what is happening to their loved ones. Knowledge about available treatment in terms of assistance remains for many a mystery.

The phenomenon of mental illness with its various manifestations is chronicled far back into antiquity. Papyri from ancient Egypt have described in rather graphic detail the symptoms of mental illness and the varying attempts that were made to deal with it. Those who are mentally ill might be considered as the "modern-day lepers" who suffer from a socially "unsanctioned illness" and who continue to be misunderstood and mistreated by society and religion alike as a consequence. I have used the designation "unsanctioned illness" to name those illnesses in society that bear the stigma of social discrimination. The consequence of stigma is experiencing a sense of "disgrace shame" that results in both denial and a conspiracy of silence, which precludes such illnesses from being treated and openly embraced, discussed, and treated.

Utilizing "leprosy" is an apt metaphor for mental illness, as the parallels between the two can be traced in the long history of discrimination endemic to both illnesses. The biblical tradition captures in varying narratives the stories of those afflicted with and affected by the dreaded disease of leprosy. Individuals who contracted this contagious disease were confined to colonies on the geographical fringe of society. Similarly, people suffering from mental illness were also for centuries sequestered away in private homes (if a family was able to afford such) or they were remanded to institutions providing custodial care that prohibited them from interacting with the mainstream of society. The debilitating effects of isolation are paramount with both diseases. Ignorance concerning mental illness has historically often resulted in brutal treatment of suffering persons, of their being fettered both literally and figuratively by the chains of helplessness and hopelessness.

Should lepers wander away from their appointed colonies, they were to announce to all who came near that they were "unclean," the stigmatization of society and the judgment of religious protocol relegating them to a less-than-human status. The biblical Holiness Code provided specific rubrics with respect to how lepers were to be dealt with in society (Leviticus 13, 14; 2 Kgs. 5:1-27). The desire to be free of this curse that plagued so many in the ancient world gives rise to the stories of Jesus healing them written in all three Synoptic Gospels. Restoration back into the community was as notable as the healing itself (see Matt. 8:3; Mark 1:42; Luke 5:12-13). People with mental illnesses have suffered parallel experiences in their lives.

People who are mentally ill often have the feeling that they are "unclean" and therefore "set apart." They frequently are pejoratively labeled with inhuman epithets, thus spawning inhumane treatment. Even though their malady is neither infectious nor contagious, they are often treated as though coming into even remote contact with them will somehow contaminate or sully the character of other people.

The stigmatization associated with both leprosy and mental illness elicits feelings of "disgrace shame" (Albers 1995) within the afflicted as well as the affected persons. These dynamics have a profound effect upon the sufferer and her or his family that prompts a devaluation of the whole family system's sense of worth and value. The net result is a progression of evaluative judgments by others, resulting in depersonalization, dehumanization, and finally "demonization" of the one afflicted. Such attitudes detract from the integrity and respect that deserves to be accorded to all people, irrespective of their diagnoses. It stands to reason that the conspiracy of silence surrounding mental illness is alive and well because the humiliation experienced in such a diagnosis exacerbates the phenomenon of denial, which in turn precludes possible treatment and care.

With these illnesses, the social reaction of "fear" is pronounced. As philosopher and theologian Martin Buber would characterize the situation, the person suffering from these illnesses is treated as an "it" rather than a "thou" (Buber 1958). Maintaining physical, emotional, and spiritual distance becomes the *modus operandi* that exacerbates the plight of the sufferers and their families. While most major religious traditions would affirm the inestimable value of human beings, both leprosy and mental illness detract from that precept, resulting in further marginalization and alienation of the sufferer.

More specifically, religious traditions have not been helpful in creating a compassionate disposition toward those with mental illness, as various sacred texts, such as the Bible, would evidence. Seeking to explain the sometimes bizarre behavior of those who were mentally ill, the origin of the phenomenon was ascribed to "demon possession." Demon possession basically meant that there were external malevolent powers loose in the world that were working in opposition to the benevolent powers of God. The fate of those so "possessed" has had a long, brutal, and bloody history perpetrated by society and religion. The marginalization of such people can be seen in the biblical narrative written in Mark 5:1-20. While the layers of that narrative are likely too thick to make a medical diagnosis, the evidence extant in the story might suggest that this man suffered from a mental illness that featured psychotic episodes, all attributed to being possessed by demonic powers. Exorcism was the singular "treatment of choice," simply because knowledge of mental illnesses as we know them today had not yet been discovered. Consequently, varying resources of current therapeutic intervention likewise were not at the disposal of human beings in ages past.

It was not until the early twentieth century that significant research was devoted to studying the etiology, symptoms, and treatment of mental illnesses. Significant progress has been made in the medical area of psychiatry, which treats these illnesses as biological phenomena, often exacerbated by environmental conditions. As with other unsanctioned illnesses such as HIV-AIDS, addiction, and dementia, it is imperative that the shroud of secrecy, shame, and silence be shattered so that the millions of people adversely afflicted with and affected by these illnesses may find a source of hope, acceptance, and new life within varying communities of society. This includes religious communities since, if someone claims a religious community, this is where they often turn for help in a time of crisis. Such was the case of the man described in the opening vignette.

The focus of this particular book is to provide a "wholistic" approach to dealing with mental illnesses. (The *w* has been added to the word *holistic* to denote that it is inclusive of the person's spirituality.) The basic assumption is that human beings are complex creatures, as exhibited in the interrelated functions of the body, mind, and spirit. In past literature, the angle of vision on mental illness reflected the specialized discipline of those who were attempting to assist those afflicted as well as those affected. Many volumes have been written with regard to the medical aspects of mental illness, but fewer books have been written relative to the social, economic, and political implications of these varying illnesses. There is an even greater paucity of literature regarding the spiritual and/ or religious aspects of mental illness.

The purpose of this book is to develop an integrated and interrelated approach that honors the work of the specialists in psychiatry, psychology, and theology. It presents this approach as a dialogue between the disciplines so that each in her or his own specialty might work in partnership and not at cross-purposes, as often has been the case in dealing with mentally ill people. The participants see each other as colleagues working in a wholistic fashion to bring to light the most relevant and helpful material for readers. The fact that representatives of both medical and religious disciplines are willing to engage in a mutual endeavor such as this is a blessing for all who are involved as we seek to articulate in clear fashion the realities that people face when dealing with mental illnesses.

The methodology for accomplishing this task was to seek out highly competent psychiatrists who have done in-depth study of the more common and most challenging mental illnesses that afflict people. Knowledge is power, and knowledge likewise is able to burst the bonds of fear that many people experience when the phrase "mental illness" is uttered. People who provide care within the context of a religious community often have little basic information regarding mental illnesses. The principal modus operandi, then, is to say, if one suspects that mental illness may be an issue, "This is beyond me, I can't do anything, I can only refer these people to others." If one is to be "wholistic" in one's approach to these illnesses, then it is imperative that referrals and conversation flow both ways between medical and religious caregivers, so as to provide the best possible opportunity for all those who provide care to do so in an effective and efficient manner. This book seeks to capture those conversations in a helpful way that can be shared with others.

The structure of each chapter is uniform, as the psychiatrist writes first about the medical aspects of the disease so as to provide accurate information about each diagnosis. As caregivers become more acquainted with the symptoms and dynamics of the illness, the caregiver is in a better position to respond appropriately to those afflicted with and affected by the illness. The logic is that one needs to know something about what is transpiring before being able to respond in an effective way.

Pastoral theologians here utilize the resources of their respective faith traditions in dialoguing with mental health providers and bringing to the table the realities of spirituality as people within faith communities experience it. For the people who claim a particular faith tradition, there are rites, rituals, traditions, and insights that are germane to assist in their healing. Their spiritual life is an integral part of who they are, and they look to their tradition for support, guidance, and care. But there are also people within faith communities who are critical of psychiatry and dismiss the important material that can be learned from psychiatric research. The hope is that with both disciplines as dialogical partners, this historical suspicion that has resulted in the internecine warfare between science and religion might be bridged in a meaningful and helpful way. In a postmodern society, human beings oppose being thought of only as biological entities or only as spiritual entities; rather, there is a hue and cry for meaningful and effective dialogue to occur so that there is mutual benefit for healing and health.

In addition to presenting a wholistic approach to the topic, it is also the intent of this volume to encourage "open dialogue" among people in varying faith communities as they seek to address effectively the agony and anguish that is often experienced when a person in the family or in the wider community is diagnosed with a mental illness. The "conspiracy of silence" is a phenomenon that is still very much with us in our society despite the fact that significant steps and progress have been made in this area of human concern. As already noted, that conspiracy of silence may be due in large part to the fact that mental illnesses are unsanctioned illnesses in many cultures. Perhaps this is true because historically there was an assumption that while other organs of the body might malfunction, it was unthinkable that the brain should ever malfunction. One of the gifts of psychiatric research is to demonstrate conclusively that in the case of mental illness, it is a result of what Nancy Andreasen names in the title of one of her books, *The Broken Brain* (1981). That title captures an important reality that helps to shape the attitude that people might have concerning mental illness. Mental illness is not a result of purely psychological or spiritual problems; it also involves the reality of a "broken brain" that can be visually demonstrated by various brain-imaging techniques.

The collective knowledge and the wisdom that this approach spawns is essential for anyone providing care to realize and understand. Mental illness is *not* about blaming the one afflicted, nor indicting those who are affected, nor attributing causation to malevolent powers; rather, it is the experience of the "total person"—body, mind, and spirit, if one chooses to use those traditional categories. Given that reality, it is judicious that the dialogue not only be initiated, but also perpetuated and expanded upon with the passing of time. Overcoming prejudices that are deeply ingrained in society, religious communities, and within each of us as individuals is no small task! There are many things that need to be "unlearned" as a result of the mythology that has taken root in the minds and hearts of people when it comes to mental illness. This can only take place through intentional educational endeavors and constant and continual dialogue between all parties involved, irrespective of the discipline. It is a dialogue that needs to take seriously the important role that all people play who with their arts, skills, convictions, and knowledge can articulate in a clear and integrative fashion what it means to be whole and what it means to be fully human.

One needs to concede that the diagnostic process is in and of itself a precarious undertaking. The *Diagnostic and Statistical Manual of Mental Disorders, Fourth Edition* (DSM-IV) (1994), in providing criteria for diagnostic purposes, makes it amply clear that acceptable behavior is predicated on what is considered as appropriate given the cultural context in which the person lives. What may be construed as bizarre behavior in one cultural setting can be assessed differently in another culture. It is impossible to be fully conversant with the idiosyncratic cultural norms in one's own context, much less those present in other parts of the globe. It is prudent for psychiatrists to exercise caution in the diagnostic endeavor, and it is incumbent upon caregivers likewise to familiarize themselves with cultures other than their own, The DSM-IV is clear in its diagnostic analysis that cultural norms are to be taken into consideration, since the manual itself is basically a product of Western society. Ministry often presents a plurality of cultures in a given community, and sensitivity to those cultural realities will hopefully preclude arrogant attitudes and alarmist actions.

Finally, the decision regarding which of the manifold illnesses should be treated in this volume was no small task. The DSM-IV presents five diagnostic categories, or "multiaxial assessments." These categories are broken down into constituent parts, and each part has varying permutations of the general diagnosis as it relates to the specificity of that illness in its varying expressions. The point is that this results in hundreds of possible diagnoses being presented, each with its particular criteria and symptoms. There are more than seven hundred pages of such material, covering scores of varying diagnoses, so it is impossible to address all of them.

A case certainly could be made for these diagnoses all meriting consideration, but since that is impossible, this book's contributors deemed it most workable to focus on nine of these diagnoses that are either most common in this society or are most challenging. For example, depression has often been called "the common cold of mental illnesses" and so will likely be the mental illness most frequently encountered in caregiving. Addiction is perhaps the next most commonly confronted illness. While there has been more written on these two subjects, we deemed it important to include them, as soft research has indicated that despite the prevalence of literature, many who provide care are not familiar enough with these diagnoses even though ample literature is available. Similarly, schizophrenia and borderline personality disorder may be two of the most challenging when it comes to mental illnesses. Thus this volume hopes to address both the most common and the most challenging so that readers have some sense of these experiences in their lives and the lives of others.

It is important to be aware that there are many people who experience "co-occurring" diagnoses; that is to say, they may be suffering from three, four, or more illnesses at the same time. For example, it is *not* unusual to see someone who is addicted to alcohol also experiencing depression and in some cases also post-traumatic stress disorder. This is where the dialogue between medicine and spirituality is so crucial so that the care of the whole person and her or his family can occur. It is possible to have enough knowledge and insight so as to do no harm, but a caregiver can also be of significant help. It is incumbent upon us all to be as prepared as we possibly can be for those occasions, because it is not a matter of *if* those opportunities will come, but *when* they will occur, for lay and clergy leaders alike.

The knock on the door can come in the dead of the night, or any time during the day. The reasons occasioning that knock, or prompting an extemporaneous conversation, or occasioning a crisis in an individual or her or his family in the vast majority of instances will be attributable to one or more of the illnesses treated in this volume. It is our hope that this volume will serve you in a meaningful and helpful way to respond in the most appropriate fashion to these inevitable encounters.

Bibliography

Albers, Robert H. 1995. *Shame: A Faith Perspective.* Binghamton, N.Y.: Haworth.

American Psychiatric Association. 1994. *Diagnostic and Statistical Manual of Mental Disorders,* 4th ed. (DSM-IV). Washington, D.C.: American Psychiatric Publishing.

Andreasen, Nancy. 1984. *The Broken Brain: The Biological Revolution in Psychiatry.* New York: Harper & Row.

Buber, Martin. 1958. *I and Thou.* New York: Charles Scribner's Sons.

Depression

William H. Meller / Robert H. Albers

1

*A distraught woman approaches her pastor after church one day.
"I don't know what to do; my husband just lies around all day. He
has quit going to work and is up watching TV most of the night.
He rarely eats. Lately he has been so morose, claiming that he is not
good for anything and life is not worth living. He won't go to church
and claims to have lost his faith. Will you go talk to him?"*

Understanding Depression

It is essential for caregivers to understand depression, not only because
it is so common and potentially serious, but also because clergy and
lay caregivers are likely to be the first people sought out by depressed
parishioners or their families. Multiple studies have shown that even
with serious mental disorders, Americans are far more likely to approach
clergy than psychiatrists or psychologists (Milstein 2003; Weaver et al.
1996). Furthermore, since depression is the most common cause of suicide, it is only a matter of time before caregivers will be confronted by a
suicidal person. We hope this chapter will help decrease the stress associated with such encounters.

Many may be shocked to learn that the World Health Organization (WHO) now reports depression is the leading cause of "burden

of disease" in the developed world and the third leading cause world-wide. "Burden of disease" is defined as "the loss of the equivalent of one year of full health" (WHO 2004). For an illness to produce such a high burden, it must be both very serious and very common. Indeed, major depression is associated with very high levels of mortality and extremely high morbidity, leading the WHO to refer to it as a silent epidemic.[1] It is the most common psychiatric condition that leads suffering individuals to seek help. Despite this reality, only 19 percent of those with depression seek treatment (Callahan and Barrios 2005).

One way to think of "health burden" is to consider how common an illness is. Put in mathematical terms, multiply the prevalence of an illness by its seriousness. Thus, "morbidity plus mortality" equals "health burden."

Morbidity, Mortality, and Prevalence

Although doing so seems coldhearted, morbidity is often measured in dollars. Very little cost has to do with treatment; by far the largest cost is caused by loss of productivity (Greenberg et al. 2003). The cost of depression in the United States in 2000 was estimated to be $52.9 billion (ibid.), second only to vascular diseases such as heart attacks and stroke. The true cost of human misery is immeasurable, and depression is one the most destructive disorders when role functioning such as parenting or effectiveness at work is considered.

The true mortality rate of depression is not known. Coroners' reports can be inconclusive or wrong. The true cause of a fatal one-car accident or death that is secondary to poorly controlled diabetes may never be known. We do know that depression is the most common cause of suicide. The most widely quoted percentage is that 15 percent of those suffering depression complete suicide (Dunner 2008). If one considers the total body count, suicide overshadows homicide, a fact seldom discussed in the current gun-control debate. Although the rate of suicide is highest among older white males, the absolute number of suicides is higher among younger people. The Centers for Disease Control (CDC) report that suicide is the second leading cause of death among twenty-five to thirty-four year olds and third among fifteen to twenty-four year olds.[2]

The devastation caused by suicide cannot be overstated: parents divorce, families are destroyed, and emotional scars are never completely healed. Suicide, however, is far from the only cause of depression-related mortality. Individuals with depression are also more likely to have heart attacks, and depressed individuals with heart attacks are more likely to die. Similarly, depression can have lethal effects on patients with diabetes, and on transplant recipients, and it can exacerbate many other illnesses (DSM-IV). Because depression is associated with poor concentration and impaired judgment, individuals with depression are at high risk for accidents. Therefore, the Department of Transportation and the Federal Aviation Administration have regulations regarding individuals diagnosed with depression driving semis or flying airplanes.

Major depression occurs in at least 10 to 25 percent of women and 5 to 12 percent of men. Although major depressive episodes are twice as common among women, depression associated with physical illness, bipolar depression, substance-induced depression, and prepubertal depression is closer to having equal prevalence among males and females.

History

Unlike other disorders that have definitions that change over time, depression has been a constant, at least since the advent of written language. Depression was described in the oldest-known medical writing, the Ebers papyrus (Andreasen and Black 1995), an ancient Egyptian document written in about 1550 BCE (however, this material was gleaned from texts that are far older) (Lyons and Petrocelli 1978). Depression was well known to the ancient Greeks and appears in fourth-century writings by Hippocrates. The Bible has numerous references to depression, particularly the psalms of lament. King Saul, in 1 Samuel 18:10ff., appears to be one of the first well-described individuals with manic-depressive disease (bipolar disorder), making David one of our first music therapists. Unfortunately, Saul, who died by suicide, reminds us of the lethality of these disorders.

In modern times, symptoms that distinguished patients with depression from normal individuals were described in a classic 1957 work by W. L. Cassidy and his colleagues (Cassidy et al. 1957). These symptoms were used to create a criterion-based diagnostic system by J. P. Feighner and others (Feighner et al. 1972; Dunner 2008), and eventually formed the basis of our current diagnostic system, the DSM-IV (see the introduction, above).

Symptomotology

According to DSM-IV, a depressive episode exists if a person experiences five of nine criterion symptoms over at least a two-week period. These symptoms must include depressed mood or loss of interest or pleasure in almost all things (anhedonia). The other symptoms include, in an abbreviated form, change in appetite or weight, change in sleep, change in psychomotor behavior (agitation or retardation), fatigue or loss of energy, feelings of worthlessness or guilt, diminished ability to think or concentrate, and recurrent thoughts of death or suicide. Many pastoral counselors keep a copy of this list in their desk, a practice that is strongly encouraged, not for diagnostic purposes, but to remind the caregiver of the stated criteria. It is clear that depression makes people miserable; saps them of energy; and ruins sleep, appetite, and even the ability to think clearly. It is an illness of intense misery.

Major depression is the most common subtype of mood or affective disorders. The depressive forms of these disorders include major depression, as described above; dysthymia, a chronic but less pervasive depressive syndrome; and a variety of mood disorders caused by medical conditions and substances. Most are beyond the scope of this chapter but can be easily researched in a DSM-IV manual.

Before focusing on manic or "bipolar" syndrome, it is important to discuss a very severe form of depression in which individuals truly lose touch with reality and become psychotic. These individuals may develop delusions of guilt, such as causing a war or perhaps somatic delusions that their "guts are rotting out." Furthermore, they may hear voices, possibly commanding them to kill themselves or telling them they are worthless. Occasionally, visual hallucinations may develop. Often these individuals may develop psychoses with religious content, thinking they are possessed by demons or controlled by the devil. All such patients should be hospitalized for safety; happily, with treatment the psychotic symptoms generally resolve.

During a Bible study in the church basement, a parishioner jumps up and begins preaching in a loud voice. He reports that he alone has been given the power to understand the true meaning of Scripture. His speech is rapid and switches from topic to topic. No one is able to get a word in. He reports that since receiving his special gift he has felt elated, and he invites everyone to join him in his "special under-standing," yet he is unable to articulate what that understanding is. His wife appears mortified and with the help of friends escorts him out of the church. Later she comes to you for help.

Mania

Mania represents a mood disorder that is nearly the mirror opposite of depression. It is less common than depression and is found in individuals who have had, or unfortunately likely will have, a depressive episode. Therefore, individuals with this disorder are referred to as bipolar, living with both "poles" of the mood-disorder spectrum. People with mania often feel "great" or "on top of the world," and are therefore unlikely to seek treatment.

Mania is defined in the DSM-IV as a "distinct period of abnormally and persistently elevated, expansive, or irritable mood lasting at least one week." Manic episodes must contain three of the following criterion symptoms, again abbreviated: inflated self-esteem or grandiosity; decreased need for sleep; rapid, pressured speech; flight of ideas or racing thoughts; distractibility; an increase in goal-directed activities; and excessive involvement in pleasurable activities that have a high potential for painful consequences. Mania may also be associated with hallucinations or delusions. Often these delusions are grandiose, for example, with patients believing they are incredibly wealthy or presidents of companies. Hallucinations may be perceived as coming from a divine source. Religiosity is a frequent symptom of mania, as in the above vignette, and can be a particular challenge to caregivers. Both depression and mania can be associated with mood-incongruent or paranoid psychotic features. These symptoms may be more difficult to treat but are less frequent.

People with mania can be extremely disruptive and a special challenge for families and coworkers. Frequently, they do not perceive that they have a problem. Prior to successful treatment modalities, mania was associated with death from exhaustion, and unfortunately continues to cause injury from accidents, excessive drinking, and other poorly considered behaviors. Mania usually responds well to treatment, typically with complete recovery. Unfortunately, it will usually recur, either as depression, mania, or both, that is, as bipolar disorder.

There are a variety of bipolar disorders, including bipolar I as described above; bipolar II, a "rapid cycling" bipolar disorder; and cyclothymia. *Cyclothymia* is an unusual form of affective disorder that is less pervasive, with lower amplitude in mood swings. Rapid cycling can occur at any time and may be exacerbated by certain psychiatric medications or physical illness. Bipolar II disorder can present in a variety of ways but often is a syndrome that includes "hypomanic episodes" or manic episodes that cause little impairment. People with this disorder are often friendly, confident, gregarious, and quick-witted. They may need little sleep and are able to pursue their ideas far into the night. These attributes can lead to tremendous creativity and accomplishment. Many of our greatest artists, writers, and composers benefited from this creativity and benefited the rest of us as well. Unfortunately, individuals with bipolar II disorder must inevitably pay with major depressive episodes.

We all should question the false myth that individuals with mental illness have little to contribute. Consider Martin Luther, who placed ninety-five theses on the Wittenberg church door—not three but ninety-five! He was able to translate the entire Bible in less than two years. Modern scholars think he did a good job in a task that would typically take a lifetime. His biographers have documented periods of extremely high energy. Luther described in his writings very deep depressive episodes, yet his creativity in both phases of the illness has led to enduring insights. There are many other truly outstanding people who have suffered from mood disorders, often creating works in times of great elation, such as Wolfgang Amadeus Mozart, Ernest Hemingway, and Vincent van Gogh. Still others, like Abraham Lincoln, developed great empathy and generativity in times of depression.

There is one other mood disorder that deserves special attention: seasonal affective disorder (SAD). Seasonal effects can be seen in both bipolar and unipolar depression. Individuals with SAD seemingly act like bears getting ready to hibernate for the winter. As the hours of sun decrease, they develop depression often associated with hypersomnia, carbohydrate craving, and weight gain, along with other criterion symptoms. SAD is more common in higher latitudes and can occasionally be treated with high-intensity full-spectrum lights (10,000 lux). Fortunately, people also can be treated with a prolonged vacation to a sunny destination (preferably with palm trees and sand beaches). SAD was once thought to be mythical but now has been well described and researched by the National Institutes of Health (Rosenthal and Blehar 1989).

Etiology and Pathophysiology

No one knows what causes depression. We do know that it runs in families and has a strong genetic component, yet we also know it can be associated with external stress, such as bereavement, or as a result of internal stress related to a stroke or heart attack. Therefore, there is a strong interaction between genetics and the environment. We also understand that affective disorders are disorders of the brain, with recent imaging studies defining abnormalities in brain areas associated with emotion, memory, and reward. Exactly why brain areas develop abnormalities and exactly how these abnormalities interact remain a mystery, but researchers continue to progress in understanding brain function. Although depression is, at its core, a brain disease, its effects in the body are far-reaching.

Our brains communicate with the rest of the body through direct nerve connections and through endocrine or hormonal communications. Both types of communication are likely disturbed in depression. For instance, the vagus nerve is a major line of communication between the brain and gut. It innervates our digestive tract, heart, and lungs. It is no wonder that patients with coronary bypass surgery, ulcerative colitis, and a variety of other gastrointestinal illnesses are likely to get depression.

More is known about hormonal abnormalities associated with depression. These can affect sexual and reproductive function, as well as the ability to metabolize glucose or respond to stress. The most well-studied abnormality involves disturbed cortisol response, a stress hormone involved in a variety of functions, including the regulation of insulin and glucose. Individuals with diabetes may need to increase insulin during depressive episodes as a result of abnormal cortisol regulation. There are many other hormonal abnormalities that can interfere with multiple body functions including thyroid issues, immune response, pain perception, and others. Therefore, people with depression often feel sick as well as depressed. To make matters worse, lack of interest can mean lack of interest in faith, making depression a true mind, body, and spirit disorder.

Treatment

There are a variety of treatment modalities available for individuals with mood disorders, and the vast majority of these individuals do very well. Treatment starts with empathetic listening, taking people seriously, and not denying or minimizing symptoms. If people say they are suicidal, they generally are. Take them seriously. It is not helpful to attempt to argue people out of their symptoms and it is far from helpful to tell them that if they just had more faith they would not feel this way. Many, many "faithful" parishioners will suffer from mood disorders, just like many will suffer broken legs or tonsillitis. It is well documented that patients derive tremendous benefit from their religion, clergy, and faith communities. Compassion rather than blaming is the preferred dynamic of caregiving.

In this chapter's opening vignette, a person with major depression has become suicidal and is terrifying his wife. If there are guns in the house the concern becomes much greater. Obviously, the man needs help, and, if acutely suicidal, needs emergency help. In such situations the police need to be called and involved.

Once a patient is protected from harm, there are three general types of treatment: psychotherapy, medication, and, in life-threatening conditions, electro-convulsive therapy (ECT), often referred to as "shock therapy." There are also experimental modalities such as transcranial magnetic stimulation, vagal nerve stimulation, or deep brain stimulation.

Psychotherapeutic techniques proven to be particularly helpful include cognitive-behavioral therapy and interpersonal therapy. Although beyond the scope of this text, there is no reason why informed clergy and lay caregivers could not become familiar with cognitive behavioral techniques that could prove very helpful in alleviating the depression. Medications will be discussed in the concluding chapter on psychopharmacology.

ECT is the most effective therapy currently available for severe, life-threatening depression. It is generally misunderstood and maligned in movies such as *One Flew over the Cuckoo's Nest*. Like so many other therapies, no one knows exactly why ECT works, but it usually works well. Prior to ECT, and currently in third world countries, people die from depression. As Lucy and William Hulme describe in their book *Wrestling with Depression*, in the severest cases, people simply lie down in a fetal position, don't eat, drink, or sleep, and just wait to die (Hulme and Hulme 1995). Obviously, these people require immediate help, as do people who attempt suicide. ECT is recommended in such cases. Other patients simply get tired of medications and request ECT, as it tends to work faster. Although we seldom think about it, nearly every major hospital in the developed world has patients who are currently receiving ECT. Many have had good success and request it during recurrence. Even before the use of anesthesia, when ECT was much more unpleasant, patients still requested ECT, as its side effects were felt to be more tolerable than depression.

Happily, with modern techniques, side effects have decreased significantly. Experimental treatments that have few side effects may someday make ECT obsolete, but for now it remains the safest and most effective treatment for people with the severest forms of depression.

Newer forms of therapy, such as transcranial magnetic stimulation, are becoming available and show great promise. New medicines are being discovered. Psychotherapies are improving. Even without any treatment, most depressions will eventually resolve on their own. Therefore, given the natural history of the disorder and the vast array of useful treatments, future prospects for treatment are hopeful. There is always genuine hope for depressed individuals, and the vast majority will recover and resume fulfilling lives.

Spiritual Dimensions of Caregiving

This chapter's opening vignette is a scenario that frequently confronts lay caregivers or clergy in ministry in all religious traditions. Given the medical realities of this illness, the question before us is how to minister most effectively to those who are afflicted with or adversely affected by this illness that has been called "the common cold" of mental illnesses. The most judicious place to start is by articulating some basic generalizations to keep in mind about depression and all mental illnesses.

General Principles of Caregiving for Those Afflicted and Affected

Every experience and expression of depression is idiosyncratic. While comprehending the basic symptoms of the illness in its varying forms is important, it is imperative to remember that each case is unique and needs to be treated accordingly. The individuals afflicted and affected inhabit a social matrix that is always varied, so the impact of the illness varies according to the culture and social location.

Caregivers are not trained as diagnosticians and so should refrain from acting in a diagnostic capacity. While there is power in knowledge, a "little knowledge" can also be a dangerous thing. Depression and mental illnesses in general are complex, and making assumptions about the illness or persons with the illness are often predicated on erroneous myths that can do harm.

Distinguish between the illness and the person. The diagnosis of the person afflicted with any mental illness does not become her or his identity. People suffer from a variety of mental illnesses, but they are first and foremost people, created in the image of God. The humanity of the person must be preserved at all costs. Labeling people as "depressive," "bipolar," or "schizophrenic" is lamentable. This is a *person* who suffers from an illness, and significant other *people* are affected by the illness.

Depression and other mental illnesses are stigmatized and therefore "unsanctioned illnesses" resulting in a sense of "disgrace shame" (Albers 1995).

The phenomenon of denial on the part of those afflicted and those affected is directly related to the nonacceptance on the part of society and religious communities who more often than not ascribe either psychological weakness or moral culpability as the cause of the illness. The hurdle of first dealing with the disgrace shame is monumental in the person afflicted as well as others who are adversely affected.

Depression is a wholistic illness and requires a wholistic approach to treatment. The historic internecine warfare between science and theology needs to be relegated to an unenlightened past! God has called all to a total ministry of the total person, which requires a cooperative effort on the part of all who are concerned about those suffering from depression and their loved ones. We have much to learn from one another in the various disciplines that we represent.

Depression should not be thought of as resulting from a lack of faith. The injunction to "have more faith," as an antidote to depression, irrespective of one's religious affiliation, is not a helpful caregiving tack. More likely is that persons first become depressed and then believe that they have lost faith, rather than that they lose faith, which then causes the onset of depression. Suggesting that an inadequate faith, improper prayer life, or questionable piety occasions depression only serves to exacerbate the sense of shame and increase the painful experience of depression.

Caregiving for all significant others affected by the depression is critical. In the vast majority of instances where a caregiver deals with depression, it comes to the caregiver's attention from a significant other, not the depressed person. Depression is a "household illness," an inclusive term signaling that all people in the social system are affected. It is *not* a communicable or contagious illness, but the depression creates an environment and ambiance that has an adverse impact on those who are close to the depressed person. Particular attention to that issue will be addressed later in this chapter.

Remember that caregivers also suffer from depression. As already noted, there are many caregivers who have experienced depression in their lives. The narrative of Elijah in 1 Kings 19:1-18 might serve as both a paradigm and a reminder of that reality for those of us who are lay or clergy caregivers. Whether or not Elijah would be clinically diagnosed as being depressed is not the salient issue. Rather, it is the admission that those who are lay caregivers, rabbis, priests, pastors, imams, or prophets are not immune from depression. What one reads in the Elijah narrative reveals his lack of energy, a negative outlook on life, preference for isolation, and his sense of being abandoned by God. All of these reactions are indicators of depression that may strike a respondent chord with religious caregivers who themselves are depressed.

Response of Those Adversely Affected

Both vignettes provided earlier in this chapter feature a significant other who is adversely affected by the illness. As with many unsanctioned illnesses, the dynamics that are often operative are predictable, though not necessarily universal.

Denial of the illness is commonplace as the affected also are resistant to the diagnosis that is made. One hears phrases like, "That can't be true, he has everything going for him." "There must be some mistake; she is just a little down and will get over it." The feeling of "disgrace shame" is exacerbated for the afflicted and the affected when the illness is labeled with pejorative terms like *crazy*, *nuts*, or *loony*, which usually results in everyone involved flatly denying the diagnosis: "We don't have depression in this family!" The sad reality is that sometimes people who require treatment do not receive it as a result of familial denial. If the diagnosis is accepted, significant others may respond by making this "the family secret" (Friedman 1985): "Don't tell anybody that Dad is depressed!" "What would people think if they knew that Mom, who is a community leader, is depressed?" The denial and secret keeping are understandable because of the social and vocational implications involving discrimination against those who have the diagnosis of depression in their medical history.

Fear is a common reaction on the part of significant others. Fear is often the result of being uninformed about the nature of depression. It behooves caregivers within communities of faith to become informed themselves and then to conduct classes or seminars in which accurate information concerning depression can be disseminated in the community, so as to break the conspiracy of silence. There is legitimate fear since suicidal ideation is a criterion factored into the diagnostic process.

Caregivers have themselves been fearful in simply "naming" the illness by calling depression something other than what it is. Suggesting that it is really something other than depression is unconscionably dishonest and potentially dangerous! Being alert to actions or language that might suggest the person is thinking about suicide needs to be articulated. Many fear that asking the person directly about suicide might "put the thought into her or his head." If the person is not suicidal, you will be told. In many instances, the depressed person is waiting for someone to name what is going on, which gives you an opportunity to verify your concern. Three questions can be used to determine the intention of the person:

1. Are you thinking of hurting yourself? (Or: Are you thinking of taking your own life?) If there is an affirmative answer, then ask:
2. Do you have a plan by which to do this? If the answer is yes, then have the person detail the plan for you.
3. Do you have the means by which to carry out this plan? If the person responds positively, then the danger level is high and the suicide likely imminent.

Call 911 (or whatever emergency number is applicable), remain with the person until help arrives, or ensure that the person is *not* left alone until assistance is available. As already indicated, if lethal means are readily accessible, calling the police is certainly in order. Fear needs to be supplanted by faith; that is, the trust that, with intervention, this is a treatable illness and appropriate action can be taken to address the depression properly.

Understanding and accepting anger. The person or persons affected may be angry with the person who is depressed. How can anyone be angry with a person who is ill? It is rather easy! As the symptoms of depression manifest themselves, significant others react to the mood, as well as to the concomitant behavior, language, and attitude that is occasioned by the depression.

"Fred" approached his caregiver and was visibly angry. He said, "My wife ('Laura') has become a real bitch! She gripes and complains

about everything, she gets nothing done, is yelling at the kids, miss-
ing work, and blaming me for everything that goes wrong in the
family." The caregiver simply said, "I can see you are really upset!"
Fred went on to explain how Laura had gotten into this foul mood
several months ago and it was just getting worse. Their intimacy
was now nonexistent; she never wanted to go the theater, which was
an activity that they both used to enjoy. He said he had about had
it and was thinking of filing for divorce because he just couldn't live
this way.

It is evident that something had changed about Laura, and the indicators are that she may be suffering from depression. The caregiver is not
a diagnostician but can plant the seed of suggestion that Laura would
benefit from having an evaluation rather than Fred simply giving up and
filing for divorce.

Understanding and accepting Fred's anger and frustration is a part of
good caregiving. Mounting frustration, waning patience, and increased
despair need to be accepted for what they are, as reactions to depression in the household. Fred would benefit from knowing something
about depression and learning to respond in more understanding ways
that would not exacerbate the problem. The situation might be amelio-
rated if his wife received treatment and both of them did some marriage
counseling.

The Experience of Grief

A sometimes hidden dynamic for those adversely affected by depression
is grief occasioned by the sense of loss that accompanies depression.
As can be easily noted from the vignette about Fred and Laura, there
is the loss of an intimate relationship, the loss of coveted companionship, and the loss of a stable and caring family environment. Opportunities are often sacrificed professionally and personally by those who
are affected. The depressed person is often unalterably opposed to any
kind of change, as the person feels her or his life is already spinning out
of control.

The fate of children is often ignored or overlooked when there is mental illness in the household, as they suffer from neglect occasioned by the depression in one or both of the parents. A child interprets the lack of interest in their lives from a depressed parent as evidence of a lack of support, care, and love. The inability to name what they are feeling and why they are feeling as they do complicates an already complex situation.

Adult children often remember what it was like to grow up with a parent who was depressed. Some state that they felt "cheated out of their childhood" and mourn those losses. Because children do not have a parental role model to emulate, they oftentimes also have problems with close and intimate relationships.

Grief is often not named as the culprit, but it can be the underlying dynamic that subverts and even sabotages the whole household. Enabling those so affected to become more fully aware of their grief and to articulate it is critical. The person afflicted with the depression often has a long laundry list of losses. The fact is that time moves inexorably onward and, as a consequence, there are many missed opportunities, which becomes an occasion for "intra-psychic" grief (Mitchell and Anderson 1983).

Theological Principles in Caregiving

In the final vignette, Fred is articulating a sense of helplessness and hopelessness, which spells despair that his situation will ever get better or return to "normal." This sense of hopelessness that pervades the whole household often takes on a life of its own. When this collective mood persists for a protracted period of time, a general malaise of despondency descends on the whole system, coloring reality with a dark hue that engulfs and threatens everyone in that sphere of influence. The reality and power of despair provides a natural segue into considering the theological implications of caregiving.

Listen attentively to the lament of despair. It is imperative to put aside the proclivity to want to "fix" the person, "straighten the person out theologically," or "rescue" the person from despair. The despair is real, and the caregiver needs to live with the uncomfortable nature of its reality. The three most important aspects in the process of caregiving are to *listen, listen,* and *listen!* The most profound sentence uttered by my spiritual director, when I was in the midst of my depression, was, "I am not afraid of your despair!"[3] Susan Muto most poignantly articulates a theological description of despair as she writes about the "dark night of the soul" as experienced by St. John of the Cross.

> It will feel at times as if one has been abandoned by God. This is so because the intellect, once full of answers, is now left in darkness, confused and unsure of the next step. The will, once eager to give all to God, once rewarded by warm, confirming consolations, now languishes in aridity. The memory, once full of sweet residues of encounters with God, once able to recall occasions of nearness to the Divine and the certitude of God's presence, now feels utterly empty. On the affective level, it seems as if all is lost. Affliction replaces affection received and given by God. Bitterness seems to cancel the beauty of a sought after and received touch of love. Anguish seems to deprive one in a cruel way of the warmth and satisfaction once obtained from a seemingly endless storehouse of spiritual blessings. (Muto 1994)

It is uncomfortable for many caregivers to enter into the dark night of the soul with those who traverse the path of despair. Walk with the despairing person and listen, rather than attempting through words to coerce the person to walk a different path. Concisely stated, it is imperative to "legitimate the lament," both for the afflicted and the affected.

The sacred texts of the Judeo-Christian tradition known as *laments* legitimate such expressions, giving voice to the agony and 'anguish of spirits in distress. Feelings of despair, anger, and hopelessness are all articulately expressed in the lament psalms (Weiser 1962). One young person expressed it in this manner: "If God is not able to accept my anger, then he [*sic*] has no business being God."[4] People who are depressed are in spiritual distress, as are those who are affected by the depression. Listen! Listen! Listen! Listen with compassion, empathy, and patience, providing a ministry of a caring presence.

Distinguish clearly between "faith" and "feeling." The fundamental meaning of the word *faith* is "to trust." Faith is not intellectual assent to a given set of dogmatic propositions, be they creeds or confessions. Faith is not obedience to an inviolate code of conduct. Faith is not equated with feelings of certitude, nor an ecstatic explosion of emotion. Faith is, rather, an implicit trust in the love of God, even when the abyss of despair looms large, threatening one's very being. It becomes evident that "faith is a gift," not something that is earned, merited, or deserved. Rather, it is a dynamic experience of grace that embraces the totality of the person when that person surrenders all efforts to create, manufacture, or induce faith.

The person adversely affected might say, "I have lost all faith in God, in my loved one, and in myself. I never had any idea that depression could be so bad!" The night is too dark, the burden too heavy, the pain too excruciating. It is only when the person affected has opened herself or himself to "practicing the presence of God" in the midst of the seeming absence of God that the flicker of faith appears. This kind of faith that borders on absurdity is what Paul Tillich would term "naked faith" (Tillich 1957).

The caregiver does not attempt to instill faith; rather, the caregiver incarnates the presence of God in listening, empathizing, and agonizing with those suffering the effects of living with a depressed person. Chrysostom said that "Patience is the queen of the virtues," and for those who live in an "instantaneous society," expecting instantaneous gratification, patience is an attribute that is in short supply. Both the caregiver and the care receiver want the pain and the problem to be instantaneously resolved. Aid the person in distinguishing between faith as trust and feelings that are legitimate, but not as the ultimate foundation for assessing the value and worth of life.

Maintain a peaceful and prayerful presence. The gift of being a "non-anxious" presence when in the company of depressed people and their adversely affected loved ones is powerful (Friedman 1985). Actions do speak louder than words, and the most meaningful action is often the seeming "inaction" of simply showing up and being available. Caregiving at its fundamental level is being acutely aware and attentive. Many of us as caregivers have spent time with distraught people who pour out their anguished spirits, and we are the calming presence in a cauldron of bubbling pain. When they know that they have been heard, it is not unusual to hear them say, "You have been so helpful. Thank you!" As the caregiver, you haven't said a word! It is my conviction that people are not so much looking for answers as they are looking for understanding. It is often our anxiety as caregivers that gets in the way of our being "truly peacefully and prayerfully present."

The gift of presence is a powerful and potent experience. What is often missed in the narrative of Job is his friends' reaction to his incredible suffering of grief, which can eventuate in despair and depression. We focus on his friends' speeches (which come later), where they try to convince Job that his calamity is connected to some "sin" that he has committed. But we miss the gift of his friends who did not recognize him because of his condition, tore their robes, and symbolically threw dust in the air as an indication of their identification of suffering with him and then, "They sat with him on the ground seven days and seven nights, *and no one spoke a word to him*, for they saw that his suffering was great" (Job 2:13, emphasis added).

This kind of presence is prayer—that is, "practicing the presence of God"—with one another. Prayer in whatever mode or form it may be utilized in a given religious tradition is being present to others, being open to the Spirit of God, and commiserating empathetically with those who suffer. Of course, prayer may be utilized in its conventional form of uttering praises and petitions to the Holy One, but at its most profound level, it is relational. Prayer is a way of living in relationship to God and others, as well as with ourselves. As such, it is an ensign of hope in the midst of hopelessness. It is more significant to have that hope incarnated in the silence of the caregiver than to have it spoken in words (Welton 2006). Andrew Lester speaks of it as creating a new narrative or a new story for the person (Lester 1995).

The caregiving key is to "wait patiently for the Lord" (Ps. 37:7), as the timing is out of our hands as caregivers. Pushing another is always counterproductive and poor caregiving practice. The caregiver *is not responsible* for effecting healing; that is finally in the province of God. The caregiver ought not "get in the way of healing" by following a self-determined agenda thought to be "good for the person" who is depressed or the depressed person's family. Incarnating hope through a peaceful and prayerful presence is our role as we accompany those who suffer.

Assure the afflicted and affected of a supportive faith community. It is my conviction that "it takes a community to heal people," an inclusive community that features the best of biology, psychology, and theology. The focus at this point is specifically the community of faith that can surround those depressed and those affected by depression with their compassion, concern, care, acceptance, and gracious love. As already noted, faith communities of all religious persuasions need to be informed and educated about depression and its effects. Accepting depression as a mental illness as opposed to a weak will or a moral failure is an important place to start. Attitudes about mental illness and all unsanctioned illnesses are deeply ingrained not only in individuals, but in the collective psyche of faith communities. Religious leaders need to work hard and tirelessly to change negative attitudes and to encourage community interest and support in ministry to the depressed and their significant others.

Those who have been afflicted or affected by depression may say, "I don't feel like going to worship." That feeling needs to be legitimated and honored. Others may say, "I can go to worship, but I don't feel like participating." That is a legitimate reaction as well, and they can be assured that the community participates on their behalf. The critical issue is that they are welcomed and accepted whether they participate or not. They are always loved and accepted for where they are in their life's journey. The old hymn says it well: "Not in our temple made with hands, God the Almighty is dwelling."[5] The visible community needs to be open and accepting of their presence, but it is equally important to remember the invisible community of people whose absence for a time is legitimated by their illness and the concomitant behavior that accompanies the illness. A gracious, loving, welcoming, and accepting community can be a salutary refuge from the rigors and isolation accompanying depression. It is imperative that the community be educated, sensitive, and aware of the importance and impact of its ministry to those afflicted and affected by depression.

Provide advocacy for the marginalized. Faith communities, irrespective of their religious persuasions, are enjoined to advocate for the invisible, the voiceless, the suffering, and the forgotten as a way to fulfill the mandate that the prophet Micah perhaps most succinctly articulated: "God has told you, O mortal, what is good; and what does the LORD require of you but to do justice, and to love kindness, and to walk humbly with your God?" (Mic. 6:8) "Doing justice" is an imperative that is a common theme in religious communities. The question of justice as equality of treatment, access to care, and compassionate acceptance for those afflicted with and affected by depression and all mental illnesses is a tall order. This kind of justice requires hard work, dedicated people, and advocacy at every level of society. Historically, it is evident that prophetic advocacy for justice is met with opposition, particularly when a society seems to value money more than people. It is too easy an answer to back away from the hard questions and decisions that are made in government and other halls of society by citing the "separation of church and state" as an excuse for inaction.

The Bible always pictures Yahweh as the champion of the oppressed. Jesus exemplified this in his life and ministry reaching out to the sick (Matt. 4:24, 14:14, 35), the lepers (Luke 17:12), and the man thought of as possessed by a demon (Mark 5:1-13). The understanding of Allah in Islam as being merciful and concerned about the poor and the dispossessed is a foundational tenet. If systemic change is to occur on behalf of those who have no power, religious groups must be the voice for the voiceless and advocate for the ideal, "justice for all," and not just for the privileged.

This mandate from the very core of religious traditions needs implementation if those with unsanctioned illnesses are to experience the abundant life referenced in John 10:10. For those afflicted with and affected by depression in its various permutations, the advocacy of all religions must sound a cooperative clarion call of justice for all.

There is help and there is hope; there is heartache but also healing. It is to that end that religious communities are called, as sisters and brothers say in Kiswahili, to stand *bega kwa bega* ("shoulder to shoulder") in effecting positive change for hope and new life.

Bibliography

Albers, Robert H. 1995. *Shame: A Faith Perspective.* New York: Haworth.
———, and William H. Meller. Winter 2001. "The Faith Factor in Wholistic Care: A Multidisciplinary Conversation." *Word and World* 21 (1): 51–60.

American Psychiatric Association. 1994. *Diagnostic and Statistical Manual of Mental Disorders,* 4th ed. (DSM-IV). Washington, D.C.: American Psychiatric Publishing.

Andreasen, Nancy C., and Donald W. Black. 1995. *Introductory Textbook of Psychiatry.* 2d ed. Washington, D.C.: American Psychiatric Publishing.

Beck, Aaron T., A. John Rush, Brian F. Shaw, et al. 1979. *Cognitive Therapy of Depression.* New York: Guilford.

Beck, Judith. 1995. *Cognitive Therapy: Basics and Beyond.* New York: Guilford.

Callahan, Christoper M., and German E. Barrios. 2005. *Reinventing Depression: A History of the Treatment of Depression in Primary Care, 1940–2004.* New York: Oxford University Press.

Cassidy, Walter L., Norris B. Flanagan, Marie Spellman, et al. 1957. "Clinical Observations in Manic Depressive Disease: A Quantitative Study of One Hundred Manic-Depressive Patients and Fifty Medically Sick Controls." *Journal of the American Medical Association* 164 (14): 1535–46.

Craig, Kenneth, and Keith Dobson, eds. 1995. *Anxiety and Depression in Adults and Children.* Thousand Oaks, Calif.: Sage.

Dunner, David L. 2008. "Major Depressive Disorder." In S. Hossein Fatemi and Paula J. Clayton, *The Medical Basis of Psychiatry,* 3d ed., 73–84. Totowa, N.J.: Humana.

Feighner, John P., Eli Robins, Samuel B. Guze, et al. 1972. "Diagnostic Criteria for Use in Psychiatric Research." *Archives of General Psychiatry* 26: 57–63.

Friedman, Edwin H. 1985. *From Generation to Generation: Family Process in Church and Synagogue.* New York: Guilford.

Greenberg, Paul E., Ronald C. Kessler, Howard G. Birnbaum, et al. 2003. "The Economic Burden of Depression in the United States:

How Did It Change Between 1990 and 2000?" *Journal of Clinical Psychiatry* 64 (12): 1465–76.

Hulme, William, and Lucy Hulme. 1995. *Wrestling with Depression: A Spiritual Guide to Reclaiming Life.* Minneapolis: Augsburg.

Jamison, Kay Redfield. 1995. *An Unquiet Mind: A Memoir of Moods and Madness.* New York: Random House.

Kocsis, James, and Daniel Klein. 1995. *Diagnosis and Treatment of Chronic Depression.* New York: Guilford.

Lester, Andrew. 1995. *Hope in Pastoral Care and Counseling.* Louisville: Westminster John Knox.

Lyons, Albert S., and R. Joseph Petrocelli. 1978. *Medicine: An Illustrated History.* New York: Abrams.

Milstein, Glen. 2003. "Clergy and Psychiatrists: Opportunities for Dialogue." *Psychiatric Times* 20 (30): 1–2.

Mitchell, Kenneth R., and Herbert Anderson. 1983. *All Our Losses, All Our Griefs: Resources for Pastoral Care.* Philadelphia: Westminster.

Muto, Susan. 1994. *John of the Cross for Today: The Dark Night.* Notre Dame, Ind.: Ave Maria.

Rosenthal, Norman E. 1993. *Winter Blues: Seasonal Affective Disorder, What It Is, and How to Overcome It.* New York: Guilford.

———, and Mary C. Blehar, eds. 1989. *Seasonal Affective Disorders and Phototherapy.* New York: Guilford.

Tillich, Paul. 1957. *The Dynamics of Faith.* New York: Harper & Bros.

Weaver, Andrew J., Harold G. Koenig, and Frank M. Ochberg. 1996. "Post Traumatic Stress, Mental Health Professionals and Clergy: A Need for Collaboration, Training and Research." *Journal of Traumatic Stress* 9 (4): 847–56.

Weiser, Artur. 1962. *The Psalms.* Philadelphia: Westminster.

Welton, David. 2006. *The Treatment of Bipolar Disorder in Pastoral Counseling: Community and Silence.* New York: Haworth.

World Health Organization (WHO). 2004. *The Global Burden of Disease.* Update. Geneva: World Health Organization.

ANXIETY DISORDERS

Thomas Mackenzie / Christie Cozad Neuger

2

Debra is a college graduate and a single mother. Her husband died unexpectedly a few months ago. She now works as an executive in a public relations firm. Recently, after her eight-year-old son leaves for school, she has started to feel very uncomfortable; she begins to tremble, perspire, and experiences a sense of impending doom. As she drives to work, she has recurrent thoughts about her son being in danger and that she will not be there to help, to provide escape or comfort. Periodically throughout the day, she will call the school, asking if her boy is safe or if he is in a state of discomfort. Debra realizes her thoughts and actions regarding her son do not make rational sense, but the thoughts intrude; she can't stop them. They produce what to her is fear for her son's welfare. The apprehension continues until she receives assurance from school personnel that all is well. Her colleagues at work are concerned that she seems very uneasy and distracted, and her job performance is suffering as the result.

Understanding Anxiety Disorders

In considering the existence of the anxiety disorders, one is immediately confronted by a semantic dilemma. Does the word *anxiety* imply pathology? Are persons who experience anxiety suffering from a disorder (the equivalent of an illness in psychiatry)? Or, can anxiety just be normal, not evidence of maladjustment?

In common usage most persons who report that they are "anxious" undoubtedly do not intend to identify themselves as psychiatrically ill. A certain amount of anxiety in anticipation of demanding, unfamiliar, uncertain events seems normal and even functional. Being anxious implies looking forward. One is anxious about the future (either immediate or remote), about something that has not yet happened but might. From this perspective anxiety that facilitates careful preparation would be more useful than anxiety so close to the event as to preclude any constructive action.

It is important to note that although anxiety is forward looking, it can be produced by what a past event predicts about the future. For example, you have completed an exam and feel that it went poorly. You feel guilty for not preparing more effectively, angry at the instructor for emphasizing the wrong material, disappointed that you are a poor student, and, perhaps most of all, anxious. The anxiety this past event generates is about consequences, such as failing the course, wasting tuition money, disappointing the instructor, and so forth.

The *Oxford English Dictionary* defines anxiety as an "uneasiness about some uncertain event."[1] There is no reference to normality or abnormality. For the remainder of this chapter, we will assume that anxiety exists on a spectrum from normal to pathological and that one of our tasks is to distinguish between the two.

Fear and Anxiety

Another semantic conundrum! Is there a difference between anxiety and fear? Many observers distinguish the two as follows: *fear* is an unconditional response to an unconditional stimulus. An event (such as encountering a tiger) universally and inevitably elicits fear. Its capacity to elicit fear is "built" or "hardwired" into the human nervous system. Anyone confronting a tiger would feel fear. Fear is a normal response to danger, present or future.

According to this conceptualization, in contrast to fear, *anxiety* develops when a stimulus that is neutral to most people becomes linked to a fear-producing unconditional stimulus and subsequently develops the capacity to elicit fear itself through a process known as conditioning.

So the difference between fear and anxiety is twofold. First, fear is normal and nonpathological (not indicative of a disorder), whereas anxiety may either be normal or abnormal (i.e., pathological). Second, the stimuli that elicit fear do so universally in humans (or at least in specific cultures), whereas the stimuli that produce anxiety are typically neutral and unique to the individual.

There is a third potential distinction. Fear and anxiety are differently responsive to experience. For example, firefighters are probably less afraid of rushing into a burning building than someone who has never done it. But both the veteran and the neophyte would have some fear. Repeated exposure has attenuated the firefighters' fear; but the fear never disappears entirely. In contrast to fear, the goal in managing pathological anxiety is to extinguish the anxiety completely.

In what ways are fear and anxiety similar? One could argue, though I do not find it convincing, that fear is an immediate response to an event, whereas anxiety is a response to an anticipated event. In other words, fear is not something you can have about the future. You must be anxious about the future, not fearful. I do not think this makes sense. If a potential future event is fearsome, for instance, a nuclear war or catastrophic climate change, then it seems appropriate to talk of being fearful about that outcome. If you are very anxious about thunderstorms and check the Weather Channel every hour about climatic conditions and won't go outside or travel if rain is predicted, we would probably say you are pathologically anxious rather than fearful.

So both fear and anxiety can be elicited by immediate or anticipated events. The proximity of the event may also be relevant. If a five-year-old is very anxious about going to college, we would consider the horizon of anxiety too remote and the anxiety, depending on its severity and persistence, potentially pathological. And, of course, if you started being anxious about college in the last semester of high school, it might be a little too late.

Both fear and anxiety can lead to avoidance of cues that provoke them. If the avoidance becomes pervasive enough, it can be the most debilitating characteristic of either fear or anxiety. The scope of avoidance can vary from avoiding a very specific, circumscribed stimulus (going to the top of a specific building) to avoiding a broad range of tenuously related stimuli (looking down from any elevated perch). The broader the pattern, the more potentially disabling the avoidance becomes.

Symptoms of Fear and Anxiety

Although the events that elicit fear and anxiety may be different, the signs and symptoms are similar. Both anxiety and fear modify our thinking and level of arousal. Thoughts may seem to speed up and/or become fragmented. The mind may go blank. Recalling even simple things may become impossible. Thought content is dominated by the event that elicits the response. Other prominent events may be completely unobserved. With variable intensity bodily functions are aroused. The heart races, breathing increases, muscles tense, eyes dilate, body shakes, and perspiration flows.

Pathological Anxiety

When is anxiety pathological? The best answer is: when it seriously degrades or compromises performance or personal potential. Gauging when this is the case requires clinical judgment. Most persons have been momentarily flustered in a way that has compromised their function. For instance, driving in a novel situation and being late for an important appointment, one might fail to see the correct exit on an interstate. While anxiety may have produced this kerfuffle, we would hardly label that person pathologically anxious solely based on that sequence.

The loss of function that corresponds to pathological anxiety is typically persistent or recurrent rather than isolated. In addition, it is generally too intense or prolonged for the situation compared to how most people would respond (or is evoked by events that are neutral to most people).

We typically conceptualize pathological anxiety as a response to discrete, recognizable events (e.g., stimuli, situations). While this typically applies to normal anxiety and fear, it is sometimes not the case for pathological anxiety. Some sufferers are not able to link their anxiety to a specific thing; there is just a persistent, unattached sense of uneasiness and tension. In such cases the anxiety is described as "free-floating."

Clinically, most sufferers of pathological anxiety realize that something is affecting their function in a negative way. Some may not use the word *anxiety* but may call it "tension," "restlessness," "a sense of apprehension," "worry," or something similar. Typically, they do not object to the application of the word *anxiety*.

Some persons resist being described as anxious or being assigned an anxiety diagnosis, perhaps because of the stigma, but also because it implies that they can't manage their emotions. In this vein, a person can be anxious *about being anxious*. Even talking about anxiety or acknowledging that one can be anxious is distressing and unsettling. This highlights an important feature of anxiety. It tends to be, at least initially, a feed-forward phenomenon. Anxiety recruits additional anxiety. Persons with pathological anxiety (e.g., those with an anxiety disorder) typically scan the environment and are hypervigilant for stimuli that might evoke anxiety and monitor themselves for symptoms of anxiety (such as rapid pulse or difficulty breathing). Such scanning and monitoring represents a state of anticipatory anxiety. This anticipation poises the person to be mobilized by any deviation from the expected.

Not only does pathological anxiety hold the person in a heightened state of vigilance; once mobilized, anxiety can produce a pattern of thinking that heightens the level of anxiety. Catastrophic thinking describes the tendency for one anxious event to mobilize an epidemic of fears that flood one's consciousness, convincing an individual that the situation he or she is facing is unmanageable and that he or she will surely be overwhelmed and fail.

Modern Psychiatric Diagnosis

The practice of medicine is contingent on accurate diagnosis, distinguishing one condition from another and selecting appropriate therapies. Accordingly, practitioners develop and update catalogues, called nosologies, which list medically valid diagnoses. Although this process has been applied to psychiatric diagnosis for two hundred years, it has become increasingly bureaucratized in the last fifty years.

The American Psychiatric Association oversees the catalogue of psychiatric diagnoses in the United States. It has composed and published a series of manuals describing those disorders that the Association recognizes as valid and reliable. Recent versions of these manuals have listed specific criteria for discerning and diagnosing conditions. Since psychiatric disorders, unlike most medical diagnoses, do not consistently show biological abnormalities, the criteria developed by expert panels are descriptive.

Before we consider the specific anxiety disorders catalogued in the DSM-IV TR (Text Revision, 2000) (DSM-V is expected in 2012), how confident should we be that modern psychiatry has collected and described the anxiety disorders in a way that distills their essence? I am skeptical. Contemporary psychiatric diagnosis is founded on description rather than etiology or pathophysiology. There is an expectation that sufficient information can be gathered to propose a tentative diagnosis in an interview lasting less than sixty minutes with an expert who has not previously met the patient.

The need to render diagnoses rapidly reflects a number of factors: the need to produce a diagnosis for insurance purposes; the expectation promoted by the mental health profession that diagnosis is straightforward and accurate; and what is perceived as a modern intolerance of complexity and preoccupation with speed.

Scales that rate items such as "anxious mood" (Hamilton Anxiety Scale) on a one-to-five severity index are used to estimate the severity of anxiety. Other instruments, such as the National Institute of Mental Health Diagnostic Interview Schedule for Children (DISC), pursue precise diagnosis by asking preformatted questions. For example, to elicit worries about school, the following question is posed, always in the same way: "In the last year, was there a time when you would worry even when you didn't need to, say [in a subject/about something at work], where you were well prepared and always did well?"[2]

Classification of Pathological Anxiety

Disorders with onset in either childhood or adulthood. DSM-IV TR contains a chapter titled "Anxiety Disorders." It specifies criteria for the following twelve disorders in which some form of anxiety is the major feature and focus of treatment.

- panic disorder without agoraphobia
- panic disorder with agoraphobia
- agoraphobia without history of panic disorder
- specific phobia
- social phobia
- obsessive-compulsive disorder
- post-traumatic stress disorder
- acute stress disorder
- generalized anxiety disorder
- anxiety disorder due to [specified general medical condition]
- substance-induced anxiety disorder
- anxiety disorder not otherwise specified[3]

Disorders with onset in childhood (may persist to adulthood). The only disorder that must have a childhood onset is *separation anxiety disorder*. Two additional entries deserve mention: (1) *adjustment disorder with anxiety* and (2) *adjustment disorder with mixed anxiety and depressed mood.*

These describe anxiety that is directly related to a stressor (e.g., learning that one has widely disseminated cancer); the symptoms must develop within three months of the stressor and must resolve within six months of the resolution of the stressor. In the event that there is no such resolution, such as the financial consequences of a bankruptcy and home foreclosure, the diagnosis may be applied for a longer period.

Before we consider the features that identify the major anxiety disorders, it is important to note that many other disorders, such as schizophrenia, depression, delirium, dementia, and anorexia nervosa, often feature prominent anxiety at some point in their course. In these instances the anxiety is not a core feature (i.e., not required for the diagnosis), but a consequence of other symptoms. For instance, a person with schizophrenia may imagine that intelligence agencies such as the CIA are poisoning his or her food. This delusional thought can elicit profound anxiety. Despite this, an anxiety disorder is not diagnosed because it is obvious why the patient would be anxious. Similarly, a person with anorexia nervosa may be panicked that she or he has gained weight and be frantically exercising and weighing her- or himself. An anxiety disorder is not diagnosed, because the anorexia nervosa diagnosis better accounts for the symptoms. So, in some cases anxiety may be very prominent, but the diagnosis of an anxiety disorder is not warranted.

The diagnostic criteria for the anxiety disorders include both inclusive and exclusive descriptors. The inclusive criteria require the presence of a specific feature. Such a feature might be a sign or symptom or the duration of the problem. The exclusionary criteria reject the diagnosis if certain conditions are met. For instance, one would not diagnose depression after the death of a spouse, because the symptoms would be better accounted for by bereavement.

Signs and symptoms are defined in terms of either their form or content. By form, I mean temporal structure and what it takes to elicit the symptoms. By content, I mean the specific thoughts generated. For instance, the *form* of a panic attack is a rapidly evolving set of symptoms that lasts about twenty to thirty minutes, which in the beginning seems to come from out of the blue. The *content* is a sense of doom and a concern that one is either dying from a physical cause (i.e,. a heart attack) or going to lose one's mind and suffer a mental breakdown.

Demographics and Etiology of Anxiety Disorders

As a rule, anxiety disorders are manifest in the second decade of life. It is highly unusual to have an onset in the fourth decade or beyond. With some notable exceptions, anxiety disorders tend to affect women more than men. The reason for this is unclear. It may be a reporting artifact, with men much less willing to acknowledge anxiety and women feeling more comfortable discussing emotional responses.

Although anxiety disorders tend to run in families, this appreciation is not decisive in making a diagnosis and to this point has not enhanced an understanding of why some people are more anxious than others. Our capacity to breed animals who acquire fear more rapidly and/or recovery from anxious situations more slowly strongly suggests that there are specific genes that contribute to a person's vulnerability to anxiety. In no case do we know of a single gene that guarantees the development of an anxiety disorder in the one who possesses it.

Core Features

Almost universally, patients with an anxiety disorder will identify one or more cues (tasks, events, situations, or objects) as capable of eliciting their anxiety. The cues run the gamut from being very potent, inevitably eliciting anxiety, to conditional, arousing anxiety on only some occasions. Expectably, the avoidance of these cues varies from mild aversion if the cue is spontaneously encountered to rigid adherence in anticipating and avoiding these cues at all costs—the latter being especially likely if the cue is very potent.

The fewer and more specific and unambiguous the cues, the easier they are to avoid. For example, a phobia of flying is easily managed—don't get on an airplane. Avoiding crowded places, such as riding in an elevator with other persons, is a much more complicated and uncertain task.

Rather than consider each DSM-IV TR anxiety diagnosis individually, I will discuss them according to the type and potency of cues that arouse them. The more specific and circumscribed a fear—such as of mice or spiders—the more likely it is to be labeled a *specific phobia*. Such phobias are extremely common in childhood—fear of the dark, fear of people wearing masks—and typically remit after puberty. If they continue into adulthood, they are likely to be permanent. Adults with phobias recognize that their fear of the cue is unreasonable; children typically do not have that insight. Adults do not make claims about the feared object that defy reality, while children may assign special powers or features to a ghost or fantasized creature. Once in place, phobias do not tend to expand or morph into something else; if one is fearful of dogs, this does not typically switch to cats or expand to include birds or other creatures. On the other hand, having one phobia probably increases the odds that one will have another.

Most specific phobias are never formally diagnosed. Only a small fraction come to clinical attention, and this is usually at the instigation of the patient. A relatively common phobia is of hypodermic needles. This is typically revealed when a treatment or diagnostic test involves insertion of a needle. In extreme form, patients may avoid visiting a doctor, even for a serious condition, to minimize the likelihood of encountering a needle stick.

Separation anxiety in children is an anxiety that something bad will happen to a caretaking figure, such as a mother or father, during a time of separation. These situations are so common that they are not represented by a single cue. Going to school or, in younger children, not being in the same room with a parent, can trigger the anxiety. Typically, the child protests or endorses symptoms, such as a stomachache, that attract concern and decrease the odds of separation. So-called school phobia or school avoidance is a manifestation of separation anxiety. There is evidence that separation anxiety in childhood predicts pathological anxiety in adulthood.

By convention cues that trigger anxiety about being scrutinized or being humiliated in public are gathered into a specific category: *social anxiety disorder* or just *social phobia*. Typically, the cue involves failure at some sort of task—making a speech, making small talk, eating, going to the bathroom—in a social context. Sufferers tend to have either a single cue, such as public speaking, or have a more generalized set of cues.

Acute stress disorder and *post-traumatic stress disorder* (PTSD) occur when recollection of a traumatic event involving a threat of harm or death is cued by ordinary circumstances. For instance, reexperiencing a serious auto accident is triggered by the sound of screeching tires or the sound of a horn. By convention a disorder cannot be considered PTSD until it has existed for four weeks after the traumatic event.

The anxieties observed in *obsessive-compulsive disorder* are triggered by situations in which concerns about safety, completeness, symmetry, cleanliness, purity, and piety are aroused. The sufferer seeks certitude that things are in order. Since certainty can be a hard standard to meet, the sufferer begins to ruminate about "what if" something is not as required and to manage this at-times unbearable anxiety by behaving in a ritualized, compulsive manner—cleaning, checking, repeating, praying, counting, and so forth. Often these activities have to be enacted in a specific manner. Unlike phobias in which the cues are circumscribed and potentially avoidable, the fears of obsessive compulsive disorder can be responsive to such a broad array of cues that the patient is essentially paralyzed, continuously engaged in either obsessional worry or compulsive ritual. Being so preoccupied is labeled *egodystonic* to reflect that the sufferer would rather not be so engaged. This differentiates obsessive-compulsive disorder from the *egosyntonic* (i.e., desirable) activity of anticipating or engaging in a pleasurable activity.

There are occasional patients who experience paralyzing anxiety unattached to any cue they can identify. Typically, however, such persons find this diffuse anxiety very aversive and become anxious about its possible appearance, anxious about becoming anxious.

Generalized anxiety disorder describes a constant burden of anxiety (also called excessive worry) aroused by situations that are ordinary in character; *Will I find a job? Will I find a partner? Can I pay my bills? Am I too old to get pregnant?* Persons with this disorder exaggerate concerns experienced by most individuals. Their concern exceeds what is useful, depleting the individual physically and emotionally.

Panic disorder is the unwarranted intrusion of signs and symptoms appropriate to an emergency in the absence of an emergency; it is a false alarm. The signs and symptoms—racing pulse, rapid breathing, tremor, sweating, dilated pupils, sense of danger—correspond to the inappropriate activation of fear centers in the brain and the release of the emergence hormone epinephrine into the circulation. Panic disorder is characterized by episodic panic attacks. They are sudden in onset, build to peak intensity within seconds, and typically last twenty to thirty minutes. During an attack the sufferer is overwhelmed by a sense of doom and is typically so preoccupied with the signs and symptoms that attention to ongoing, instrumental behavior is impossible. The attacks, which can come "out of the blue," are so aversive that sufferers often attempt to predict their appearance, intending to avoid the situation or retiring to a safer place, at the first hint of an attack. A common tactic is to avoid the physical place where an attack occurred. In assigning significance to the place, the sufferer imbues it with the capacity to elicit an attack if approached (called anticipatory anxiety). A more general strategy is to avoid places that would be hard to retreat from, such as elevators, small spaces, restricted access roadways, tunnels, bridges, and so forth. This pattern of avoidance and the fear that these cues elicit is called *agoraphobia* and is a common companion of panic disorder; hence, the term "panic with agoraphobia."

In addition to monitoring their physical location, sufferers from panic disorder may monitor their own physiology for fluctuations. So, noticing that one's pulse quickens after navigating a flight of stairs may be interpreted as an indication that a panic attack is imminent. Of course, imagining this to be the case increases the odds of such an outcome.

Symptoms of anxiety can be produced by medical conditions (*Anxiety disorder due to a general medical condition*) that increase physiological arousal. Like panic disorder, hyperthyroidism, pheochromocytoma, and insulinoma mimic an emergency by releasing a substance into the circulation that jolts the body into an emergency mode, confusing the patient by generating symptoms of arousal when there is no danger. Fortunately, these conditions can be detected with assays for the substance that is being overproduced.

In seizure disorders, specific brain structures spontaneously become active and in so doing replace functional brain activity. If the seizure involves the entire brain, it is called a grand mal seizure. In this case the victim is rendered unconscious during the seizure. If the seizure involves only selected areas, it is called a partial seizure. The symptoms associated with some partial seizures include experiencing anxiety. This would be considered anxiety disorder due to a general medical condition.

Substance-induced anxiety is related to consumption of a substance or withdrawal (e.g., discontinuation) from a substance. Consumption includes prescription medications, over-the-counter medicines, and alcohol/drugs. Notably, a number of the modern antidepressants, such as fluoxetine, can produce an agitation early in treatment. Anxiety caused by discontinuation is usually confined to sedative hypnotic substances, such as alcohol and benzodiazepines. Acute withdrawal from these substances not only can produce anxiety, but can be life-threatening if it includes seizures. Withdrawal from alcohol tends to appear within twelve hours of cessation. If the individual were a heavy and chronic user, however, the severest symptoms may peak forty-eight to seventy-two hours after discontinuation.

As implied by the name, an *adjustment disorder with anxiety* is a short-term disturbance triggered by a jarring life event. For example, if one receives a phone call describing a severe stroke in a heretofore robust but aging parent, it would not be unusual if the following anxiety would interfere with work and typical routines. If one had to put a label on it, adjustment disorder would be appropriate.

Comorbidity

The diagnostic boundaries between the anxiety disorders are porous; the disorders frequently overlap. Based on criteria, individuals often qualify for several discrete diagnoses. Rather than assign several disorders, diagnosticians select *anxiety disorder NOS* (NOS = not otherwise specified) to capture the clinical presentation.

Treatment

The treatment of anxiety disorders rests on two approaches. Psychotropic medications aim to alter the nervous system so as to mute anxiety. The goal is to modify neurotransmission so that stimuli that elicit anxiety are rendered neutral. To pretend that we have sufficient knowledge of the nervous system to explain how this happens is arrogant. We know medications that enhance serotonergic function or potentiate the effects of gamma-amino butyric acid (GABA) are superior to placebos in treating anxiety disorders. It would follow that the neurotransmitters serotonin and GABA are important in experiencing anxiety. Beyond that recognition, we have a limited understanding of why these medications work.

The second arm of treatment is to modify how an arousing stimulus is processed. This can be done in two ways: first, by repeatedly presenting the stimulus to an individual until its ability to elicit anxiety is exhausted—this is called *behavioral therapy* and aims to extinguish the potency of a cue in eliciting anxiety. The theory is that with multiple presentations a neutral stimulus will eventually lose its ability to generate anxiety. The second method is to systematically explore and correct inaccurate psychological conclusions held by the individual regarding her or his anxiety. Typically, the patient considers him- or herself helpless in face of an overwhelming situation. These ideas are challenged using a method known as *cognitive-behavioral therapy*.

Pastoral Theological Reflections on Anxiety

One afternoon, Pastor Jim Williams receives a call from Amanda, a twenty-six-year-old parishioner, who asks if she can meet with him for a problem she's having. When she arrives she seems nervous and hesitant to tell her story, but slowly it emerges that Amanda is having trouble with panic attacks. It all started when she wasn't feeling well one day at school a couple of years earlier. She got dizzy, left the classroom, and passed out in the hallway. The health center checked her out and said that she might have had a panic attack. A few weeks later, she had the same experience on a bus, was terribly embarrassed by it, and since then has been unable to ride buses. Gradually, she got more and more worried that she would have another episode, and so she dropped out of graduate school. Over time, she has begun to have trouble participating in various things—going to shopping malls, driving long distances, sitting in a movie theater, and so on.

With some gentle reflective listening, Pastor Williams encourages Amanda to talk about what else is going on in her life. Amanda says that she is very torn about what to do. She has two small children on whom she knows she should focus, but she also wants to finish graduate school and have a meaningful career. Her husband says that she has to make her own decision about what to do, and he will support any decision that she makes. He is, however, getting frustrated with her anxiety and her indecision. She gets more anxious as she tries to explain her psychological and moral dilemma about these hopes and responsibilities. She says that she has been enrolling in school, staying for a semester, and then dropping out for a semester to stay home with her children because of her feelings of guilt. Now that she's dropped out entirely, she feels relieved but sad and frustrated. In addition, she says that she thinks God is disappointed with her because she isn't a more committed mother and is punishing her with the panic attacks. She finds herself having difficulty sleeping, worrying that she'll encounter God in a dream, and she feels very frightened. She has stopped praying for the same reason. She also says she knows that this is a bit crazy and doesn't know what to do about it. She ends by saying, "Pastor Williams, you've got to help me!"

Theological and Psychological Reflections on Anxiety

We'll revisit Amanda shortly. Her experiences of panic attacks, general anxiety, feeling paralyzed, a sense of dread, and difficulty moving forward are not uncommon. Caregivers frequently encounter people struggling with all forms of anxiety, with or without religious and/or moral dilemmas attached to them.

Anxiety, as an aspect of the human condition, has been a key focus in modern theology and psychology. In the eighteenth century, Søren Kierkegaard found anxiety to be so fundamental to human life that he made it the focus of a major treatise, concluding that the key to developing selfhood was learning to live productively and dynamically in the tensions of freedom and anxiety. Over a hundred years later, Paul Tillich wrote *The Courage to Be*, suggesting that the fact that human beings are self-transcendent and thus can contemplate their own nonbeing/death, creates an anxiety that is central to our lives. In 1973 anthropologist Ernest Becker wrote a Pulitzer Prize–winning book, *The Denial of Death*, in which, following Kierkegaard and others, he wrote that human beings live in the dilemma of both creatureliness and self-transcendence, which generates immense anxiety—the simultaneous anxiety of living and of dying. Because of that anxiety, Becker suggests that human beings tend to arm themselves with a variety of denial strategies so that they can live with less anxiety. Yet the consequence is a life that is less honest and self-aware than it could be. He proposed another option. Human beings, he says, can let themselves fully experience the anxiety of existence, going to the edge of despair and giving themselves over to the experience of God, who creates meaning in the midst of despair. This is how Becker sought to address the paradox of human life. In a deathbed interview with Sam Keen a few months after his book was published, he made his philosophical claims more personal and theological when he said, "I believe in God, and this allows me to feel a great sense of relief and trust that eggs are not hatched in vain. Beyond accident and contingency and terror and death there is a meaning that redeems: redeems not necessarily in personal immortality or anything like that, but a redemption that makes it good somehow. And, that is enough. . . . I think it is very hard for secular people to die" (Keen 1974). Becker found what might be called a trans-finite solution for allowing him to live in the midst of existential anxiety.

Much more recently, theologians and psychologists have been thinking and writing about the "new anxiety" or the post–September 11 anxiety in which contemporary Americans live. Pastoral theologian Kirk Bingaman, in his book *Treating the New Anxiety: A Cognitive-Theological Approach*, brings theology and psychology together to explore living in this new anxiety of our world. He sizes up the situation by saying:

> The present age of anxiety is characterized by pressing concerns about the threat of terrorism, global warming, the beginning of the end of oil, immigration and pluralism, the widening economic gap between those who have and those who have not, and the outsourcing of American jobs. These concerns are legitimate, and they will demand our and our children's undivided attention for years to come. The anxiety that we feel is compounded daily or, in some cases, hourly by skilled fear entrepreneurs who know how to push our buttons. As if the issues listed here, eliciting legitimate concern and anxiety were not enough, some fear entrepreneurs introduce a host of potentially threatening crises that keep us constantly on edge. (Bingaman 2007, 17)

Bingaman goes on to say that this new anxiety shares many features of generalized anxiety disorder (DSM-IV TR) but is more than that. He writes:

> Rather, it is a collective phenomenon affecting a people and a nation, the manifestation of which is in the excessive worry and apprehensive expectation of one who comes to therapy looking for a place to make sense of a world in transition. . . . The new anxiety, simply put, cannot be reduced to a mental problem inside the head of a particular client. In a super-modern, post-September 11 world, the new anxiety reflects a collective disease with a world that we have not even begun to learn how to look at. (Ibid., 79)

To summarize in colloquial terms Bingaman's point—it would be nuts not to be anxious in today's world.

All this is to say that anxiety in people's lives, in and of itself, is not an aberration from the normal. It is, at some level, at the heart of the human condition. Between our own existential reality of self-transcendence in a finite form, the cultural realities of rapid change, and an investment in "selling" anxiety as part of the media's participation in an age of information overload, it would be hard to imagine a self-aware but anxiety-free life. As Dr. Mackenzie stated in the first part of this chapter, our work is not to assume immediately that anxiety implies pathology. The concern for those of us who seek to support and care for people who are struggling is to assess and address how anxiety is functioning in people's lives and how to help people live with anxiety in ways so that it doesn't control them. Certain levels of anxiety are appropriate to contemporary culture, but when anxiety gets in the way of people being able to engage in a productive and desired life, it is appropriate that caregivers respond in the most effective ways they can. To that end, people's self-assessment of how anxiety is operating in their lives is helpfully seen in the contexts of the human condition, the age of anxiety-producing events and information, and their personal experiences of threat and harm. All of these contexts work together to shape core beliefs and systems of meaning-making in people's lives that have a direct impact on the way they generate anxiety.

Meaning-making is at the heart of human experience. Narrative counseling theory helps us to make sense of this process. Narrative theory assumes that people make meaning in their lives through stories—in other words, we provide narrative links between events in our lives (storying them) in order to make sense of them. Since our lives are multilayered, we could tell many stories about them in many ways. Yet only a small percentage of our life experiences get storied. Most get lost or obscured by the more dominant story lines of our lives. The way we understand our lives, the way we have storied them, becomes a lens on the way we see life and the way we give ourselves identity. The stories through which we understand our lives (personal, familial, cultural, contextual) become the realities that we live out. In other words, the way we interpret the events in our lives and who we are in the midst of those events comes from the way we have made meaning over time— our "stories" of our lives—and this is "reality" for us. Nonproductive anxiety is generated when the meaning we make out of the events in our lives creates a sense of threat inherent in our future. The dominant story line for interpreting the events of our lives has become one of danger. Other, nonthreatening story lines have become obscured by the anxiety story line. Both cognitive-behavioral therapy, with its proven track record in effectively helping people who are struggling with nonproductive anxiety, and narrative therapy focus on assessing whether the way we are interpreting or making meaning is the most helpful way to understand what's happening or if there is a better, more accurate, or more resource-rich way to do so in this particular context. People who struggle with various kinds of troubling anxiety tend to make meaning along a story line that predicts more trouble, a loss of control, or grave risk. In most situations, there are a variety of ways to interpret or "story" the experience. But most people who struggle with nonproductive anxiety story their experience in ways that are frightening. Counseling with cognitive-behavioral methods has to do with helping people assess whether their meaning-making processes are the most useful and accurate ways to think about this situation. Narrative-therapy strategies similarly invite people to see alternative story lines (based in other experiences they have had) as useful in storying the particular events that are generating frightening future stories.

Pastoral Care Reflections on Anxiety

As noted above, the care strategies for people who are struggling with nonproductive anxiety involve helping them to look at the ways in which they are interpreting the events in their lives and where that interpretation is leading to high levels of anxiety, and to see whether a different interpretation or an alternative story line would be more helpful, more accurate, or more resourceful for them. To this end, cognitive therapy, for example, helps people conduct "thought experiments" that help them assess the accuracy/usefulness of their interpretative framework. It is not uncommon for people who seek pastoral help for their anxiety that some of the interpretive framework is based in religious beliefs. We can see this in the case of Amanda described above. Amanda had a core belief or narrative about her relationship with God that was primarily judgmental and punitive. The meaning she made of her current dilemma was literally "damned if I do and damned if I don't." This caused both panic attacks and a growing belief that nowhere was safe except staying in her "stuckness" (staying at home). Clinically, this would be diagnosed as agoraphobia, although we tend to lose much of the richness of the story in the diagnostic label. The pastor had a number of choices about how to address this situation. He could have instructed her that, in order to be more attuned to God, Amanda should let go of her anxiety (since there are Bible passages that tell believers not to be worried) and that not to let go of the anxiety would be sinning. This pastoral approach to people with anxiety problems is often seen in religious self-help books (for example, *Let It Go!* by Tony Evans). My sense is that this approach would have strengthened Amanda's belief in a judgmental God who found her inadequate and a failure, since it's not so easy to "let go" when one is struggling with a pattern of panic attacks. Instead, Pastor Williams invited Amanda to reflect on whether this view of God as judgmental and punitive fit with her wider experiences of God and with her own sense of moral rightness. Since he had known Amanda for some years, he had a sense that she had other beliefs about God that might be useful to "try on" again at this time in her life. This generated a productive conversation that helped decrease the fear that she was experiencing in sleeping and praying. He also referred her to a counselor who used cognitive-behavioral methods so she could assess some of her other fear-producing belief systems. Finally, he invited her to make some pastoral calls on a few elderly parishioners, which served the dual purpose of expanding Amanda's ever-narrowing world (facing the fear so as to reduce it) and helping her engage in activities that generated a different sense of partnership with God's work of loving care, a value she had expressed many times. Over the course of a few months, Amanda's nonproductive anxiety decreased to where she had full access to the life she wanted to lead and only rare experiences of panic, which she was able to handle with her new cognitive skills generated through the counseling work.

A situation like Amanda's is one way in which caregivers may encounter people struggling with anxiety. Certainly it is a fundamental part of a pastor's responsibility to assist people in exploring their religious belief systems and how those are having an impact on their lives and relationships. Since religious beliefs are often more complex and multilayered than other kinds of automatic thoughts or core assumptions, they often can't be "tested" for validity in the same ways. Yet they can be explored for consistency and usefulness in light of the counselee's experience, history, and faith tradition. Often problematic religious beliefs are inconsistent with the person's larger frame of reference and with other important values in his or her life. This was certainly the situation with Amanda. And, in addition to helping a counselee decrease the anxiety associated with the problematic religious belief, a pastoral counselor can also help to revitalize a person's faith, which may have foundered due to stagnant or incompatible beliefs. A pastoral conversation where problematic or inconsistent beliefs can be collaboratively explored may well enliven other aspects of the person's faith life as well as invite the person to question other kinds of taken-for-granted "truths."

Let me offer another short case study as an example of how a situation of unproductive anxiety may be raised for pastoral counseling.[4]

Pastor Sara Wilson and Nancy Smith were straightening up after a women's fellowship meeting. Upon being asked how things were going, Nancy told the following story. The whole family (Nancy, husband Mike, and two children in their late teens) were supposed to go to a wedding, about four hours away by car. Nancy was very eager to go to this wedding but Mike was saying that he couldn't possibly take a car trip that was that far away. She explained that Mike got anxious on car trips, not wanting to be so far from home. As the story continued, Pastor Wilson discovered that Mike had many worries, and all the family members worked to support him and make his environment as "safe" as possible. Nancy concluded, "Sometimes I feel like I have three children. I can't go out during the times he is at home unless one of the kids is there. Jason stopped dating his girlfriend because he felt that Mike needed him in the evenings, and Ellen fights with her Dad all the time because of the restrictions he puts on her activities so he doesn't have to stay alone. Is it too much to ask that we go to this one event?" Pastor Wilson asked if it would be okay if she made a home visit to talk with all of them about the family situation, and Jane welcomed the suggestion. Mike became angry when he discovered that his "secret" had been told but agreed to the visit, as did the children. Over two counseling sessions the family was able to negotiate a way to support Mike enough to where he felt comfortable to go on the trip. However, the family confronted Mike on how his anxiety was affecting their lives, effectively putting the kids' lives on hold as well as damaging the marriage. Mike agreed to participate in a program the pastor knew about, a structured group therapy program designed to offer behavioral strategies and cognitive resources for people who struggle with anxiety. The pastor continued to follow up with supportive pastoral care. At six months the family was doing well. In particular the group component of Mike's therapy program had really helped decrease his complete dependence on the family for his social support.

In both of these pastoral counseling cases, the pastor was well informed about appropriate referral resources as well as how to do initial assessment and short-term counseling. The pastors were also able to move back into an appropriate pastoral care role following the pastoral counseling sessions. These are essential skills for effective parish-based pastoral counseling.

Anxiety issues may come to the pastor's and congregation's attention in other ways than counseling requests. For example, people who have certain forms of anxiety may develop difficulties in entering and remaining in a worship service due to discomfort with being in a crowded environment. Obviously, when a congregation is aware of those kinds of difficulties, offering gracious support and a nonjudgmental presence makes it more likely that people can face their fears by continuing to enter the worship environment.

Finally, to come full circle, it's important to realize that people and communities may well experience general anxiety and worry that is, in fact, proportional to the threats in their lives. As Bingaman suggests, this is a time of rapid cultural change that includes threats to individual and communal well-being. Congregations need to be helped to support one another in hard times and to engage in the kinds of discussions that help people face their fears and mobilize their resources. One therapist reported on a case in which the parents brought in for counseling their six-year-old child who was experiencing significant anxiety symptoms. They had already pathologized his experience, given his age and his anxiety symptoms. By the counselor openly inviting him to talk about his experience, however, the young boy was able to reveal the appropriate proportionality of his anxiety given that he overheard, from his bedroom, the newscasts to which his parents listened every night. He had legitimate concerns about his own personal safety and the safety of his parents and community, given what he heard on the news. Encouraging his family to discuss these local and world events together and to offer credible reassurance to the child helped reduce his anxiety. We all need support in this new age of anxiety and "fearmongering."

Suggestions for Pastors and Congregations

Each situation of pastoral need requires its own analysis and strategies. However, there are some general suggestions for pastors and congregations that may help them better to support people and families who have experienced the effects of various kinds of nonproductive anxiety, especially general anxiety disorder, panic attacks, and agoraphobia.

First, caregivers should have and continue to develop appropriate knowledge and skills for pastoral counseling. There is data that suggests that pastors do not experience improvement in their pastoral counseling through gaining more experience. This is probably because pastoral counseling is such a private ministry without opportunity for significant feedback. So pastors need to engage in continuing education in order to continue to improve and update their pastoral counseling skills. Pastors do not really have a choice about whether they do pastoral counseling, only about how well they do it. The National Institute of Mental Health found, in 1999, that clergy were more likely than psychologists or psychiatrists combined to have a person with a psychiatric diagnosis seek them out for help. Clergy confirm these numbers when they report that they spend between 10 percent and 20 percent of their working time in pastoral counseling, on average six to eight hours per week (Milstein and Bruce 2000). There are many benefits to pastors doing counseling. They are visible, accessible, financially affordable, able to see the big picture, and able to take initiative in follow-up care. Their limitations are also significant. They have limited training, limited time, multiple roles that require very careful boundary setting, few resources directed at helping them, and a lack of confidence in providing counseling to parishioners. This means that all pastors doing any counseling must have accountability partners and a clinical consultant (from outside the parish) to help them manage the limitations. Nonetheless, given the number of people who seek out clergy for problems in their lives and the current difficulties people have finding affordable counseling help, it is important that clergy are as prepared as possible to offer appropriate help while at the same time knowing their limitations and being able to make good referrals. Pastors have to walk the fine line of not getting in over their heads in trying to provide pastoral care and counseling for their parishioners (which must always be short term, well boundaried, and nonintrusive) while being responsible and responsive to their needs and concerns.

Second, and related, caregivers need to gain basic information about the dynamics of anxiety and its impact on individuals, families, and communities. It can be very hard for people who have never struggled with nonproductive anxiety to understand or empathize with this kind of problem. In addition, pastors should gain basic information about the principles of cognitive-behavioral therapy so that they have a basic understanding of what their parishioner might be experiencing in therapy (if referred to this kind of therapy).

Third, caregivers need to have a well-developed and up-to-date list of referral resources for people struggling with anxiety (and other kinds of emotional and psychological difficulties). Bingaman points out that, despite the significant empirical evidence that the most effective therapeutic approach to anxiety problems is cognitive-behavioral, a relatively small number (around a third) of people who went to counseling for this problem were treated with cognitive-behavioral methods. Many were treated with methods (psychodynamic, primarily) that may do more harm than good (Bingaman 2007, 51). Given this, pastors need to know effective resources for people struggling with anxiety. That means interviewing and evaluating counselors about their approach to the problems they treat before making referrals to them.

Fourth, caregivers need to be willing and able to invite counselees into a conversation about their religious beliefs. This means that caregivers need to be skilled in engaging in theological reflection and familiar with their own theological positions so as not to impose those unwittingly on their counselees.

Fifth, it can be very helpful for caregivers periodically to use illustrations in their sermons that demonstrate their awareness of and openness to persons who struggle with emotional and psychological issues like anxiety. It is important to recognize that using a sermon illustration like this is likely to result in people seeking the caregiver out to discuss the problem as it exists in their lives.

Sixth, it's important for church libraries and sitting areas to have up-to-date books and resources that appropriately inform people about problems like anxiety and panic. These resources should be reviewed and evaluated before being purchased so that resources that give inappropriate "help" aren't included.

Seventh, it is helpful for congregations to have opportunities to discuss those things that generate anxiety for them as individuals and as a community. Challenges such as economic downturns, job losses, political polarization, ecological threats, and so on need to be a part of communal conversation and support. When a congregation experiences a particular challenge (such as having high unemployment), special supportive resources can be generated. One church, for example, runs a job-loss group that serves as both a social support and a networking opportunity. Support groups of various kinds in congregations can be very helpful.

These are a few of the many possible strategies that caregivers and congregations can adopt to support people struggling with anxiety (and other problems). Pastors can empower congregations to be aware of these kinds of problems and to be creative in their potential responses. The church can be a powerful resource for people who struggle with emotional and psychological problems. Developing the church as a caring community should be a top priority for today's congregations.

Bibliography

American Psychiatric Association. 2000. *Diagnostic and Statistical Manual of Mental Disorders*, 4th ed., Text Revision (DSM-IV TR). Washington, D.C.: American Psychiatric Publishing.

Becker, Ernest. 1973. *The Denial of Death*. New York: Simon & Schuster.

Bingaman, Kirk A. 2007. *Treating the New Anxiety: A Cognitive-Theological Approach*. Plymouth, U.K.: Jason Aronson.

Keen, Sam. 1974. "The Heroics of Everyday Life: A Theorist of Death Confronts His Own End." *Psychology Today* (April): 71–80.

Milstein, Glen, and Martha Bruce. 2000. Abstract 5495, "Mental Disorders Prevention and the Clergy," in 128th *Annual Meeting of American Public Health Association Proceedings*.

Psychotic Disorders

Stephen Olson / Joretta L. Marshall

3

Pastor Wilson was surprised when Megan, a woman in his congregation about thirty years old, approached him after services and asked if she could meet with him to talk about "a personal matter." He knew little about Megan or her parents, who kept to themselves and only attended the Sunday service. She seemed very shy and barely responded when he had greeted her on occasion in the past. He had heard she was active in the youth group when in high school but was rumored to have had a "nervous breakdown."

When they met, Megan explained that her therapist had suggested she talk with a clergy to "clear up some questions" about God and her faith. Megan said, "You see, I have schizophrenia, and it's really messed up my beliefs about God and the church." She went on to explain how she started having problems with mental illness while she was away at college ten years ago. It started very gradually at first, with her feeling out of place with the other students then thinking that they were whispering and making fun of her in class. She dropped out of school and didn't tell her parents of her concerns.

She tried to get a part-time job, but things got even worse when it seemed that everyone was reading her thoughts and making faces at her when they disapproved of what she was thinking about. "The worst of it was in church. Whenever there was a silent prayer, I felt like everyone knew what I was thinking, and then I heard their thoughts and prayers, all mixed together, and sometimes I heard God talk to me, saying I was bad and should be punished." Sunday services became overwhelming for Megan, and she said at times she thought she herself must be God, because "who else hears everyone's prayers?" She stopped going to church, or even going out at all, until she attempted to overdose on pills and was hospitalized on a psychiatric unit. Megan then was diagnosed with schizophrenia and given medication, but she didn't believe she was ill and stopped taking it shortly after she was discharged. "I certainly didn't think I had a mental illness. I thought I had a gift, maybe I was God, maybe someone else, but other people knew about it and were trying to mess me up." She went in and out of the hospital and sometimes did get better but stopped taking the medication because she didn't feel she needed it. "I got real confused about God because I kept hearing him all the time, talking to me, sometimes nice, but mostly mean and awful things. I thought he was mad at me because I had some powers like him." She was unable to work due to her confused thinking and lack of motivation.

Several years ago, she began working with a psychiatrist and therapist who educated her about schizophrenia, stabilized her with medications, and arranged her involvement in community rehabilitation. Part of her recovery involved resuming activities she had enjoyed and found meaningful before her illness and to understand how her psychosis affected her belief in God. She began attending church again but struggled with her inner confusion and the sense of awareness of others' thoughts. Megan said she was learning to better block out the voices and ignore them, and she knew other people couldn't really know what she was thinking. She wanted to go to Sunday school classes and expressed interest in helping in the nursery. She said, "I don't know if other people know I have mental illness and if they are scared of me or wouldn't want me near the children. I realize now that was part of my illness, and I just want to be able to love God and be a part of the church again."

Understanding Psychotic Disorders

Schizophrenia is the most common of the *psychotic disorders* in which disturbances of thinking are predominant. *Psychosis* is an impairment in the brain's ability to perceive accurately and interpret the world around in a way consistent with how others see things. The most obvious symptoms of psychosis are *delusions* (false beliefs) and *hallucinations* (false perceptions). Schizophrenia and its related disorders are highly variable from person to person, and from time to time in the same person, and encompass a wide range of symptoms and behaviors beyond the psychosis itself.

Although this chapter will focus on schizophrenia, much of what will be said can apply equally to other forms of serious mental illness, particularly where psychotic symptoms occur. These include bipolar disorder and depression, where psychotic symptoms frequently arise during the course of an acute episode but generally go away when a person recovers. Other psychotic disorders include schizoaffective disorder, delusional disorder, and psychosis due to nonpsychiatric causes, such as drugs or medical illness. Because psychosis alters the person's ability to assess reality accurately, including the recognition that they are experiencing a mental illness, frequently the affected person rejects help until the situation has reached a crisis.

Psychotic Symptoms

Delusions are fixed ideas and beliefs that do not follow logically from evidence that others would consider reasonable. Common themes include persecution (e.g., believing one is being spied on or is in danger of being killed), somatic or body-related ideas (e.g., having cancer or mechanical body parts), grandiosity (e.g., being someone famous or having superpowers), or depressive beliefs (e.g., one is bankrupt or has committed an unforgivable sin). The belief is not understandable based on the person's cultural background, so a Haitian who believes his or her belly pain is due to voodoo influences may not be delusional, whereas a suburban American office worker who has the same belief likely would be considered so. In fact, it is the process of arriving at the delusional belief that is abnormal, so individuals tend to hold tenaciously to their ideas, even in the face of what everyone else believes to be overwhelming evidence to the contrary, including simple common sense. The consequence of this in dealing with a delusional person is that it's not generally possible to argue them out of their beliefs—in most cases, it is better to "agree to disagree" nonjudgmentally on the content of their beliefs and attempt to connect on some other level, for example, empathizing that it must be stressful to be in constant danger yet have no proof that one can take to the authorities.

Hallucinations are false perceptions without actual sensory stimulus. The most common form, experienced by 75 percent of persons with schizophrenia at some time during the illness, is hearing voices that others do not hear. Sometimes these are mumbled and indistinct, like overhearing a conversation across the room, but they can be as loud as normal conversation or even shouted. Persons with psychosis usually describe them as negative, calling them names or telling them to do bad things, but this is not always the case. At the height of the psychosis, most individuals with hallucinations attribute them to something other than mental illness, such as God or the devil, telepathy, or electronic devices. In this way, hallucinations often lead to and reinforce delusional beliefs. Hallucinations can occur in other senses, such as seeing visions, feeling bugs on the skin, or smelling or tasting something strange.

Other symptoms of psychosis include disorganized thinking and conversation such that the individual has trouble communicating clearly because her or his language is vague, rambling, illogical, or fragmented. Some patients may exhibit abnormal motor behavior, or catatonia, in which they become mute, stop eating and drinking, have little or no spontaneous movement, and sometimes assume awkward or bizarre postures.

Schizophrenia

Schizophrenia is a complex brain disorder characterized by psychotic symptoms as described above, but also affecting emotions, personality, behavior, and cognition. Most patients show the first symptoms between the ages of fifteen and twenty-five, and most continue to be affected to a variable degree for the rest of their lives. The term *schizophrenia* literally means "split mind," referring to the disorganization of thinking and the disconnection between thought and emotion. The term is unfortunate, because the general public often confuses this with "split personality" or Dissociative Identity Disorder, an extremely rare condition in which there are multiple personalities or "alters" that can take over control of the individual. That misunderstanding, and media attention to sensational crimes committed by persons said to be mentally ill, contribute to stigma by associating schizophrenia with unpredictable and savage violence. Although untreated mental illness, especially if there are paranoid delusions, can lead to violence including homicide, the vast majority of people with schizophrenia are nonviolent and passive, and more likely to be victimized by violent crime than to perpetrate it.

Schizophrenia affects about 1 percent of the population worldwide during their lifetimes, and can be found in every culture. It is a major public health problem, accounting for 3 percent of health-care costs and total societal cost of $70 billion annually in the United States, where 2.5 million people live with a schizophrenia-related disorder. Between 6 and 10 percent of individuals with schizophrenia die by suicide, and their average lifespan is fifteen to twenty-five years shorter than the general population. Most people with schizophrenia are disabled occupationally and socially to some extent, although partially this reflects the lack of comprehensive community mental health services in many areas. A large proportion of the persistently homeless population, numbering several hundred thousand in the United States, suffers from severe mental illness, often complicated by chemical dependency.

The course of schizophrenia over time varies considerably. Some persons have a gradual onset over years; others may be perfectly normal one week and floridly psychotic the next. Sometimes there is an attack with a full recovery, but more often, especially after several episodes, it's more likely to have continuing symptoms, even with treatment.

Delusions and hallucinations, as described above, represent just the "tip of the iceberg" as far as all of the manifestations of schizophrenia. They are referred to as *positive symptoms* because they represent something abnormal "added on" to the mental state. There are also *negative symptoms*, which refer to decreased behaviors that are "subtracted from" normal experience, including low motivation, lack of enjoyment, reduced emotional expression, and decreased socialization. Most patients with schizophrenia have significant *cognitive impairment* of attention, memory, and problem-solving functions, which are more responsible for their difficulty in employment and living independently than the delusions and hallucinations are. There are often signs of depression, some of which are similar to the reaction to other chronic illnesses, but sometimes become quite severe and can lead to suicide. In general, the positive symptoms tend to fluctuate more over time and are more responsive to treatment, whereas the negative and cognitive symptoms are more persistent and stay even when hallucinations and delusions may be in complete remission.

Schizophrenia is a *disorder of brain development* that becomes evident when the brain is in the late stages of maturation. The cause is multifactorial, meaning that in each individual case there are likely many contributing factors. Schizophrenia is not a single disease entity but, like mental retardation, is an outcome of various conditions affecting brain development. The most important risk factor is genetic, or inherited. The immediate family members of a person with schizophrenia are five to fifteen times more likely to have schizophrenia than someone unrelated, although most people affected do not have schizophrenia in their family. Persons who have an identical twin with schizophrenia have a 50 percent chance (fifty times greater than the general population) of developing schizophrenia themselves. But, since identical twins have identical DNA, the fact that the concordance is not 100 percent tells us that there are nongenetic factors involved as well.

Some of the nongenetic factors clearly relate to early brain injury, such as maternal illness during the pregnancy or difficult labor and delivery. Head injury early in childhood is another such factor. There is now clear evidence that regular use of marijuana in adolescence increases the risk of later developing schizophrenia by two- to fivefold. Other known associations are still mysteries—persons born in the winter months have a slight increase in risk, as do people raised in central urban areas before the age of ten. In fact, the risk drops steadily from inner city to suburb to small town to rural areas. Immigrants have been known for decades to be at greater risk for psychosis. There is no support for the antiquated notion that parenting style or poor communication is the cause of schizophrenia, a belief that led to unwarranted blame by professionals and subsequent shame on the part of parents. There is some evidence that severe physical or sexual abuse may contribute to the development of auditory hallucinations in persons who later develop schizophrenia, as well as those who do not, but instead deal with depression or post-traumatic stress disorder. Neuroscientists believe that most people who have schizophrenia have both genetic and nongenetic risk factors that interact to result in schizophrenia.

The early stages of the illness provide an opportunity for intervention and education that may improve the overall outcome for persons with psychosis. There is compelling evidence that the longer a young person remains psychotic without being treated, the more the condition progresses and becomes more difficult to treat. It stands to reason that being psychotic cannot be psychologically healthy, but it is an entirely different matter if remaining psychotic has a toxic, irreversible effect on a vulnerable, developing teenage brain. Early intervention programs in Australia, Europe, and Canada have been very successful in educating persons who interact regularly with teens and young adults to recognize the early symptoms of mental illness and refer them to a specialty program for a definite evaluation. This includes school counselors, coaches, employers, and those in youth ministry in a position to identify young people who are showing changes in their behavior, emotions, and especially thought process that could be an early sign of mental illness. These signs include gradual changes, such as decline in school performance, worsening self-care and grooming, withdrawal from usual social activities, or new odd and eccentric behavior. Referral to a mental health professional, especially a program designed for psychosis prevention, will sort out age-appropriate teen behavior from drug use, depression, or possible early psychosis and will recommend treatment.

The treatment of schizophrenia starts with a comprehensive medical and psychiatric evaluation. Prescription or street drug abuse must be ruled out, as well as a variety of medical conditions that can mimic mental illness. There are no specific biological tests or brain imaging that can be used now for the diagnosis of a specific mental disorder, but such tests, as well as genetic testing to assist in the selection of a safe and effective medication regimen, are being studied in research centers. The cornerstone of treatment of schizophrenia is *antipsychotic medication*, which works to regulate the balance of neurotransmitters in the brain, particularly dopamine, which is overactive in parts of the brain during a psychotic episode. Antipsychotics, also called neuroleptics, include aripiprazole (Abilify®), risperidone (Risperdal®), quetiapine (Seroquel®), clozapine, and many others. These medications primarily reduce the intensity and emotional reaction to hallucinations and delusions, and allow the patient to behave in a more appropriate manner. When optimally effective, these medications can result in full recovery and allow the return to usual activities in a few weeks or months, although only about 25 percent of patients have such a good result. Unfortunately, about the same percentage derive very little benefit, or refuse to take medication unless forced to do so under court order. That leaves about half the population with schizophrenia who partially improve with medication but continue to have negative symptoms and cognitive impairment that make their lives difficult. Other medications, such as antidepressants and mood stabilizers, can be used in selected cases to address other symptoms. Once the acute episode has been resolved, it is still necessary in most cases to continue the antipsychotics to prevent a relapse of symptoms. Unfortunately, most patients have difficulty remaining on medication for long periods of time for a variety of reasons. These include lack of insight, troubling side effects, cost, and limited access to care, among others.

Besides medication treatment, other interventions are also very important to maximize the quality of life and function of a person with schizophrenia. Counseling and psychotherapy play an important role in helping patients cope with their illness and its effect on their lives. In the early stages, psycho-education directed at the family is critical in helping everyone understand the nature of their illness and how to deal with the changes associated with having a family member with a new and often frightening condition. Specific kinds of psychotherapy such as cognitive-behavioral therapy can help patients to rethink their beliefs, question their assumptions about hallucinations, and use others to help distinguish what's real from what's not. Traditional intensive psychodynamic ("Freudian") therapy is not helpful and may actually make things worse by encouraging deep intrapsychic exploration by patients already confused and anxious about their inner experience.

Persons with schizophrenia may need months to recover slowly from an acute psychotic episode before they can return to school, work, or all of their previous activities. It is necessary to manage their, as well as their families', expectation about the speed of their recovery, and strike a balance between pushing for too much, too soon versus not expecting or encouraging any recovery. Patients, family members, and friends will need to differentiate negative symptoms (lack of motivation, social withdrawal, and inactivity) from depression or side effects of medications. Many persons lack *insight*, or awareness that they are ill in any way, and may refuse treatment or hospitalization. Xavier Amador has written extensively about this as another aspect of a malfunctioning brain, that is, one that cannot accurately perceive its own malfunction, and on how to engage such a person constructively and identify what their motivation to get help might be (Amador 2007). If the individual continues to have active psychotic symptoms, or stable negative and cognitive deficits that interfere with recovery, it will be necessary to engage community mental health resources to provide rehabilitation. Personnel in various disciplines can be brought onto the care team, depending upon resources and availability in the community. Case managers are helpful in identifying what services are needed and how to access their providers. They may include Social Security benefits workers, housing specialists, chemical dependency counselors, vocational trainers, or independent living specialists. All of these individuals may work together on an Assertive Community Treatment (ACT) team, including a psychiatrist and nurse, who together provide comprehensive care to persons with schizophrenia and other serious mental illnesses living in the community.

Pastoral Responses to Persons with Schizophrenia and Their Families

A case study of Megan introduced this chapter. In this section, we will hear also from Dana, a sister of one of the authors of this chapter.[1] In talking with the members of her church school class, Dana notes that living with schizophrenia is like "having a radio playing in your head that you can't turn off or down." She represents a group of those living with this chronic illness whose lives are marked by meaningful recovery.

Clergy and friends in the church school class are interested in learn-ing from her; she is articulate and thoughtful as she talks about what it means for her and her family to live with a mental illness that will, most likely, not disappear during her lifetime.

As has been noted in the previous section of this chapter, schizo-phrenia is a unique disorder that disrupts the lives and plans of those affected by it in a myriad of ways, but it also has a major impact on their families, friends, and caregivers. The changes that occur in some-one can be frightening, and tremendous uncertainty is shared by all. At times, persons living with psychosis do not even believe they have a problem, even when their entire lives are dominated by bizarre and con-fused thinking. How can pastors, family members, caregivers, friends, and church members seek to respond theologically to this particular manifestation of mental illness, encouraging people toward health and wholeness?

Theological and Pastoral Responses to a Diagnosis

Leaders who provide care, family members, and faith-community friends can become pivotal conversation partners for Dana and her family as they discern how to put the experiences of this illness into some kind of perspective. Responses from those in the faith community can support and empower persons on their journey of recovery or create roadblocks and difficulties. For example, when Dana reports hearing voices, it can be incredibly damaging to suggest to her that those voices are "God's words" or are simply figments of her imagination, or to deny the way they can be problematic to living. Likewise, it can destroy movements toward health to propose that prayer is the only avenue for healing or that a steadfast and faithful person would not need to rely on medication. Connecting a disease of the mind to sins from the past or present to the will of God or to some kind of internalized demonic presence can nega-tively alter a person's relationship to self, God, family, and community. Appropriate caregiving and theological responses, on the other hand, can provide space for persons living with schizophrenia, their families, and friends to ask questions, reflect on possibilities, and discover ways to move toward greater wholeness through recovery.

Historically, theologians and religious leaders have attached a variety of meanings to those who hear voices, see hallucinations, or experience the constellation of symptoms presented earlier in this chapter. As noted historian and theologian Rosemary Radford Ruether notes, "hearing voices" has a rich history in religious tradition, including within Scripture (Ruether 2010). Faithful people have talked about seeing visions and hearing the call of God throughout time; indeed, hearing the voice of God, listening to the ancestors, or having an "out-of-body experience" are revered and valued in contexts where such occurrences are considered to be part of religious experience (ibid., 49–54).[2] Daniel B. Smith writes of historical figures, including Joan of Arc and Socrates, who heard voices but, rather than becoming incapacitated by them, turned their experience into inspiration and leadership (Smith 2007).

Psychiatrists have only recently recognized that perceptual distortions and outright hallucinations are reported in community surveys by people who never seek care or have the disability or distress associated with mental illness. There is a community of "voice-hearers" who shun any implication that they have an "illness" or "disorder." Certainly among these people are some whom clinicians would identify as potentially benefiting from treatment, but likely not all. Psychosis represents a state of disordered salience, the process of attributing significance to events in the world around us. A person who is developing psychotic thinking may find significance and a personal message in every minutiae of their environment, whether a random gesture, facial twitch, or license-plate number. Religious revelation may also be partly based on the same brain mechanisms, finding higher meaning and significance in the seemingly random natural world.

What, then, makes the hearing of the voices or seeing of visions for those who live with schizophrenia something distinct? Most significantly, in the experience of those with active schizophrenia, the visions and voices are often self-destructive or violent. In discerning how to respond to suggestions that the voices and visions are of God, it is helpful to assess whether the voices and visions are life giving or death dealing. Is the individual functioning "normally," or are there other signs of mental disturbance?

Theologically, the presence of schizophrenia in our world represents nothing different from the presence of any other illness with which someone is born or that is experienced during a lifetime. God does not will for people to suffer with schizophrenia any more than God wills for people to die from floods or cancer. When all is said and done, the experience of voices can bring positive value—not in a way that distorts or honors the destructive potential of the voices—but in a way that reminds us that there is a diverse richness of experience in our world that cannot yet be explained. Pastoral theologian Kathleen Greider notes that there is a wisdom that can be drawn from the experiences of those who live with voices and visions. In reading the memoirs of the "soul-suffering," or people who experience schizophrenia, mania, or depression, she notes that "profound questions of ultimate meaning and value emerge explicitly and implicitly throughout their reflections" (Greider 2007, 8). This ought not to be interpreted as overly optimistic or in denial of the incredible anguish and pain that emerges in the midst of the symptoms of this disease; rather, it suggests only that persons who hear voices and have visions have something theologically to teach us about the meaning and value of life itself.

Religious leaders and others connected to the faith community may be among those who first wonder about whether something extraordinary is happening to someone. They may be told about the voices or hallucinations by the one experiencing them, asked questions about whether they are real or not or whether they are evil, or they may wonder about a speech pattern that is marked by odd transitions and what feels like nonsensical rationality. Those are precisely the times for careful and thoughtful initiatives by those who surround an individual. Being alert to some of the manifestations of a disease can help individuals in the community discern how best to respond. Maintaining connections with a psychiatrist or counselor who can help with appropriate referrals is essential. Knowing the various resources for support—National Alliance on Mental Illness (NAMI), another local organization, or books on the shelves in the church library—can be incredibly helpful to individuals and families.[3] There is nothing more devastating and isolating to a family than knowing that others saw something that "didn't make sense" but did not follow up or pursue with questions or concerns out of a sense of fear or lack of knowledge.

Diagnosis, as we have learned, is not a simple science. There may be long periods between the onset of symptoms, the changing of symptoms, and the time when a health-care professional offers a "diagnosis." These can be frustrating, painful, and chaotic times when families and the persons experiencing the symptoms feel helpless or hopeless. Yet, to be diagnosed as someone living with schizophrenia can be a powerful experience, carrying both positive and negative consequences. For some, coming to understand the way in which schizophrenia is an illness much like other kinds of illnesses offers individuals, family members, and communities a way to see something as more "normal." Having a language and a concrete name provides a broader sense that there are others who experience this illness, not just one individual who is identified in the culture as "crazy." A more negative consequence of diagnosis is when schizophrenia becomes a totalizing label from which one cannot escape. In other words, when someone's self-understanding is centered only on the disease, or when someone is treated as if she or he are only a disease and not a person, a diagnosis can be destructive.

The language we use is incredibly important. Dana notes that "to say you *are* schizophrenic means that schizophrenia owns you; to say you *have* schizophrenia means you can own the illness." She understands herself as someone who lives with a chronic mental illness, not as a schizophrenic whose primary identity is captured by a diagnostic category. For someone who has been diagnosed with schizophrenia, it is important to help the individual, family, and community understand that this is not the only—nor perhaps the most important—thing to know about someone. People who live with the disease ought not to be seen as or limited to self-understandings that are defined by the disease; they continue to be children of God who are called by their own name in God's richness and grace.

Once diagnosed, or in the process of treatment, families or individuals may turn to the community or pastoral leader for support or for assistance in asking difficult questions. Why did God allow this to happen? Am I supposed to learn something from this? Why aren't my prayers being answered? Do I not have enough faith? At other times, persons may distance themselves from the community out of fear of rejection, difficulty of explaining what is happening, or because of the shame that many carry about mental illness. Or, as Dana has expressed, while church can sometimes be a place for building good relationships, at other times the stimulation of a worship service and the engagement of so many other voices can be too much. Religion, a rich spiritual life, and an experience of God can be supportive, comforting, and life giving. The community that stands with persons and their families in the abyss of not knowing precisely what is going on or what will happen into the future, embody a rich symbol of God's ability to stand with us. Listening carefully, responding nondefensively, not overinterpreting the cause or meaning of someone's illness, supporting healthy religious experiences and understandings of God, and engaging persons directly in the questions that have no answers can help people move from feeling helpless and hopeless toward recovery. Just as there is not one response that everyone makes to any crisis or experience, there is not a universally faithful response that people who live with chronic mental illness have in response to God, faith, spirituality, or community.

A special word needs to be said about communities, families, and pastoral leaders in diverse contexts, such as more rural areas of the United States or among communities who simultaneously experience racism or poverty, who have no insurance, or who live in states with poorer mental health options. The lack of local resources and options may sometimes create a greater sense of feeling overwhelmed and alone in a moment that is unpredictable and chaotic. Some individuals and communities find it difficult to accept help due to a genuine fear of authority structures that may have brought harm in the past out of indifference or a lack of knowledge, or familial shame of being identified with mental illness. Marked by a lack of trust in public health-care systems or the "outsiders" who offer help (including psychiatrists and other counseling specialists), such fear or shame can exacerbate violence or chaotic behavior (Woolis 2003, 224–28). Advocating for training by physicians and police who are often first responders to families and persons experiencing the symptoms of schizophrenia can be part of the work of the church and the pastoral leadership. Similarly, while there may not be a local NAMI in rural communities, connecting with others who experience some kind of issue related to mental health and accessing information and resources through websites and the Internet can be a tremendous support. In the midst of chaos and the complexity of schizophrenia and its symptoms, church leaders can encourage life-giving responses.

Treatment and Medication as a Theological Issue

Faith communities and pastoral leaders who can positively and honestly address the spiritual and faith concerns of the symptoms, causes, and treatment of schizophrenia are more likely to be helpful in encouraging individuals and their families to live a life that is meaningful. The complexity of diagnosis can be attested to by physicians and psychiatrists as they wrestle with an illness that is embodied in many different symptoms and forms. While the causes of schizophrenia are still under investigation,[4] what is clear is that treatment by caring and competent counselors, physicians, spiritual caregivers, families, and friends can make the difference between someone being caught alone in the downward spiral of self-destructive impulses and someone who can move toward recovery with the support of others. Treatment that takes account of the wholeness of a person and draws upon the resources of one's community, faith, and spirituality, as well as competent counseling and helpful psychiatric and medical treatment, can be positive markers in not allowing the disease to be the only word in someone's life.

Living with a chronic illness such as schizophrenia means being involved with the psychiatric and medical community in an ongoing way. Depending on the severity of the symptoms and one's ability to work and provide health insurance, this often means connecting with public health-care systems. The historical difficulties in providing public treatment options for those living with the symptoms of schizophrenia have been well documented (Ruether 2010, 103–35; Earley 2006). The hope for the future is that we will continue to find ways to address the needs of those who live with chronic mental illness in ways that are more just and equitable for all.

The realities of schizophrenia require multiple kinds of interventions and responses. In the last several years, the pharmaceutical industry has continued to develop medications that address the symptoms of this disease.[5] Yet these drugs also have complicating side effects that make it difficult for some persons to see them as a positive resource in the treatment of their illness. The drugs tend to make people feel lethargic and less alive. Often there is weight gain or other side effects connected with some of the medication that require constant medical attention. For some, medication is experienced as something intrusive and unwanted (Woolis 2003, 30–31). And some people resort to theological reasons for not wanting to take medications, holding on to the assumption that such intervention is a sign of weakness or a way of not trusting the power of faith and prayer to heal. For others, medication is understood to be an unnatural way to alter one's brain or behavior. All of this does not mean to suggest that people ought not take their medication because they don't like to; it does suggest, however, that people have a right to be concerned about what is happening to their brains and their bodies as a result of the medication. Good pastoral care requires attentive conversation in these moments.

Resistance (in a negative sense) and compliance are two words used to describe the attitude persons with schizophrenia have in their response to drug therapy. Those who do not stay on their medications are often labeled as *resistant*, while those who take their medications are understood to be *compliant*. Both of these words place emphasis on behavioral or attitudinal perspectives rather than focusing on understanding why someone may choose to take—or not take—medications that have been prescribed. It is not uncommon for persons to be coerced into taking medication and then, when given the option, no longer use the pills that have been given to them. This back-and-forth behavior often leads persons to be labeled as "resistant." The bias in this language is that those who do not stay on their medication do so out of irrational choices rather than resistance to the side effects of the drugs or the feeling of losing control over their choices. "Nonadherence" (a less pejorative term) can be based on a rational weighing of the risks and benefits, but this should not be confused with a lack of awareness of illness. It is difficult to see how one who not does recognize behavior as abnormal or inappropriate can make an informed choice about taking or not taking a medication. In reading the biographies of people with schizophrenia, it is clear to see how the issue of taking medication plays a part in their resistance and fear of losing a vital, creative, and vibrant sense of their being. Sometimes the resistance is not to the medication alone, but to the systems around them or to the way in which they are being treated. Even while encouraging people to "stay on their medications," this kind of resistance ought not to be determined as completely negative.

Religious leaders who have a theological way to understand and talk about the use (and abuse) of medication can offer persons of faith an alternative vision. Not taking medication because of a belief that it is not part of God's will, or that one does not have enough faith, does not provide the kind of spiritual care that is most helpful. Listening and responding to the concerns of the person taking the medication offers a more faithful way of responding. While there are many who do not see the use of drugs as a panacea for a serious illness, it is also possible to understand them as part of the gift of God's wisdom embodied in the minds and knowledge of those within the medical profession. For those who struggle to live on medication because it takes away their creativity or their sense of "aliveness," it is important that religious leaders reflect on the importance of such creativity in human existence.

Working with the person, the family, and the medical profession might provide some alternative interpretations of living on medication for the rest of one's life. Increasing a sense of agency for those living with the disease means working with them around their experiences of medication and treatment. And recognizing that counseling and appropriate pastoral care can have a positive impact on one's use of any medication is also a gift in the process. After years of struggling with medication, Dana now understands that "meds are a means to an end; in other words, meds allow me to live a life of hope, and being in treatment is a way to ensure I remember that." Her attitude may not be universal, but working with a counselor alongside a psychiatrist has increased her sense of the importance of both medications and a larger treatment plan that includes her spiritual life.

One of the significant issues related to treatment for family members, friends, pastoral leaders, and caregivers is that of discerning when to intervene and when to let someone make decisions for one's own life that may, in the end, not be helpful or beneficial for recovery. Should one, for example, be forced to take medication? Or when should family members determine that it is not safe for their loved one to live on the streets and force him or her into a hospital or psychiatric facility? These are complicated questions with no single answer. Increasing someone's ability to make decisions on their own behalf is critical, yet this does not mean that one is left to make decisions all alone. Instead, it suggests that in the context of supportive community (whether it be in a treatment facility, with a psychiatrist and counseling, in a semi-independent living situation, or with family members), individuals who live with schizophrenia can be encouraged to make more decisions that are life giving for themselves while, at the same time, recognizing that need for safety of self and others. What is clear is that there will always be a healthy tension between encouraging individuals to make their own decisions while, at the same time, watching out for their safety and health as well as the safety and health of those around them (Ruether 2010, 130, 150; Woolis 2003, 222–23). Because violence toward self or others is so often part of the disease, it is important that care be taken in working with individuals and their families.

Recovery, Meaning Making, and Hope for the Future

Over the years, Dana has shifted her perception from one of surviving schizophrenia and seeing only the limitations it places on her life to one of recovery. She says, "Recovery is a long road interrupted by lots of detours that marks a continuous improvement in the quality of living." The authors of *The Complete Family Guide to Schizophrenia* note that recovery is a

> process rather than an outcome. . . . When you focus all your efforts on overcoming a major illness, you make yourself responsible for an outcome over which you don't have total control—a demoralizing and depersonalizing prospect. The process view of recovery, on the other hand, allows you to focus on making whatever difference you can in your daily experience of mental illness, its consequences, and related hardships. (Mueser and Gingerich 2006, 35)

Drawing on the language of recovery does not suggest that schizophrenia can be cured; rather, it notes that there are ways to shift our perspective on those living with this disease to "see them as competent human beings struggling to live productive lives and experiencing many different kinds of needs" (Woolis 2003, 219).

There are many aspects to recovery that can be significant in the lives of those most closely affected by schizophrenia. Social worker Rebecca Woolis suggests these "five sets of experiences from which they need to recover":

> 1) The symptoms of the illness. 2) Traumas occurring before or during the onset of symptoms. Sometimes these traumas are restimulated when people are restrained, arrested, or mistreated during the course of getting care. 3) The problematic effects of getting no treatment, inadequate treatment, or the wrong type of treatment. 4) The stigma and discrimination associated with mental illness. 5) Ineffective patterns of behaviors developed to cope with the other four. (Ibid., 220)

And, as Woolis notes, such recovery includes attending to "spirituality, feeling connected to something bigger than themselves and their illness."

Different levels of symptoms and differing abilities suggest that there are various ways to move into recovery. Assisting persons as they set realistic goals for their lives is an important part of this process and is a place where caregivers, friends, and families can sometimes be helpful. Developing social relationships, attending to places for work (either paid or volunteer), and planning for the future are some of the concrete aspects of living long term with this disease. Even basic needs—shelter, food, and meaningful health care—can become obstacles for living into the future. The number of persons who have little or no public safety nets around them can be witnessed by those who live on the streets, in the jail systems, or in other kinds of emergency-care facilities. Without community support, it is often impossible for those living with schizophrenia to access the various bureaucracies necessary for lifelong care.

Currently, Dana experiences some security because she lives in a family household; yet there are times when it takes everyone in the household to discern how to navigate state and federal mental health and health-care systems. She is unique in many ways because of the ability of family members to be able to support her. Parents who are the sole providers or who are aging often face mind-boggling fear as they recognize a public mental health system that is broken and cannot provide meaningful options for their children into the future.[6] Similarly,

Peter Earley's jarring examination of how the streets, jails, and emergency rooms become places to house persons living with schizophrenia is a sobering and challenging reminder of the need for more adequate health-care systems (Earley 2007). Finding "creative environments" (Ruether 2010, 161) for those living with schizophrenia is a challenge not simply for that individual or for the family, but for the communities in which we all live.

Recovery is important not only for the individuals who experience schizophrenia, but also for families and friends who are closely connected to the individual. Families, for example, may need to recover from their extreme sadness, frustration at the systems around them, feelings of helplessness and hopelessness, an experience of violence, the grief of seeing someone you love seem out of control, or the shame of living with mental illness in a family. Reading the stories and biographies of individuals and families offers glimpses into how much the disease can be an all-consuming, lifelong endeavor. These same stories offer moments of transcendence, however, as both those living with the disease, as well as their family and friends, turn from letting the disease be in charge of life to "self-responsibility, empowerment, and self-determination" (Woolis 2003, 221; Greider 2007). Increasing a sense of agency is important not only for those living with the disease itself, but for those of us who surround that person.

Recovery looks different for each individual and family. For some, recovery is being able to live in ways that promote independence, including having a place to live and a job. For others, recovery becomes a way to talk about finding meaningful relationships and engagement in the world, even within the limits of a lifelong disease. The chronic nature of schizophrenia requires a recovery process rather than simply hoping that people can exist or maintain a sense of "sanity."

The Need for Public Theology

Religious leaders and members are called upon to act as advocates in the more public face of a disease that strikes so many individuals and families. Speaking up, organizing for change, and participating in public conversations around mental health care are part of what it means to be a church in the world. Let us suggest three ways in which congregations and pastoral leaders can become part of a larger conversation that makes a difference in the lives of many.

First, the importance of education about mental health cannot be overstated. Conversations about schizophrenia belong in religious classes and in other places where people gather to think about the meaning of life and connect it to the bigger reality of spirituality. Having a good library that people can access, knowing resources in the community for support groups and mental health care, and inviting mental health professionals to think with a congregation about what they might be helped in knowing does a lot to offer care to individuals and families who experience schizophrenia. Those who live with the disease can be teachers, yet we ought not to be dependent on them for our knowledge. Understanding this disease in its complexity and providing a place to think theologically about its meaning in the context of faith is a primary starting place.

Second, challenging the "stigma" of mental illness during sermons or talking about persons whose lives are marked by psychosis with a sense of deep respect and dignity becomes part of the public voice of pastoral leaders. The inaccurate generalizations and preconceived beliefs about the mentally ill are largely based on ignorance or fear. Carrying a "stigma" is a visible and invisible mark of disgrace that can easily lead to discrimination. The church should be leading the way to model an acceptance that those living with mental illness just have another brain disorder, like those with Alzheimer's or epilepsy or a stroke.

Third, voicing concerns and talking about mental health issues in general from the pulpit, in worship, and in other aspects of a community's life can do a great deal to break the shame and silence that often greet individuals and families who live with this disease. Interpreting the struggle and pain of a public act of violence that was the result of someone hearing voices is one way to help people come to new awareness about the tragedies of schizophrenia. Because people do not know how to talk about "voices" and "visions" in complex ways, we tend to avoid the topic altogether until there is an opportunity to talk about only good voices and visions. Helping congregations think about what it is like to live with any chronic and lifelong disease, including schizophrenia, can help members know how to respond in caring ways rather than out of fear or anxiety.

Finally, it is important that the church be involved in the public conversations about health care, alternative living spaces for those with schizophrenia, and responding to the needs of those who are slipping through the cracks and ending up on the streets or in jails. By engaging in the collaborative efforts of others who are working toward restoration and recovery, pastoral leaders can make a difference in the lives of many. Members of faith communities and those engaged in pastoral care can learn much about recovery and living fully by listening carefully and deeply to the experiences of those living with schizophrenia and to their families.

Bibliography

Amador, Xavier. 2007. *I'm Not Sick, I Don't Need Help! How to Help Someone with Mental Illness Accept Treatment.* Peconic, N.Y.: Vida.

Capps, Donald. 2005. *Fragile Connections: Memoirs of Mental Illness for Pastoral Care Professionals.* St. Louis: Chalice.

Earley, Peter. 2006. *Crazy: A Father's Search through America's Mental Health Madness.* New York: Berkley.

Greider, Kathleen J. 2007. *Much Madness Is Divinest Sense: Wisdom in Memoirs of Soul-Suffering.* Cleveland: Pilgrim.

Horwitz, Allan V. 2002. *Creating Mental Illness.* Chicago: University of Chicago Press.

MacDonald, Angus W., and S. Charles Schulz. 2009. "What We Know: Findings That Every Theory of Schizophrenia Should Explain." *Schizophrenia Bulletin* 35 (3): 493–508.

Mueser, Kim T., and Susan Gingerich. 2006.*The Complete Family Guide to Schizophrenia.* New York: Guilford.

Ruether, Rosemary Radford, with David Ruether. 2010. *Many Forms of Madness: A Family's Struggle with Mental Illness and the Mental Health System.* Minneapolis: Fortress Press.

Saks, Elyn R. 2007. *The Center Cannot Hold: My Journey through Madness.* New York: Hyperion.

Smith, Daniel B. 2007. *Muses, Madmen, and Prophets: Rethinking the History, Science, and Meaning of Auditory Hallucination.* New York: Penguin.

Temes, Roberta. 2002. *Getting Your Life Back Together When You Have Schizophrenia.* Oakland: New Harbinger.

Torrey, E. Fuller. 2006. *Surviving Schizophrenia: A Manual for Families, Patients, and Providers.* 5th ed. New York: Harper.

Van Os, Jim, and Shitij Kapur. 2009. "Schizophrenia." *The Lancet* 374 (9690): 635–45.

Woolis, Rebecca. 2003. *When Someone You Love Has a Mental Illness: A Handbook for Family, Friends, and Caregivers.* Exp. and rev. ed. New York: Jeremy P. Tarcher/Penguin.

PERSONALITY DISORDERS

Donald W. Black / Janet Ramsey

4

Tom Myers, senior pastor of St. John's Lutheran Church, has called his synod office with a request for emergency help—the first time in fifteen years of ministry. He needs assistance coping with a parishioner who is not only impeding the congregation's care programs, but also causing him and his family distress. When Amy first began attending worship at St. John's a year ago, she was a welcomed addition. Her intense enthusiasm was appealing to Tom, leading him to suggest that she participate in several programs, including the lay visitation care team, and he welcomed her warmly whenever she unexpectedly stopped by his office. Amy told him of her difficult childhood and dramatic religious conversion experience, and he was quite moved by her story. A physically attractive woman, she was obviously wanting a close relationship, and he couldn't help being pleased by her referring to him as "the best pastor I've ever met." She told him that she had, at first, really liked the pastor at her previous church in another state but later began to dislike him because "he is such a hypocrite! He just pretended to care about me."

Soon things changed dramatically. First, Amy requested individual pastoral counseling, and then she started calling both the church office and the pastor's residence several times a week to relay a new insight about her past. One day, during a counseling session, she told Tom, with tears and great intensity, that she was in love with him, and that she could tell that he had the same feelings for her: "We can both feel it; we have a special connection." She didn't seem able to hear his gentle but firm denial of romantic feelings for her, and responded with a smile, "I can understand why you can't say you love me, since you are married and my pastor." A few days later, when he failed to return one of her phone calls immediately, she became angry, screamed at the church secretary on the phone, and called Tom's wife to tell her that Tom was in love with her. Several days later, when members of the care committee did not agree with one of her requests, she stormed out of that meeting.

In the weeks that followed, Amy continued to come to worship services and criticized the pastor publicly, hinting to congregational members that she and their pastor were having an affair. She also revealed private information about both care committee members and some of the persons she had visited. Finally, she wrote a long letter to the pastor, implying that she had thoughts of suicide in response to his rejection.

Pastor Myers now tells his bishop that he feels that he is in the midst of a nightmare. He knows he has to confront Amy about her behavior, see how serious she is about self-harm, and make a referral to a mental health professional—but he fears being alone with her. He needs help understanding what is going on and guidance for how to proceed. His ministry and the congregation's life together are at stake.

Clinical Understanding of Personality Disorder

Amy, the fictional parishioner in our case study, has a form of mental illness that differs from many others described in this book. She is clearly not simply depressed or anxious or abusing a substance, although all or none of these may be true—she has a personality disorder (PD), most likely borderline personality disorder (BPD). According to the DSM-IV TR, personality disorders (PDs) represent an enduring pattern of inner experience and behavior that "deviates markedly from the expectations of the individual's culture, is pervasive and inflexible, has an onset in adulthood, is stable over time, and leads to distress or impairment" (DSM-IV TR, 686). As a general rule, PDs represent long-term functioning and are not limited to episodes of illness, for example, a person in the midst of an episode of major depression.

These disorders are divided among three "clusters," each characterized by observable disorders whose criteria overlap (see Table 4.2, page 98). Cluster A ("odd cluster") consists of paranoid, schizoid, and schizotypal personality disorders and is characterized by a pervasive pattern of abnormal cognition (e.g., suspiciousness), self-expression (e.g., odd speech), or relating to others (e.g., seclusiveness). Cluster B ("dramatic cluster") consists of borderline, antisocial, histrionic, and narcissistic personality disorders; it is characterized by a pervasive pattern of violating social norms, impulsivity, excessive emotionality, grandiosity, or "acting out" (e.g., tantrums, self-abusive behavior, angry outbursts). Cluster C ("anxious cluster") consists of avoidant, dependent, and obsessive-compulsive personality disorders. They are characterized by a pervasive pattern of abnormal fears involving social relationships, separation, and need for control. Few persons have a "pure" case in which they meet criteria for only one PD. For example, a person with borderline personality disorder may also have narcissistic traits, as appears to be the case with Amy.

DSM-IV TR has a multiaxial coding system. Using that system, PDs are coded on Axis II in order to separate them from major mental disorders, which are coded on Axis I. A person, such as Amy, may have both Axis I and Axis II diagnoses. The most frequently diagnosed Axis I disorder in persons with PDs is major depression.

Research shows that 10 to 20 percent of the general population have a PD, with especially high rates in psychiatric samples, and in special populations such as offenders or substance abusers. Younger persons are at greater risk for a PD than older individuals, as prevalence diminishes with advancing age (Coid et al. 2006; Grant et al. 20042; Moran et al. 2006). PDs are often first evident in adolescence or early adulthood, and some PDs are more frequent in men (e.g., antisocial), while others are more frequent in women (e.g., borderline). PDs are generally considered stable and enduring, but recent follow-up studies reveal a more complex picture (Grilo et al. 2004; Shea et al. 2002; Zanarini et al. 2005). Over varying lengths of follow-up, fewer people will meet criteria for a PD, yet most will remain impaired in interpersonal, occupational, and other life domains. Follow-up studies also suggest that PDs tend to wax and wane in severity over time, often in response to significant or stressful life events (Grilo et al. 2000). PDs contribute to impaired social, interpersonal, and occupational functioning, as family life, marriages, and academic and work performance suffer. Rates of unemployment, homelessness, divorce and separation, domestic violence, and substance misuse are high in persons with PDs. As a group, individuals with PDs are at risk for early death from suicide or accidents.

The Origins of Personality Disorders

Early views held that PDs occurred when a person failed to progress through appropriate stages of psychosexual development. For example, fixation at the oral stage was thought to result in a personality characterized by demanding and dependent behavior (i.e., dependent personality disorder). More recent formulations suggest that PDs result from the interplay of genetic and environmental factors. Research shows that some PDs run in families (e.g., antisocial, borderline), but that as a group PDs have high heritability, as do certain personality traits, such as callousness or intimacy problems (Livesley et al. 1993; Torgerson et al. 2000; Cadoret et al. 1995). Risk for PD has been related to childhood maltreatment and is thought to cause difficulty in developing trust and intimacy—two dominant traits of people with a PD. An early home environment in which domestic abuse, divorce, separation, or parental absence occurs also can contribute to the risk of developing a PD.

Modern neuroimaging methods have shown that persons with BPD and antisocial personality disorder (ASPD) have alterations in brain structure and function (Lieb et al. 2004; Raine et al. 2000; Kiehl et al. 2001). For example, in borderline patients positron emission tomography has shown altered metabolism in prefrontal regions, including the anterior cingulate cortex, and reduced frontal and orbitofrontal volume has been reported, while antisocial persons have reduced prefrontal gray matter. Because these brain regions help regulate mood and behavior, impulsive aggression or emotional instability characteristic of these disorders could stem from functional abnormalities in these areas.

Cultural factors may also affect the development and expression of a PD. The best evidence comes from cross-cultural research showing very low rates of ASPD in Taiwan, China, and Japan. Paris points out that family structure in these East Asian cultures maintains high levels of cohesion (Paris 1996). Similarly, low rates of ASPD occur in Jewish families, presumably because of their strong family structures.

Assessment

The diagnosis of a PD requires a thorough personal and social history and a careful mental status examination. Structured interviews and self-report assessments are available to help with diagnosis but are mainly used in research. People with PDs often have little insight into the difficulties their maladaptive traits create for others and themselves. The clinician's task is to help the patient understand how the maladaptive traits contribute to ongoing difficulties, such as chronic depression, poor work performance, and interpersonal problems, and to help the patient to modify them.

The patient's history forms the most important basis for diagnosing a PD. For example, a clinician might ask about problems in interpersonal relationships, sense of self, work, affects, impulse control, and reality testing.

- How often do you have days when your mood is constantly changing?
- How do you feel when you are not the center of attention?
- Do you frequently insist on having what you want right now?
- Are you concerned that certain friends or coworkers are not really loyal or trustworthy?
- Are you concerned about saying the wrong things in front of other people?
- How often do you avoid getting to know someone because you are worried he or she may not like you?

Collateral information is important to obtain when possible. For example, a person with ASPD may deny criminal activity or minimize its significance, whereas information from relatives, the police, or a parole officer can be helpful in confirming its severity and extent.

One concern is that the PD diagnosis not be made prematurely. Patients with major depression can be socially anxious and dependent on others, traits that tend to recede or disappear altogether when the depression lifts. For that reason, caution needs to be exercised in making the diagnosis.

A Difficult Personality Disorder

Amy, in the opening case study, suffers from BPD, a PD that tends to draw more attention than others. Perhaps the high level of interest results from the tendency of some PDs to create interpersonal chaos. BPD is directed inward as the individual copes with feelings and affects through self-destructive or self-harm behaviors. Below we discuss the symptoms and manifestations of this disorder, reflect on our case study, and discuss implications for both clinical management and pastoral care.

Borderline personality disorder was introduced in DSM-III in 1980 to describe individuals having a pervasive pattern of mood instability, unstable and intense interpersonal relationships, impulsivity, inappropriate or intense anger, lack of control of anger, recurrent suicidal threats and gestures, self-mutilating behavior, marked and persistent identity disturbance, chronic feelings of emptiness or boredom, and frantic efforts to avoid real or imagined abandonment (see Table 4.1, page 97). Some patients experience transient paranoid ideation or dissociative symptoms. Early theorists considered BPD to be a precursor of schizophrenia, and the term *borderline schizophrenia* was created to describe people who experienced transient episodes of psychosis during periods of regression or during psychotherapy.

The diagnosis of BPD overlaps with many other PDs, especially the schizotypal, histrionic, and antisocial types. One of the more common PDs among psychiatric patients, its frequency in the general population has been estimated at 1 to 2 percent (Swartz et al. 1990; Lenzenweger et al. 2007).

Up to three-quarters of borderline patients engage in deliberate self-harm (e.g., cutting, burning, overdoses), and 10 percent eventually kill themselves (Black et al. 2004; Soloff et al. 2000). Better long-term outcome is associated with higher intelligence, self-discipline, and social support from friends and relatives. Anger, antisocial behavior, suspiciousness, and vanity are traits associated with poor outcome. Patients frequently have co-occurring (additional and secondary) disorders, including major depression, dysthymia, and various anxiety and substance-use disorders.

There is little agreement on the appropriate treatment for BPD. While individual psychotherapy has been the mainstay of treatment for borderline patients, the focus of this treatment has gradually moved from psychodynamic to cognitive-behavioral models. Patients with BPD can form an intense transference, and countertransference therefore can be a problem, because these patients often stimulate intense feelings of frustration, guilt, or anger in their therapists. There is an unfortunate irony in the fact that individuals with BPD fear abandonment from others, and yet they react to perceived signs of being abandoned in a manner that alienates those who try to be supportive.

Cognitive-behavioral therapy (CBT) has been used with borderline patients and may be effective in correcting dysfunctional attitudes and ambivalent perceptions of others and oneself. There are now several evidence-based group treatments. Dialectical Behavior Therapy (DBT) is the most widely discussed group treatment, and is delivered in an intensive year-long program that includes both individual and group therapy formats. There are other group treatments, including a program called STEPPS, which is also based on CBT principles and is relatively easy to teach and administer; mentalizing therapy, which is based on psychoanalytic principles; and schema-focused therapy, which is a hybrid of psychoanalytic principles and CBT (Zanarini 2004; APA 2001; NICE 2009; Lieb et al. 2010).

Because there are no standard or proven medications for BPD, pharmacotherapy tends to focus on the patient's target symptoms. Selective serotonin reuptake inhibitor antidepressants such as fluoxetine may be helpful in treating coexisting depression. Antipsychotics can help to treat perceptual distortions, anger dyscontrol, and suicidal behaviors. Mood stabilizers, such as lithium or valproate can be useful in treating mood instability. Because suicide attempts are frequent in these patients, physicians should be cautious about prescribing any medication that can be dangerous in overdose. Benzodiazepine tranquilizers should be avoided, except perhaps for short-term use (e.g., days to weeks), because they can cause behavioral disinhibition and may be habit forming.

The case study of Amy above is consistent with many aspects of BPD. She displays lack of control over her anger, displays emotional intensity and impulsivity, and experiences turbulent interpersonal relationships characterized by alternately overidealizing and devaluing other persons—in this case, her pastors.

Pastoral Caregiving Understandings of Personality Disorders

The difficulties PDs present to pastoral caregivers are implicit in the definition offered by Black above, namely their enduring, inflexible, pervasive, counterintuitive, and highly distressing nature. It is typical to feel moved and overwhelmed when caring for and counseling these persons, or even when attempting to integrate them into the life of a congregation, since the impact of their behaviors extends far beyond the context of their individual psychology. As Amy's story exemplifies, the results for both religious leaders and their congregations can be dramatic and dangerous. A resulting unhealthy climate in a religious community, together with the distress of congregational caregivers, can, in turn, result in stagnated programs, interpersonal conflict, and clergy burnout. An entire community can be sabotaged through the crises that are created, both those that are visible and those occurring behind closed doors. Ironically, professionals in religious organizations, whose "basic stance of empathy, charity, and unrequited giving" (Ciarrocchi 1993, 18) often find that their compassionate personalities are themselves barriers to effective management of BPD. Clearly, Tom wanted to be helpful to Amy and was intrigued by her story. Yet because Amy misinterpreted this interest, Tom's empathy only exaggerated her problematic behavior.

As a seminary professor with a background in both parish work and marriage and family therapy, I have found that most seminarians are eager to learn about people with PDs. They recognize their need to understand the dynamics created by persons who seem to bring disorder into a congregation simply by being present. Yet seminaries typically require only a few classes in pastoral care and in no way prepare clergy to work clinically with these seriously impaired persons. Congregational life is such that public leaders cannot avoid interactions with those who display a wide range of mental health impairments, including PDs. In fact, while some PDs, such as schizoid and ASPD, tend to be less common in religious groups, others, including BPD, appear to be increasingly prevalent—not only in members of these congregations, but also in their leaders (Sperry 1998).

Becoming aware of the dominant features of each disorder, and of PDs in general, is a crucial first step. It is also important to become knowledgeable about potential theological issues involved with each disorder, and to learn what pastoral interventions and attitudes are more likely to be helpful than others (see Table 4.2, page 98). The goal for any professional caregiver must be to first do no harm, and only secondly to discern how best to offer continued pastoral accompaniment after a referral has been made. Caring for the partners, friends, and family members who are seriously affected by living with those with PDs (and who are more likely to seek our care) is another crucial part of this ministry.

Theological Issues

A handout I give seminary students begins by acknowledging my theological perspective on personality disorders: "We are all children of God, who are unique and cannot be adequately described by clinical language. Neither do we fit neatly into a diagnostic box. Whatever our personality and/or emotional health, we are all capable of change and stand in need of God's love and forgiveness." As are many pastoral theologians, I am always a bit uncomfortable with diagnostic labels, even as I recognize their usefulness. I also recognize that, as Black reports, diagnoses are now understood as fluid over the course of the lifespan.

But the faith issues facing persons who have a PD are far more challenging for them than any we encounter as their caregivers. The theological shelter they try to build must be constructed precisely during the emotional and spiritual tornado that is their everyday life. Furthermore, an openness to belief change so important for spiritual formation and spiritual resiliency in people of faith (Miner 2007) is often not available to these persons. For persons with BPD, issues of splitting (vs. integration) and fear (vs. trust) are particularly problematic, impeding the development of a healthy theology. A third deficiency, rigid defenses, and thus a lack of imagination (Lewin and Schulz 1992), reflects a fractured inner world and, among other costs, impedes the healthy use of religious transitional objects as sources of hope, playfulness, and comfort.

Paradox

The reconciliation of apparent opposites, including hope and reality, change and rootedness, closeness and distance, has been described as a vital aspect of spiritual resiliency (Ramsey and Blieszner 2011). This ability to integrate, or at least to tolerate, apparent paradox (e.g., dynamics and change, destiny and freedom, integration and differentiation [Tillich 1967]) is simply not available to those with a BPD. Rather, an all-or-nothing vision results from a lifelong tendency to split off black and white, good and bad, true and false (Lewin and Schulz 1992). This radical splitting hinders the ongoing formation of a mature faith and destroys the fruits of the Spirit valued in all religious traditions, such as patience, forgiveness, and peace. In all religions, the capacity to hold on to visions of gratitude, peace, and love are crucial goals, but clergy working with persons with BPDs soon discover a very different way to be in the world. Here each day is dominated by disappointment, anger, and fear—particularly fears of losing someone or of fusing with them. Like other defenses, especially in persons with BPD, this splitting is a lifelong pattern (albeit if less intense in the later years) and results from a pattern of disorganized attachments (Holmes 2004). It is not difficult to imagine how this can lead to spiritual exhaustion.

Nevertheless, mature and knowledgeable pastoral counselors can provide a kind of holding environment that, over time, serves as a bulwark in the storm and a testimony to God's faithful and constant love. If the religious environment is also a place where firm limits have been set and stability endures, one hopes that gradual progress toward more wholeness can be achieved over time (Sperry 1998) and as one part of a more inclusive program of care.

Trust

As Black states, two dominant traits of persons like Amy are difficulties in developing trust and intimacy—probable results of childhood traumas. Since trust is foundational for the formation of religious beliefs and behaviors (Küng 1966), an individual with BPD who is motivated to participate in the thought and practices of a religious community is challenged in core ways. Like therapists, pastoral counselors' efforts to develop a trusting relationship are appropriate—if for no other reasons than to assist the person to begin to trust God. Yet a seemingly endless series of crises, present for many years, make this a precarious process.

Transitional Religious Objects

One of the most important ways that religious traditions contribute to the art of living is through providing traditional transitional objects—crosses, prayer shawls, the star and crescent in Islam. Persons with BPD, however, may not be able to make inner use of these objects, or even secular transitional objects such as those in arts, because they remain stuck at more concrete levels of development.

In their exploration of BPD from an object relations perspective, Lewin and Schulz write, "By a lack of creativity, we do not mean a deficiency in the ability to paint, sculpt, dance, or write . . . rather we are . . . referring to the inner process that weaves the garb that the world of subjective experience wears for each individual . . . that everyday all-day long process of creativity that gives living its special flavor for each individual" (Lewin and Schulz 1992, 64). Perhaps this lack of creativity is the most serious problem facing religiously inclined persons with a PD, and particularly those with BPD.

Implications for Pastoral Care: Boundaries

The need to maintain clear and consistent boundaries with someone who has a PD is less complicated in a noncongregational (e.g., clinical) setting. In the life of a congregation, where persons frequently come together socially as well as for worship and community service, boundaries can be easily confused, especially by the person suffering this disorder. The congregational leader's task, therefore, must be to navigate this complex environment with wisdom, tact, and consistency. Avoiding intimate environments, for example, not inviting the distressed person into one's own home and keeping the door open in the church or synagogue office, are important first steps. But avoiding personal topics and in no way allowing the person with a PD to become the one who meets the clergyperson's needs for friendship and/or intimacy, are also crucial.

Boundaries are more easily maintained when a pastoral counselor receives consultation from others. Pastor Tom Myers might have called his religious resource center or adjudicatory office earlier or simply picked up the phone and consulted with a mental health professional with expertise in this area. In attempting to avoid doing harm, clergy and lay caregivers should be aware that the *interior* nature of issues in persons whose personalities have lead to lifelong impaired thoughts and behaviors are, ironically, often echoed in the *interior* lives of those who care for them. Beyond lack of basic knowledge of the disorders, a pastoral caregivers' own hidden needs and anxieties (his "countertransference") may well present the biggest challenge in coping with these relationships. Countertransference typically results in confusion, fear, wanting to rescue, or, conversely, wanting to run, sexual attraction, and anger (Frances 1987). Too often, a Savior complex, a need to fix and to rescue, leads to a need to see quick and obvious results—which is never possible with this population, even for those with psychiatric training. Another need, to control the behavior of others, inevitably sets caregivers up for failure in these relationships and leads to early burnout. Emotional exhaustion and enmeshment are more common in clergy with neurotic needs (Miner 2007). Thus a caregiver finds herself anxious and/or depressed, and, like Tom, wondering how it all happened. Even a more seasoned pastor can display signs of anxiety and burnout when he is trying to "go it alone" and meet needs he does not really understand—needs in both himself and the person with a PD.

In the case of BPD, and because of the personality types of persons drawn to ministry, there is always the danger that can lead to the worst possible outcome—pastoral sexual abuse, which Pamela Cooper-White calls "soul stealing" (Cooper-White 1991). Our need to be loved and affirmed by those we serve, and our unawareness of our own susceptibility, combine to make pastoral caregivers highly vulnerable to either unethical misuses of power or to the appearance thereof, as Tom Myers discovered. Caregivers, including clergy, must be self-aware, knowledgeable, and proactive. Also important is the caregiver's spiritual grounding—a firm sense that personal identify that is dependent, not on the affirmation or attention of others (such as Amy's praise), but through a mature, vocational sense of who and whose we are, in relationship to God.

When I teach a seminary class on personality disorders, I show the students the familiar scene from the movie *Fatal Attraction* in which Alex (played by actress Glenn Close) changes, without warning, from passionate lover to enraged, knife-bearing enemy. My hope is that, at the very least, students will be frightened enough in watching this scene to resist any temptation to become romantically involved with someone with a BPD! I also hand out a sheet describing challenges for church leaders related to other PDs (see Table 4.2, page 98).

Implications for Pastoral Care: Suicide Prevention

In addition to boundary issues, suicide, particularly with BPD, is a very real risk, as Black notes. Mortality rates are high, and this is particularly true when there is comorbidity with a major depressive episode (Black et al. 2004; Paris 2002). Pastor Myers may either overestimate or underestimate Amy's veiled suicide threats, depending on his own personal defenses and educational background (every pastor should know the warning signs and at risk factors for suicide prevention). Too often clergy are reluctant to ask directly about someone's plans for self-harm. A caregiver can simply ask, without being overly dramatic or naïvely apologetic, "How bad does it get for you?" or "Have you ever thought about hurting yourself?" The myth that people will become suicidal simply by being asked if they are having suicidal thoughts is absurd, yet it often prevents persons without clinical experience from asking these basic and life-saving questions. Being direct is simply part of what all professionals must and can do, including those of us in ministry settings.

Making Referrals

Because most caregivers are not prepared to counsel persons with severe PDs, it is always wise to refer these persons to someone with appropriate educational background and clinical experience, such as a psychiatrist, clinical psychologist, a licensed therapist, or a certified pastoral counselor. These professionals may also suggest group therapy or support, which can be helpful especially when the other persons in the group have a similar PD (Pompili et al. 2005).

Making a successful referral can itself be difficult, however, since projective defenses (that is, imaging negative qualities in another person rather than in oneself) are often dominant in persons with PDs. Encouraging someone with BPD or another serious PD to seek professional help takes wisdom, sensitivity, and awareness of the common defenses associated with each disorder. In the case of persons such as Amy, it is easy to see how the process of referral could easily be interpreted as rejection—Tom will need to be prepared for an angry reaction.

When a pastoral caregiver does offer formal pastoral counseling to a person with BPD, in addition to maintaining boundaries and making a professional referral, it is best to focus on one specific issue, such as a theological problem that has arisen in the person's life. It is also best to limit the number of formal sessions and to remember to consult and to refer.

A final caveat: I have found that clergy and future clergy can become overly interested in PDs and be tempted to diagnose everyone from their mother-in-law to church council presidents. It is important not only to discourage this behavior (I do that playfully in class), but also to remember the very real difference between traits and disorders. Most of us have, for example, narcissistic, borderline, and dependent traits at one time or another in our lives, especially during times of crises, but fortunately these traits do not dominate our personalities or make it impossible to live full and healthy lives. For persons whose lives are persistently and extensively colored by one or more of these disorders, however, life is very different. Caring for these persons in ways appropriate to our particular vocation, whether as a psychiatrist or as a pastoral care provider, is part of our responsibility as members of a humane society, even if we are not members of a particular religious tradition. It is thus an endeavor for which we must prepare—psychologically, educationally, and spiritually.

Table 4.1. DSM-IV-TR Diagnostic Criteria for Borderline Personality Disorder

A pervasive pattern of instability of interpersonal relationships, self-image, and affects, and marked impulsivity beginning by early adulthood and present in a variety of contexts, as indicated by five (or more) of the following:

(1) frantic efforts to avoid real or imagined abandonment

(2) a pattern of unstable and intense interpersonal relationships characterized by alternating between extremes of idealization and devaluation

(3) identity disturbance: markedly and persistently unstable self-image or sense of self

(4) impulsivity in at least two areas that are potentially self-damaging (e.g., spending, sex, substance abuse, reckless driving, binge eating)

(5) recurrent suicidal behavior, gestures, or threats, or self-mutilating behavior

(6) affective instability due to a marked reactivity of mood (e.g., intense episodic dysphoria, irritability, or anxiety usually lasting a few hours and only rarely more than a few days)

(7) chronic feelings of emptiness

(8) inappropriate, intense anger or difficulty controlling anger (e.g., frequent displays of temper, constant anger, recurrent physical fights)

(9) transient, stress-related paranoid ideation or severe dissociative symptoms

Table 4.2. Core Features of DSM-IV Personality Disorders and Summary of Related Pastoral Issues

Cluster A: The Eccentric Disorders

Paranoid   • Distrust, suspiciousness—"I don't believe you!"   • Possible problems for the church leader: negative projections, marital issues often present, difficult to refer.   • Suggestions: check up on stories (e.g., spouse's infidelity?). Don't argue or agree with illusions.
Schizoid   • Social detachment, restricted emotions—"I don't want to be with you."   • Possible problems for the church leader: few interactions; concerned family more likely to seek care and counsel.   • Suggestions: don't personalize detachment; develop a formal relationship if possible.
Schizotypal   • Interpersonal deficits, cognitive distortions, eccentricities—"You don't understand me!"   • Possible problems for the church leader: how to relate to the person in the back row who is acting in a bizarre way.   • Suggestions: combine compassion and realism.

Cluster B: The Dramatic Disorders

Antisocial   • Disregard for rights of others, irresponsibility—"I'll get what I want, no matter what."   • Experience no guilt for violating the rights of others; reckless; no sense of remorse.   • Possible problems for the church leader: monitor possibilities for theft; counsel and care for their victims.

- Suggestions: don't assume understanding of or concern for morality; be direct in confrontations; seek support from law authorities when necessary.

Borderline
- Emotional instability, impulsivity—"I love you; I hate you; don't leave me."
- Possible problems for the church leader: idealize or demonize authorities; seductive behavior; test boundaries constantly; high rates of suicide.
- Suggestions: highly structured and limited relations; consult often and refer as soon as possible; clear and consistent communication. *Special warning: Always work closely with a mental health professional because of the constant danger of boundary violations and/or suicide.*

Histrionic
- Attention-seeking, shallow emotions—"Look at me!"
- Possible problems for the church leader: expect seductive self-dramatization and seductive attempts for rescue and attention.
- Suggestions: maintain firm boundaries; remain matter of fact and realistic; make short-term pastoral counseling commitments only.

Narcissistic
- Grandiosity, need for admiration—"I'm special."
- Possible problems for the church leader: initiate power struggles; expect you to see them at their convenience; expect lots of recognition for even minor contributions.
- Suggestions: remain empathetic yet honest; keep relationship rather formal; give credit as appropriate; stay focused on the immediate problem; build rapport slowly.

Cluster 3: The Anxious Disorders

Avoidant
- Social inhibition, inadequacy, hypersensitivity to negative feedback—"I'm afraid of you."
- Possible problems for the church leader: will avoid activities that involve significant interpersonal contact (e.g., teenager in the youth group who can't join in).
- Suggestions: allow opportunities for church work that permits contribution with limited social contact; don't force group participation; use gentle praise and be a safe friend.

Dependent
- Need to be taken care of—"Save me! Help me!"
- Possible problems for the church leader: common disorder among religious people; highly other-directed, so need constant reassurances; may agree with you and volunteer for projects to receive your approval; abandonment and/or separation issues may make difficulties during clergy relocation; may need extra support during breakups.
- Suggestions: refer for relaxation education; give limited practical help but avoid becoming the rescuer; model independence and assertiveness; suggest self-confidence building activities such as travel, a new job.

Obsessive-Compulsive
- Orderliness, perfectionism, control—"I must be perfect and perfectly organized."
- Possible problems for church leaders: challenging on committees, especially finance or property; not team players; have change, hold on to money; come to see you to complain about others' incompetence.
- Suggestions: don't make chair of your finance or pastoral relationships committee; find a spot where he or she can work alone, where details matter most; make use of your authority but avoid power struggles.

Bibliography

American Psychiatric Association. 2000. *Diagnostic and Statistical Manual of Mental Disorder.* 4th ed., Text Revision (DSM-IV TR). Washington, D.C.: American Psychiatric Pub.

———. 2001. "Practice Guideline for the Treatment of Patients with Borderline Personality Disorder." *American Journal of Psychiatry* 158 (suppl. 1): 1–52.

Black, D. W., N. Blum, B. Pfohl, et al. 2004. "Suicidal Behavior in Borderline Personality Disorder: Prevalence, Risk Factors, Prediction, and Prevention." *Journal of Personality Disorders* 18 (3): 226–39.

———, J. Allen, D. St. John, et al. 2009. "Predictors of Response to Systems Training for Emotional Predictability and Problem Solving (STEPPS) for Borderline Personality Disorder: An Exploratory Study." *ACTA Psychiatrica Scandinavica* 120 (1): 53–61.

Buchsbaum, Monte S., Stanley Yang, Erin Hazlett, et al. 1997. "Ventricular Volume and Asymmetry in Schizotypal Personality Disorder and Schizophrenia Assessed with Magnetic Resonance Imaging." *Schizophrenia Research* 27 (1): 45–53.

Cadoret, Remi J., William R. Yates, Ed Troughton, et al. 1995. "Genetic-Environment Interaction in the Genesis of Aggressivity and Conduct Disorders." *Archives of General Psychiatry* 52: 916–24.

Capps, Donald, and Nathan Steven Carlin. 2007. "Mental Illness Publication in Major Pastoral Care Journals from 1950–2003." *Pastoral Psychology* 55 (5): 593–99.

Caspi, Avshalom, Joseph McClay, Terrie E. Moffitt, et al. 2002. "Role of Genotype in the Cycle of Violence in Maltreated Children." *Science* 297 (5582): 851–54.

Ciarrocchi, Joseph W. 1993. *A Minister's Handbook of Mental Disorders.* Mahwah, N.J.: Paulist.

Clarkin, John F., and Kenneth N. Levy. 2006. "Psychotherapy for Patients with Borderline Personality Disorder: Focusing on the Mechanisms of Change." *Journal of Clinical Psychology* 62 (4): 405–10.

Coccaro, Emil F., Richard J. Kavoussi, Yvette I. Sheline, et al. 1996. "Impulsive Aggression in Personality Disorder Correlates with

Tritiated Paroxetine Binding in the Platelet." *Archives of General Psychiatry* 53 (6): 531–36.

Coid, Jeremy, Min Yang, Peter Tyrer, Amanda Roberts, et al. 2006. "Prevalence and Correlates of Personality Disorder in Great Britain." *British Journal of Psychiatry* 188: 423–43.

Cooper-White, Pamela. February 20, 1991. "Soul Stealing: Power Relations in Pastoral Sexual Abuse." *The Christian Century*, 196–99.

Crowe, Marie. 2004. "Never Good Enough—Part 1: Shame or Borderline Personality Disorder?" *Journal of Psychiatric Mental Health Nursing* 11: 327–34.

Fonagy, Peter, and Anthony W. Bateman. 2007. "Mentalizing and Borderline Personality Disorder." *Journal of Mental Health* 16 (1): 83–101.

Frances, Allen J. 1987. *DSM-III Personality Disorders: Diagnosis and Treatment.* New York: BMA Audio Cassettes.

Grant, Bridget F., Frederick S. Stinson, Deborah A. Dawson, et al. 2004. "Co-occurrence of 12-month Alcohol and Drug Use Disorders and Personality Disorders in the United States: Results from the National Epidemiological Survey on Alcohol and Related Conditions." *Archives of General Psychiatry* 61: 361–68.

Grilo, Carlos M., Thomas H. McGlashan, and Andrew E. Skodol. 2000. "Stability and Course of Personality Disorders." *Psychiatric Quarterly* 71 (4): 291–307.

———, Charles A. Sanislow, John G. Gunderson, et al. 2004. "Two-year Stability and Change of Schizotypal, Borderline, Avoidant, and Obsessive-Compulsive Personality Disorders." *Journal of Consulting and Clinical Psychology* 72 (5): 767–75.

Hoffman, Perry D., Alan E. Fruzzetti, and Ellie A. Buteau. 2007. "Understanding and Engaging Families: An Education, Skills and Support Program for Relatives Impacted by Borderline Personality Disorder." *Journal of Mental Health* 16 (1): 69–82.

Holmes, Jeremy. 2004. "Disorganized Attachment and Borderline Personality Disorder: A Clinical Perspective." *Attachment and Human Development* 6 (2): 181–90.

Janis, Irene Belle, Heather Barnett Veague, and Erin Driver-Linn. 2006. "Possible Selves and Borderline Personality Disorders." *Journal of Clinical Psychology* 62 (3): 387–94.

Kernberg, Otto F. 1984. *Severe Personality Disorders*. New Haven: Yale University Press.

Kiehl, Kent A., Andra M. Smith, Robert D. Hare, et al. 2001. "Limbic Abnormalities in Affective Processing in Criminal Psychopaths as Revealed by Functional Magnetic Resonance Imaging." *Biological Psychiatry* 50: 677–84.

Küng, Hans. 1966. *On Being a Christian*. Garden City, N.Y.: Doubleday.

LaMothe, Ryan. 1999. "Trauma and Development: A Faith Perspective." *Pastoral Psychology* 47 (5): 373–87.

Langley, G. C., and H. Klopper. 2005. "Trust as a Foundation for the Therapeutic Intervention for Patients with Borderline Personality Disorder." *Journal of Psychiatric Mental Health Nursing* 12 (1): 23–32.

Lenzenweger, Mark F., Michael C. Lane, Armand W. Loranger, et al. 2007. "DSM-IV Personality Disorders in the National Comorbidity Survey Replication." *Biologic Psychiatry* 62 (6): 553–64.

Lewin, Roger A., and Clarence Schulz. 1992. *Losing and Fusing: Borderline Transitional Object and Self Relations*. Northvale, N.J.: Jason Aronson.

Lieb, Klaus, Mary C. Zanarini, Christian Schmahl, et al. 2004. "Borderline Personality Disorder." *The Lancet* 364: 453–61.

Lieb, Klaus, Birgit Völlm, Gerta Rücker, et al. 2010. "Pharmacotherapy for Borderline Personality Disorder: Cochrane Systematic Review of Randomised Trials." *British Journal of Psychiatry* 196: 4–12.

Livesley, W. John, Kerry L. Jang, Douglas N. Jackson, et al. 1993. "Genetic and Environmental Contributions to Dimensions of Personality Disorder." *American Journal of Psychiatry* 150 (12): 1826–31.

Miner, Maureen H. 2007. "Burnout in the First Year of Ministry: Personality and Belief Style as Important Predictors." *Mental Health, Religion, and Culture* 10 (1): 17–29.

Moran, Paul, Carolyn Coffey, Anthony Mann, et al. 2006. "Personality and Substance Use Disorders in Young Adults." *British Journal of Psychiatry* 188: 374–79.

National Institute for Health and Clinical Excellence (NICE). January 2009. "Borderline Personality Disorder: Treatment and Management." http://guidance.nice.org.uk/CG78.

Paris, Joel. 1996. *Social Factors in the Personality Disorders: A Biopsychosocial Approach to Etiology and Treatment.* Cambridge: Cambridge University Press.

———. 2002. "Chronic Suicidality among Patients with Borderline Personality Disorder." *Psychiatry Services* 53 (6): 738–42.

Pompili, Maurizio, Paolo Girardi, Amedeo Ruberto, et al. 2005. "Suicide in Borderline Personality Disorder: A Meta-Analysis." *Nordic Journal of Psychiatry* 59 (5): 319–24.

Raine. Adrian, Todd Lencz, Susan Bihrle, et al. 2000. "Reduced Prefrontal Gray Matter Volume and Reduced Autonomic Activity in Antisocial Personality Disorder." *Archives of General Psychiatry* 57: 119–27.

Ramsey, Janet L., and Rosemary M. Blieszner. 2011. *Spiritual Resiliency and Aging: Hope, Relationality, and the Creative Self.* Amityville, N.Y.: Baywood.

Scarpa, Angela, and Adrian Raine. 1997. "Psychophysiology of Anger and Violent Behavior." The *Psychiatric Clinics of North America* 20 (2): 375–403.

Shea, M. Tracie, Robert Stout, John G. Gunderson, et al. 2002. "Short-Term Diagnostic Stability of Schizotypal, Borderline, Avoidant, and Obsessive-Compulsive Personality Disorders." *American Journal of Psychiatry* 159: 2036–41.

Soloff, Paul H., Kevin G. Lynch, Thomas M. Kelly, et al. 2000. "Characteristics of Suicide Attempts of Patients with Major Depressive Episode and Borderline Personality Disorder: A Comparative Study." *American Journal of Psychiatry* 157: 601–8.

Sperry, Len. 1998. "The Borderline Minister." *Human Development* 19 (4): 21–26.

Swartz, M. S., D. Blazer, L. George, et al. 1990. "Estimating the Prevalence of Borderline Personality Disorder in the Community." *Journal of Personality Disorders* 4 (3): 257–72.

Tillich, Paul. 1967. *Systematic Theology.* Chicago: University of Chicago Press.

Torgerson, Svenn, Sissel Lygren, Per Anders Øien, et al. 2000. "A Twin Study of Personality Disorders." *Comprehensive Psychiatry* 41 (6): 416–25.

Trestman, Robert L., Richard S. E. Keefe, Vivian Mitropoulou, et al. 1995. "Cognitive Function and Biologic Correlates of Cognitive Performance in Schizotypal Personality Disorder." *Psychiatry Research* 59 (1-2): 127–36.

Vaughan, Richard P. 1994. *Pastoral Counseling and Personality Disorders.* Kansas City, Mo.: Sheed & Ward.

Zanarini, Mary C. 2004. "Update on Pharmacotherapy of Borderline Personality Disorder." *Current Psychiatry Reports* 6 (1): 66–70.

———, Frances R. Frankenburg, John Hennen, et al. 2005. "The McLean Study of Adult Development (MSAD): Overview and Implications of the First Six Years of Prospective Follow-up." *Journal of Personality Disorders* 19 (5): 505–23.

SUBSTANCE-USE DISORDERS

Sheila Specker / Robert H. Albers

5

Mary, fifty-eight years old and a prominent member of your faith com-munity, approaches you with a concern about her husband, Dan. She wants help in deciding what to do. She is embarrassed and upset and tells you that her husband has been under a lot of stress and has been drinking too much. He has resisted her attempts to talk to him and instead blames her for contributing to his stress. Mary has noticed a personality change in Dan over the past several months. She does not want to meet friends socially because she is afraid that he might embar-rass her and them. There is no one she feels comfortable talking to but is hopeful that you might be helpful since you know her husband.

Understanding Substance Use and Addiction

This scenario is common, as it highlights some of the typical issues of someone with an alcohol problem: a concerned spouse who feels dis-traught; distress when discussing the alcohol problem with her husband; the progression of the problem in her husband; his resistance in acknowl-edging a problem; and his blaming. In addition to the drinking, stress has presented itself as a possible mental health problem. The dilemmas of this situation constitute a major issue for caregivers in ministry, since the phenomenon of addiction is pervasive in faith communities as well as in the whole of society.

Brief History of Alcohol

Records of alcohol use date back to at least nine thousand years ago in the Middle East and China. Alcohol was made from rice and various grains and was consumed as part of a daily diet as well as for medicinal or religious purposes. It is the most commonly abused psychoactive substance, and its use is governed by societal and religious beliefs. Dr. Benjamin Rush, in the 1700s, was the first American physician to chronicle the progression of the disease of alcoholism (called drunkenness) and claim that proper medical treatment could restore health. Although the characteristics of biological predisposition, tolerance, and disease progression were already noted in the 1800s, "treatments" were provided in inebriate asylums and consisted of enforced abstinence, medication-assisted detoxification, and lengthy convalescence. The "modern alcoholism movement" was initiated by the birth of Alcoholics Anonymous (AA) in 1935. Community-based residential treatment was pioneered by Minnesota treatment programs at Willmar State Hospital, Hazelden, and Pioneer House in the late 1940s and 1950s. This "Minnesota Model" was based on education and professionally led peer groups in a residential setting. The emergence of addiction medicine as a specialty occurred through the establishment of two professional organizations now called the American Society of Addiction Medicine, established in 1967, followed by the American Academy of Addiction Psychiatry.

Definitions

The terms *addiction*, *substance dependence*, *alcoholism*, and *chemical dependency* are often used interchangeably. These terms refer to a severest stage of the illness of substance-use problems. The DSM-IV manual categorizes substance-use disorders into substance abuse and substance dependence and includes both alcohol and drug use disorders. The term *abuse* is often used incorrectly to refer to any substance-use problem. For alcohol, use is on a continuum, with one end being abstainers and low-risk drinkers. These constitute 7 percent of the population. Social drinkers are included in this category of drinking; drinking is usually not the focus of the occasion and is not problematic. Social drinking also occurs in a cultural context with some societies more or less permissive than others. A drink is defined as twelve ounces of beer, five ounces of wine, or one and a half ounces of 80-proof liquor. The National Institute of Health has defined low-risk drinking by daily and weekly amounts: no more than three drinks a day for women, four drinks per day for men; and no more than seven drinks per week for women and fourteen drinks per week for men. Greater than these amounts constitute "at-risk" drinking and increases the likelihood of having alcohol abuse or dependence from fewer than one in one hundred for low-risk drinkers to almost one in two for those who exceed both the daily and weekly limit. It also increases risk for developing medical problems. Notably, lower levels of drinking or abstinence are indicated in certain medical or psychiatric conditions, in older people, or in the presence of certain medications. The term *dependence* can be confusing: it may either refer to a physiological state produced by continuous use of certain medications or the presence of an addiction. The former scenario should be called "physiological dependence" and not be classified under DSM substance dependence if it does not have the other components of addiction (see Diagnosis, below).

Epidemiology

Alcohol-use disorders are extremely common according to the National Epidemiologic Survey on Alcohol and Related Conditions (NESARC). Lifetime prevalence of alcohol abuse and dependence, as described in the DSM-IV, is 17.8 percent and 12.5 percent, respectively (Hasin et al. 2007). For drug abuse and dependence, the lifetime prevalence is 7.7 percent and 2.6 percent, respectively. The gender ratio for lifetime prevalence of alcohol dependence is more than two to one, male to female: 20.1 percent in men, 8.2 percent in women. Men also have higher lifetime prevalence of drug-use disorders. The highest prevalence rate occurs in youth. Early use is associated with an increased risk for dependence on alcohol and an increased risk of injury. Early use of drugs is associated with an increased risk for developing alcohol or drug problems (Dewit et al. 2000). It is also thought that early onset of drug or alcohol problems contributes to a poorer prognosis and tends to be more associated with a greater family history of drug or alcohol problems.

High rates of comorbid (or co-occurring) psychiatric disorders occur in persons with drug or alcohol problems. It is estimated from the National Comorbidity Study of 1990–1992 that 41 to 65 percent of those with a lifetime history of addiction have at least one other mental health disorder; rates are higher among women than men. Of women with addiction, 86 percent had lifetime drug or psychiatric disorder versus 78 percent of the men (Kessler et al. 1997). The most common psychiatric disorders occurring in persons with addiction are major depression, dysthymia, mania, hypomania, social and specific phobias, panic and generalized anxiety disorder, as well as personality disorders.

Etiology

As is true for most of the other mental health disorders, addiction is described as a bio-psycho-social illness with serious physical, psychological, social, and spiritual consequences. The hallmark of the disorder is an intense desire for the substance, with an impaired ability to control urges to use the substance despite adverse consequences. While individuals may begin to use the substance for its pleasurable effects, with repeated exposure and an underlying vulnerability, certain individuals will progress to addiction. Substances are used for varying reasons, including social pressure, changing of mental states, self-medication of various disorders, peer pressure, and improving performance. After time and repeated exposure to substances, these reasons give way to compulsive use of substances with subsequent loss of control.

Diagnosis

DSM-IV TR divides substance-use disorders into abuse, dependence, and substance related (such as substance-induced mood disorder). The criteria are the same regardless of the substance used. There needs to be repeated occasions within a twelve-month time period resulting in impairment or distress and criteria are met. Under the current diagnostic criteria, the criteria for *substance abuse* are met if there are recurrent interpersonal, work, social, or legal problems or use in situations that could be physically dangerous, with the latter typically referring to drinking and driving. A relatively small percentage of individuals meet criteria for alcohol abuse and go on to develop dependence. The criteria for abuse are summarized as follows:

A. A maladaptive pattern of substance use leading to clinically significant impairment or distress with one or more of the following criteria recurring over a twelve-month period:
    a. Failure to fulfill major role obligations at work, school, or home.
    b. Use in situations in which it is physically hazardous (e.g., driving).
    c. Legal problems (e.g., disorderly conduct).
    d. Social or interpersonal problems caused or exacerbated by the substance (e.g., arguments with spouse).
B. Never-met criteria for dependence.

Substance dependence, in contrast to abuse, encompasses other aspects: impaired control of the substance, increasing importance, physiological adaptation, and it must result in distress and/or impairment. Specifically, the criteria are summarized:

C. Maladaptive pattern of use, leading to clinically significant impairment or distress with three or more of the following criteria met within a twelve-month time period:
    a. Tolerance (need for increased amounts to achieve the same effect).
    b. Withdrawal (characteristic substance-specific withdrawal).
    c. Substance taken in larger amounts or over longer time than intended (i.e., loss of control).
    d. Persistent desire or unsuccessful efforts to cut down or stop use.
    e. Time consuming: obtaining, using, recovering from the substance.
    f. Important activities decreased or given up because of use.
    g. Continued use despite physical or psychological problems created or exacerbated by the substance.

Various tools and screening instruments exist to aid in the identification of a substance use problem that caregivers can utilize when there is a question of an alcohol problem. A brief screening tool is the CAGE, a set of four questions asked by the screener and designed to identify possible problematic alcohol use (Ewing 1984). These questions are: Have you tried to *cut* down? Has anyone been *annoyed* by your drinking? Do you feel *guilty* after drinking? and Do you ever use alcohol as an *eye-opener*? An affirmative response to any of these questions merits follow-up questions that can begin the discussion and highlight the need for further help. Such follow-up questions may include:

1. Cut down: When did you cut down and why? How did it work?
2. Annoyed: Who made comments and what kind of comments? Why do you think they made those comments?
3. Guilty: What happened? What made you feel bad?
4. Eye-opener: Do you drink when you try not to? What happens if you don't drink in the morning?

These questions can also be adapted to inquire about other drug use. Of note, the last question about using a substance as an eye-opener is probably the least sensitive question, since it implies a more chronic pattern, possibly evidencing withdrawal. In the vignette at the beginning of this chapter, the spouse is providing information that points to her husband's possible difficulty cutting down as well as her concern (annoyed). Information from concerned persons is extremely valuable in determining if there is a problem and also for subsequent counseling. Since denial is the defense mechanism that prevents the individual from recognizing the addiction, the collateral information is critical in determining the extent of the problem.

Treatment: Stages of Change

Just as there is a continuum of alcohol use, there needs to be a continuum of treatment options. The intervention must match the category of drinking. An individualized approach rather than "one size fits all" is essential and must address other mental health and medical problems, the person's level of motivation, and treatment preferences.

Enhancing motivation is a critical aspect of intervening and providing guidance (Prochaska and DiClemente 1983; Prochaska et al. 1992). This is elaborated on in the "stages of change" listed below, the process that must occur for an unhealthy behavior to change. The premise is that change occurs over time through a series of stages: precontemplation, contemplation, preparation, action, maintenance, and termination. Identifying the stage that a person is in with regard to a behavior such as drinking will aid in developing specific feedback and advice. While these stages apply to any behavior changes, we will apply it to alcohol use.

- *Precontemplative stage.* Here the person does not have any interest in making a change in her or his drinking, usually because the person does not see it as a problem. The husband in the vignette at the beginning of the chapter may fall into this category since blaming and lack of insight are often associated with this stage.
- *Contemplative stage.* The individual is weighing the benefits versus risks of change. Ambivalence and procrastination are features of this stage.
- *Preparation.* A stage in which the individual has made a decision to stop or reduce drinking or change behaviors and intends to do so in the immediate future. The individual may have a plan to contact a counselor or a physician, look up locations for AA meetings, and so forth.
- *Action stage.* The person makes clear changes in behavior: beginning a treatment program, attending an AA meeting, or ceasing to drink.
- *Maintenance stage.* This is necessary to continue the changed behavior and may last months or years. The individual works to maintain recovery but not as intensely as in the action stage. This will typically include attending regular AA meetings and contact with sponsor.
- *Termination.* The stage where the individual has no temptation and is 100 percent effective in his or her change. In the field of alcoholism, however, recovery is lifelong, and it is most likely that individuals thus remain in the maintenance phase.

Motivational enhancement therapy is a type of approach that caregivers could utilize in encouraging change and action of individuals with drinking problems. Counseling follows from the identification of the stage of change. For persons in the *precontemplative* stage, one would strive to increase awareness of alcohol effects and consequences, provide direct feedback, observations, and education. In the *contemplative* stage, one would assist the person in weighing the benefits of changing versus the reasons to continue drinking. For the *preparation* stage, providing encouragement that the person can be effective and presenting them with options is desirable. Support and problem-solving obstacles to making changes would occur in the *action* stage. Education about the importance of ongoing activities and commitment to recovery is appropriate for the *maintenance* stage. Periodic contacts to monitor self-efficacy and any possible return to unhealthy habits are indicated for the *termination* stage.

Treatments by Risk Status

One goal is early identification of problem drinking and providing the appropriate level and type of treatment or intervention. In the continuum of care, individualized treatments must not only recognize the stage of change but the severity of alcohol use. In those who are vulnerable to develop problem drinking because of a strong family history of alcoholism or co-occurring problems such as bipolar disorder or conduct disorder, the clinician would provide primary prevention with counseling about risk. For at-risk drinkers, education regarding the adverse effects of alcohol and advice on reducing use to National Institutes of Health guidelines can be very effective. Brief motivational counseling reduces drinking by 25 percent in the following year (Whitlock et al. 2004). The majority of persons in the abuse category are there because of driving while intoxicated. The most effective treatment approach for this category is less clear; typically court-enforced education and monitoring occur. Alcohol abuse does not always develop into dependence; many persons will stop or modify drinking and not progress into serious problems and loss of control.

Most studies on treatment have been done among those with alcohol dependence. The majority of those who develop dependence do so during adolescence or young adulthood, yet only 25 percent continue with a chronic course (Hasin et al. 2007). For those who have serious problems or have not responded to brief intervention or self-change attempts, referral to addiction-treatment programs is indicated. Decisions need to be made regarding setting (e.g., inpatient vs. outpatient), duration of treatment (e.g., short-term or long-term, such as six months), intensity of treatment (concentration of hours per week), amount of treatment (total number of hours), and treatment modalities (e.g., group vs. individual).

In general, research does not support the efficacy of residential/inpatient treatment over outpatient treatment, although those with severer alcohol problems do benefit more from an initial episode of inpatient or residential treatment (Tiet et al. 2007). Therefore, matching patients to the appropriate level and type of treatment is important. The American Society of Addiction Medicine (ASAM) has developed criteria for matching patients to different levels of care: (1) early intervention, (2) outpatient treatments, (3) intensive outpatient, (4) residential/inpatient, and (5) medically managed inpatient. Decisions of levels of care are based on need for detoxification, acute medical conditions, psychiatric conditions, treatment acceptance/resistance, relapse potential, and recovery/living environment.

After primary treatment, continuing care is essential to maintain recovery. The most prevalent form of continuing care is AA. There is now evidence on the effectiveness of AA: those who frequently attend AA do better than those who do not (Tonigan et al. 2000). Specific components of treatment include cognitive-behavioral therapies, introduction and facilitation of twelve steps, drug counseling, psycho-education, group therapy, family and couples therapy, and medications. The goals of these therapies are to teach, model, and support positive behaviors, and to provide motivation and hope. Abstinence is the goal for most individuals with dependence. It is beyond the scope of this chapter to provide an in-depth discussion of these components.

Medications are an effective treatment and usually are adjunctive to behavioral treatments. Three medications with different mechanisms of action are approved for the treatment of alcohol-use disorders: disulfiram, naltrexone, and acamprosate. Disulfiram (Antabuse®) was approved in 1949; it is an aversive agent that produces an unpleasant reaction if alcohol is consumed. It acts by inhibiting a liver enzyme that is necessary to metabolize alcohol and results in accumulation of a toxic substance. Although there are few control studies as an adjunct to treatment and supervision, it has been shown to be effective (Chick et al. 1992). Several neurotransmitters in the brain are involved in the reinforcing effects of alcohol: opioids, serotonin, dopamine, and excitatory amino acids (glutamate).

Many medications have targeted these chemicals in the hope of affecting alcohol consumption, but only a few have shown efficacy in research trials. Naltrexone blocks the opioid receptor (antagonist) that has a role in the pleasurable experience of alcohol. Many studies have provided support for its efficacy in reducing the number of drinking days and relapse, less craving for alcohol, and less progression during a relapse to heavy drinking (Volpicelli et al. 1992). Despite the promising research, the overall effect was modest in general populations. It is more likely to show benefit in subgroups of alcoholics who experience more craving or genetically have a particular encoding on the opioid receptor. Acamprosate (Campral®) stabilizes the balance of the excitatory neurotransmitter, glutamate, and the inhibitory transmitter, gamma-aminobutyric acid (GABA), which is thought to be responsible for the drug's effect on drinking. The evidence for acamprosate's efficacy is less convincing than that for naltrexone; the large multicenter U.S. trial did not find an improvement over those who took a placebo (Anton et al. 2006), despite European trials that showed it to be effective. It may be more effective in the person who is motivated for abstinence.

In summary, there are medications that can improve drinking outcomes but should be used in conjunction with psychosocial treatments. Unanswered questions include what subtype of alcoholic will respond to a specific medication, optimal dose, and which treatment combination is the best.

Spiritual Dimensions of Addiction

Mary and Dan, in the opening scenario of this chapter, alert the caregiver to two significant aspects of addiction. First, the initial effort at change is most often made by an affected significant other who is sick and tired of being sick and tired (Hansen 1971). Second, resistance to change is the most frequent response of all the people in the system. It is critically important for the caregiver to know something about this illness, its progression, and the final outcome in order to be of assistance to both the afflicted and the affected.

Addictions are classified in two ways: those involving mood-altering substances and those addictions that are termed behavioral or process addictions, such as gambling, the Internet, sex, shopping, or any behavior that is compulsive in nature and where the power of choice is gone (Clinebell 1998; Fassel 2000). This chapter is devoted principally to addiction to mood-altering substances, with beverage alcohol being by far the most prevalent form and therefore used as the paradigm for other addictions.

When meeting with concerned others (or the person with addiction) in a caregiving situation, only four options for resolution present themselves:

1. Death: Addiction is a progressively fatal disease and, if not addressed, will result in premature death.
2. Incarceration: The majority of prison sentences are linked with committing crimes that involve the use or sale of mood-altering substances.
3. Institutionalization: The deleterious effects of addiction to mood-altering substances can result in irreparable brain damage (e.g., Korsakoff's Syndrome), requiring in some instances permanent institutionalization. These substances can induce other mental disorders such as cognitive disorders, psychosis, mood disorders, anxiety, sexual dysfunction, and sleep disorders (DSM-IV, 192ff.).
4. Recovery: This involves not only a cessation of use, but an intentional shift in lifestyle for those afflicted *and* those affected in order to restore some semblance of sanity in the social system.

In caregiving, truth telling in love is absolutely essential so as to begin breaking through the nearly impenetrable wall of denial on the part of those afflicted and affected. Theologically framed in the Christian tradition, this is "tough love," that is, the courage to be "speaking the truth in love" (Eph. 4:16) as a way of discovering the veracity of the promise "that you shall know the truth and the truth will make you free" (John 8:32). A parody of this verse from John, seen in a treatment center, poignantly expresses this kind of tough love and the pain endemic to such truth telling: "You will know the truth and the truth will make you free, but first it will make you damn miserable!" Breaking the denial and coming to terms with the reality of the illness is paramount for the whole household if health and recovery are to prevail.

Truth telling and tough love are what distinguish caregiving with those afflicted and affected by addiction from other caregiving situations. Caregivers normally provide gentle comfort, empathic identification, and encouraging assurance. In dealing with addiction, telling the truth and confronting the problem is paramount. The caregiver needs to "detach with love," so as not to become enmeshed in the dysfunctional system and thus become a part of the problem, rather than a potential source for solving the situation. In this process, the caregiver can anticipate resistance, fear, anxiety, anger, and a host of other negative emotions. As with other illnesses dealt with in this book, addiction is an "unsanctioned illness," beset with the power of disgrace shame (Albers 1995a). This intensifies the denial and exacerbates the defense mechanisms that are put in place for all participating persons.

General Principles Related to Caregiving with the Afflicted and Affected

Addiction Constitutes a Spiritual Crisis for the Whole Person and Social System. The physiological and medical aspects of this illness have already been articulated. Addiction is a wholistic illness that results in the deterioration of every facet of human life: physical, emotional, social, and spiritual. The spiritual dimension of the illness involves a variety of factors, only a few of which can be dealt with in this limited context.

A search for meaning and purpose in the midst of the realities of life is a key spiritual issue. The devastation wrought by addiction has the addict and significant others asking about the meaning of life and if life itself is governed only by the addiction. Physical healing and emotional healing are imperative, but they are insufficient for total healing until the spiritual dimension of the illness is brought to the surface. This basic spiritual need is poignantly expressed by Holocaust survivor Viktor Frankl in his book *Man's Search for Meaning* (Frankl 1968). Why am I here? What purpose is there in life? How can I deal with suffering? These are fundamental spiritual questions.

The feeling of emptiness is articulated in a phrase often uttered by people in treatment: "I feel like I have a hole in the gut!" The emptiness of life was poignantly expressed by a person dying of alcohol addiction, who said, "I know that it is the booze that is killing me, but at this point, it doesn't really matter. My life is empty. I know I am dying, and that is what I want."[1] A few days later he died of his illness. He believed his life was empty and death was preferable to life.

The reality of isolation and loneliness plagues the beleaguered addict and the lives of others around the addict. This isolation can be either self-imposed, because of the feeling of "disgrace shame" (Albers 1995a, 29ff.), so that the person does not want to be seen. Or it can also be created by others who no longer wish to associate with the person whose drinking has resulted in embarrassing behavior. This prompts others to shun the addict as a pariah and consign the addict to social exile.

We have been created for relationship with God, creation, others, and ourselves. The illness carries great personal and social import, to the point that the isolation and loneliness exacerbates the drinking. Beverage alcohol has become the only reliable friend and companion that the addict has in life. Spouses, partners, family members, and friends can also isolate themselves in utter disgrace shame.

The reality of relational alienation and estrangement is ubiquitous. This was evident in this chapter's opening vignette. Relationships are damaged and deteriorate exponentially as the ravages of the disease tear at the very fabric of the relational network for everyone involved.

Paul Tillich defines sin as "alienation and estrangement" (Tillich 1957, 51–59). He uses a technical term, "concupiscence, that is, the unlimited desire to draw the whole of reality into one's self" (ibid., 52). This is comparable to the "big ego" referred to in *Alcoholics Anonymous* (AA 1955), which sees that hubris or pride results in estrangement with others when relationships are forfeited as a result of self-gratification.

Within a household, at work, and in the larger social arena, estrangement is paramount as the addict evokes anger and resentment in those surrounding her or him and all of life falls apart. Estrangement that damages or ruins relationships is transferred to one's relationship with God, thus forming the nexus of a powerful spiritual problem. If this issue is not addressed, it exacerbates the illness and feeds it like a fuel cast into the flames of discontent. The hope for reconciled relationships fades like mist on a summer morning. When the estrangement is not addressed, it incites anger, evokes resentment, and exacerbates the demise of an already deteriorating system.

Addiction issues require an interfaith perspective and mutual participation. The most salient feature about ministry with those addicted and affected is the attitude demonstrated by the faith community in relationship to the illness. The track record historically in faith communities has not been stellar. It has improved as concentrated education about and greater awareness of the predilection for the disease and its pervasiveness has grown.

There are principles in at least the three major Western religious traditions—Judaism, Christianity and Islam—that can be affirmed. These affirmations are taken from the curriculum developed by the National Association of Children of Alcoholics for caregiving training in theological schools (Albers 2010).

1. *The divine desire for healing and health.* Religious traditions affirm this truth in their sacred writings and spiritual practices. The divine is thought of as a benevolent force operative in the world that represents an unqualified and inexpressible love for every created creature to experience healing and health.

2. *The proclivity for developing false "gods" in this life.* Here the word *god* is defined as that which commands one's total life, attention, and energy. Both those afflicted and those affected have to admit readily that the addiction has supplanted "God" in their spiritual lives.

3. *The reality of human imperfection.* Imperfection is endemic to the human condition. Another way of stating this is to admit the

reality of brokenness in one's life (Moyers 2006). Perfectionism is the humanly devised antidote to the issue of imperfection, whereas admitting one's humanity, imperfection, and brokenness can be the starting place for true spirituality and healing (Kurtz and Ketcham 2002).

4. *The mandate to care for the marginalized.* This is integral to all major religious movements. Those afflicted with and affected by addiction have been summarily relegated to the margins of society. They become the voiceless, the invisible, the neglected, as evidenced by the large cohort of street people who suffer from addiction and/or co-occurring mental illnesses of varying varieties.

5. *The rites, rituals, and sacred traditions and writings of religious groups.* These enjoin religious followers to change their attitude toward those who are less fortunate and to exercise action on behalf of them and their welfare.

6. *The centrality of hope.* Amid the seemingly hopeless situations that millions of people find themselves in when it comes to alcoholism, hope is a beacon of light in the dark world of addiction. The possibility of hope requires the will of society and caring individuals to actualize opportunities for people to recover. This involves advocating for the oppressed and marginalized of the world, so that new life is able to rise up from the ashes of addiction like the phoenix.

It is evident that, given the magnitude of the problem and social and ecclesiastical denial about it, coupled with the reality that alcoholism and addiction are unsanctioned illnesses, these disorders present an immense problem for faith communities. The message and mission of the varying faith traditions must address the spiritual realities of people if religion is to gain any sense of integrity and viability. Concerted efforts for advocacy, training, intervention, and prevention need to prevail if this persistent and pervasive problem of addiction is going to be addressed effectively by the religious communities, irrespective of what faith tradition is represented.

Specific Caregiving Roles in Dealing with the Afflicted and the Affected

There are a plethora of roles that caregivers can provide for addiction. The role played is contingent upon a multiplicity of factors, including cultural and religious realities that need to be factored into the decision-making process. The attitudes and ideas about addiction in your faith community need to be examined to see if they are commensurate with the purpose of the community's stated mission. The following roles were developed as normative for caregivers by the National Association of Children of Alcoholics (Albers 2010).

1. *Catalyst for change.* Caregivers are in a unique position to effect change in a household system where addiction is an issue. My definition of addiction is that it is a *"lifestyle disorder,* comprised of physical, psychological, social and spiritual components, that brings dis-ease to the individual and her or his social system" (Albers 1982, 13). That it is a lifestyle, or a way of life to which people have adjusted, readjusted, and finally maladjusted, is a reason why change is so difficult. People who are enmeshed in this social system are often not cognizant that something is amiss, because they have become accustomed to the way they live and cope.

It is understandable why the afflicted and the affected are so resistant to change. Change requires effort and energy, and they have accommodated to a way of life that has become normative for them, even if it may be painful. "Naming" the elephant in the room—addiction—raises the anxiety level, which in turn exponentially exacerbates the fear when change is suggested. Therefore, being a catalyst for change involves risk, as the reality of denial and resistance to change have the upper hand.

The caregiver needs to inquire about the behavior that is causing disruption and *to link that always to the drinking or using.* It is critical to point out what occurs when a mood-altering substance enters the equation. The caregiver is in a unique position to advocate for attending twelve-step meetings or to consider a possible intervention. The system is self-sustaining and self-perpetuating, thus maintaining homeostasis. It often takes an outsider to name what is happening and to strategize for change so as to realize a preferred future for all who are involved.

2. *Coordinator of available resources.* The caregiver needs to provide available resources that are immediately accessible for persons who are in an addictive system. Alcoholics Anonymous, Al-Anon, Al-Ateen, or other suitable twelve-step groups can provide immediate help. There are numerous materials, such as books, brochures, periodicals, and other publications directly related to the issue of addiction. Many caregivers have found the materials from AA and Al-Anon to be fitting resources because they are succinct, straightforward, and simply written so that almost anyone can read and understand them. If the person is unable to read, then recordings of these materials can be offered.

Some caregivers have developed a referral list for those who need assistance with addiction. If you are serving in an area where resources are not readily available, find out where they can be accessed. This is a fatal illness, and unless the addictive cycle is broken, devastating consequences will occur for all.

Awareness of where intervention specialists might be secured is also valuable. An intervention is a threatening experience for the addict as well as those adversely affected, so caregiving support is essential. An intervention is only as strong as its weakest link, so adequate preparation for this event is imperative.

The most effective resource I have found for caregiving is to engage a person in the faith community or in the wider community who has experienced long-term sobriety and is willing to talk with the addict or those affected. This person can be a veritable treasure trove of help, because this person knows the ins and outs of the illness. She or he can speak as an insider who knows the reality of denial, deceit, and deception.

Those who have been affected are often unwitting "enablers" in the process and can develop a phenomenon that is referred to as "codependency." A working definition of codependency is "a primary lifestyle disorder occasioned by adaptation to and enmeshment with an unhealthy relationship or relationships which results in the loss of a person's sense of self or a group's sense of identity" (Albers 1995b, 2). The "adaptation" and "enmeshment" to an "unhealthy relationship" in addiction is experienced by significant others who are adversely affected. Caregivers need be aware of their own codependent proclivities so as not to complicate further already confused and complex relationships. There is a spate of literature that addresses the impact of addiction on children, as well as materials that deal directly with codependent relationships.[2]

3. *Correlator and integrator of spiritual questions.* Theologian Paul Tillich used the word *correlation* to indicate the process of integrating or correlating the spiritual questions that are asked in order to discover possible resolutions that can emanate from one's religious tradition. Caregivers need to be aware of the attitude and posture of their religious tradition to determine if the religious tradition aids or deters the process of recovery. In some religious traditions, the question of "sin or sickness" seems to still hold sway. For those traditions that still view addiction as a moral failure, the possibility of recovery is drastically reduced. The addict and those affected have already endured the scorn of others, and to hear further judgment, accusations, and condemnation exacerbates the disgrace shame, often resulting in the addict using even more and significant others experiencing the despair of hopelessness. Evaluating your own tradition might include the following questions:

- What is your tradition's teaching concerning *the divine* or a higher power? Is God thought of as punishing, vindictive, and condemning, or is God thought of as gracious, beneficent, and loving? This is a concern of great import if the person afflicted and the persons affected are to embrace your tradition.

- How does your tradition view *humankind?* Are humans thought of as intrinsically evil, of little worth or value because of their illness; or are human beings seen as created good (Gen. 1:31), that is, of inestimable worth and value? Are human beings categorized in a hierarchical fashion so that males dominant females, children are to be invisible, heterosexuality is normative, the rich are preferred to the poor, or the healthy elevated over those who are ill? Addicts and those affected have finely tuned sensors with respect to attitudes that are either overtly or covertly expressed in word and deed.

- What disposition prevails with respect to *the function of relationships and community?* Recovery from this illness is predicated on healthy, loving, and accepting relationships on the part of others. Tried, true, and trusting relationships are endemic to most religious traditions. Asserting that truth, and implementing it as a lived reality, may be quite a different matter. Religious communities can be the source of contention, strife, power, control, and bigotry, as opposed to being a safe haven and a harbor of tranquility in the midst of the storms of life, where genuine care and concern are experienced in deep relationships of love and acceptance. This is why many people in recovery will eschew the idea of being "religious" and prefer to speak of themselves as "spiritual," because peace is not found in the maelstrom of a community where power struggles and prejudice prevail. Rather, they seek a community where one can be "loved back to health," as one of my recovering friends expresses it.

- How does your religious community view issues of *advocacy and justice* as it relates to the marginalized of the world? Once again, the foundational consideration is focused on attitudes that prevail. Does the community see its mission as being advocates for the underprivileged, the oppressed, the sick, and the dying? Addicts and their loved ones quickly perceive the integration of religion with human and civil rights. Advocacy speaks volumes to those whose lives have been consigned to the ash heap of society because of their unsanctioned illness. Loving attitudes result in living actions that exemplify the radical nature of acceptance and inclusion of all people, irrespective of who they might be, where they may have been, and what they might have done or not done. The caregiver can be a vital force as a representative of a given religious persuasion provided that the spirit of care, love, and acceptance is commensurate with the understanding of divine intention for human beings and the world.

4. *Confessor who listens to the story.* Fundamental to all caregiving is the ability to listen and not just hear. Theodor Reik wrote of *Listening with the Third Ear*, since communication involves interpretation not only of words, but also of body language that is observed (Reik 1948). Every addict and every person adversely affected by the addiction has a story to tell and their narrative reveals the level of panic and pain that is being

experienced. The story will often reveal everyone in the system's frustration of attempting to *control the addiction* in some fashion.

Generally speaking, it takes approximately seven years from the onset of the addiction before someone or something in the system precipitates some kind of action for change. The story of addiction has often fallen on deaf ears and consequently has been sublimated, but its dynamics are daily lived out in the lives of the persons afflicted and affected. Listening with attention, patience, and a degree of objectivity is important as the story pours out in varied form. It is critical that the caregiver listen and *not attempt to fix, solve, or rescue* the person seeking help. Rather, the caregiver can draw on the resources previously cited in this chapter and participate in a mutual plan and strategy to effect a change.

The best available resource known as of today are the twelve-step groups. If a person is a part of AA or Al-Anon, the caregiver may also function as a "confessor" should the person ask you to "listen" to a fifth step! The fifth step states: "Admitted to God, to ourselves and *another human being*, the exact nature of our wrongs" (AA, 59). The caregiver may be the person to whom the one addicted or the one affected chooses to listen to her or his fifth step. One acts as a confessor not in the sense of "hearing confession" per se and then being expected to provide absolution. Rather, the fifth step is a way for the person to be honest about the carnage left on the highway of life as a consequence of the addiction. For those affected, it is a way to come to terms with the negative attitudes and actions that have occurred as a result of "reacting to the addiction." Literature and training sessions regarding fifth-step work are available for the caregiver. The best way to prepare for hearing a fifth step is to do a fourth-step inventory and then do *one's own fifth step* as a caregiver to understand more fully the reality and power of this process as integral to a new life and sense of freedom.

5. *Conciliator for damaged relationships.* If a caregiver has specific training in counseling, she or he may continue a follow-up ministry with members of the household in effecting reconciliation wherever that may be possible. If the caregiver does *not* have those skills, then she or he can function in the role of catalyst and refer the person or persons to competent professionals who can assist in a conciliatory process. An important caveat in all of this is that many times the relationship is so

severely damaged that reconciliation in terms of repair is not possible. Then it is important to reconcile to the fact that reconciliation is not going to occur. Acceptance of that reality can be a painful consequence that requires special care.

Candidly speaking, recovery most often does not occur, and the addict dies. The complicated grief that ensues for those affected often requires a prolonged period of mourning in order to sort out the ambivalent feelings that are experienced. Professional counseling for such situations is strongly encouraged. Whether you or another professional provide that as a caregiver, it is critical to maintain contact and to be prepared to listen to the deeply painful stories that need to be both shared and heard if healing is to occur.

Another unfortunate aspect of this illness is that "relapse" or a "slip" (traditional AA language) is a disconcerting reality with this illness. This often evokes optimal negative reactions on the part of the addict, who feels like a failure, and by significant others, who feel their convictions that the illness is hopeless have just been confirmed. Caregivers can point out that "relapse" happens with other illnesses as well. We take them in stride, celebrate whatever length of sobriety was experienced, determine what precipitated the relapse, and how one can learn from it. Discouragement is the greatest enemy of recovery. The reality of relapse must be addressed and embraced.

A poignant experience is to observe the incremental but gradual healing of relationships over time that can bring health and harmony to a household. It is critical to remember that the problem did *not* develop over night and, consequently, it is not resolved in a brief period of time. Reconciliation is not like "fast food" or "instant banking"; it requires patience, time, grace, faith, and, above all, a quality of mercy and love that is truly indicative of a healthy spirituality where the past is not forgotten but is integrated into a new lifestyle where all who have been touched by this insidious illness can experience sobriety with serenity.

In providing care for those afflicted with and affected by addiction, health and healing is possible, and that is good news! The wise words of the apostle Paul from the Christian tradition could likely be spoken by people of other religious traditions as well. In summing up the quintessential core of Christian living, Paul offers these words: "And now faith, hope, and love abide, these three; and the greatest of these is love" (1 Cor. 13:13). Faith as trust is imperative if people are to recover from this devastating illness and its prolonged effects. Hope is necessary, lest the addiction take down everyone with its cunning, baffling, and powerful force. Love is absolutely essential if healing, health, and harmony are to be experienced. This is why the universal prayer of those in recovery is the "Serenity Prayer," attributed to the theologian Reinhold Niebuhr:

> God, grant me the serenity to accept the things I cannot change,
> The courage to change the things I can,
> And the wisdom to know the difference.
> Amen.

Bibliography

Albers, Robert H. 1982. *The Theological and Psychological Dynamics of Transformation in the Recovery from the Disease of Alcoholism.* PhD dissertation. Ann Arbor: University Microfilms International.

———. 1995a. *Shame: A Faith Perspective.* New York: Haworth.

———. 1995b. "Codependency: Characteristic or Caricature?" *Journal of Ministry in Addiction and Recovery* 2 (1): 1–7.

———. 2010. *A Seminary Curriculum Based on "Core Competencies for Clergy and Other Pastoral Ministers in Addressing Alcohol and Drug Dependence and the Impact on Family Members."* Kensington, Md.: National Association of Children of Alcoholics, and Washington D.C.: U.S. Department of Health and Human Services, Mental Health Services Administration, Center for Substance Abuse Treatment. Expanded version available online at http://www.Kenrickparish.com/nacoa.

Alcoholics Anonymous (AA). 1955. New York: Alcoholics Anonymous World Services.

American Psychiatric Association. 1994. *Diagnostic and Statistical Manual of Mental Disorders.* 4th ed. (DSM-IV). Washington, D.C.: American Psychiatric Publishing.

Anton, Raymond F., Stephanie S. O'Malley, Domenic A. Ciraulo, et al. 2006. "Combined Pharmacotherapies and Behavioral Interventions for Alcohol Dependence: The COMBINE Study: A Randomized Controlled Trial." *Journal of the American Medical Association* 295 (17): 2003–17.

Beattie, Melody. 1987. *Codependent No More: How to Stop Controlling Others and Start Caring for Yourself.* Center City, Minn.: Hazelden.

Black, Claudia. 1982. *It Will Never Happen to Me.* Denver: M.A.C.

Chick, J., K. Geogh, W. Falkowski, et al. 1992. "Disulfiram Treatment of Alcoholism." *British Journal of Psychiatry* 161: 84–89.

Clinebell, Howard J. 1998. *Understanding and Counseling Persons with Alcohol, Drug, and Behavioral Addictions.* Nashville: Abingdon.

Dewit, David J., Edward M. Adlaf, David R. Offord, et al. 2000. "Age at First Alcohol Use: A Risk Factor for the Development of Alcohol Disorders." *American Journal of Psychiatry* 157 (5): 745–50.

Ewing, John A. 1984. "Detecting Alcoholism: The CAGE Questionaire." *Journal of the American Medical Association* 252 (14): 1905–07.

Fassel, Diane. 2000. *Working Ourselves to Death.* Lincoln: Authors Guild.

Frankl, Viktor. 1968. *Man's Search for Meaning.* New York: Washington Square.

Hansen, Philip. 1971. *Sick and Tired of Being Sick and Tired.* Lake Mills, Iowa: Graphic.

Hasin, Deborah S., Frederick S. Stinson, Elizabeth Ogburn, et al. 2007. "Prevalence, Correlates, Disability, and Comorbidity of DSM-IV Alcohol Abuse and Dependence in the United States: Results from the National Epidemiologic Survey on Alcohol and Related Conditions." *Archives of General Psychiatry* 64 (7): 830–42.

Kessler, R. C., R. M. Crum, L. A. Warner, et al. 1997. "Lifetime Co-occurrence of DSM-III-R Alcohol Abuse and Dependence with Other Psychiatric Disorders in the National Comorbidity Survey." *Archives of General Psychiatry* 54 (4): 313–21.

Kurtz, Ernie, and Katherine Ketcham. 2002. *The Spirituality of Imperfection and the Search for Meaning.* New York: Bantam.

Moyers, William Cope. 2006. *Broken: My Story of Addiction and Redemption.* New York: Viking.

O'Malley, S. S., A. J, Jaffe, S. Rode, et al. 1996. "Experience of a 'Slip' among Alcoholics Treated with Naltrexone or Placebo." *American Journal of Psychiatry* 153 (2): 281–83.

Prochaska, James O., and Carlo C. DiClemente. 1983. "Stages and Processes of Self-Change Smoking: Toward an Integrative Model of Change." *Journal of Consulting Clinical Psychology* 51: 390–95.

——, ——, and John C. Norcross. 1992. "In Search of How People Change: Applications to the Addictive Behaviors." *American Psychologist* 47: 1102–14.

Reik, Theodor. 1948. *Listening with the Third Ear.* New York: Grove.

Tiet, Quyen Q., Mark A. Ilgen, Hilary F. Byrnes, et al. 2007. "Treatment Setting and Baseline Substance Use Severity Interact to Predict Patients' Outcomes." *Addiction* 102: 432–40.

Tillich, Paul. 1957. *Systematic Theology,* Vol. 2. Chicago: University of Chicago Press.

Tonigan, J. Scott, Radka Toscova, and William R. Miller. 1996. "Meta-Analysis of the Literature on Alcoholics Anonymous: Sample and Study Characteristics Moderate Findings." *Journal of Studies on Alcohol and Drugs* 57 (1): 65–72.

——, Gerard J. Connors, and William R. Miller. 2000. "Participation and Involvement in Alcoholics Anonymous." In Thomas F. Babor and Frances K. DelBoca, eds., *Treatment Matching in Alcoholism,* 183–204. New York: Hollis.

Volpicelli, Joseph R., Arthur I. Alterman, Motoi Hayashida, et al. 1992. "Naltrexone in the Treatment of Alcohol Dependence." *Archives of General Psychiatry* 49 (11): 876–80.

Warner, Lynn A., Ronald C. Kessler, Michael Hughes, et al. 1995. "Prevalence and Correlates of Drug Use and Dependence in the United States: Results from the National Comorbidity Survey." *Archives of General Psychiatry* 52 (3): 219–29.

Whitlock, Evelyn P., Michael R. Polen, Carla A. Green, et al. 2004. "Behavioral Counseling Interventions in Primary Care to Reduce Risky/Harmful Alcohol Use by Adults: A Summary of the Evidence for the U.S. Preventive Services Task Force." *Annals of Internal Medicine* 140 (7): 557–68.

Woititz, Janet. 1990. *Adult Children of Alcoholics.* Deerfield, Fla.: Health Communications.

EATING DISORDERS

William Yates / Diana Thierry

6

A parishioner named Mary called the pastor's office asking for an appointment to speak about her daughter, Olivia. Pastor Jones, a recent seminary graduate, scheduled an appointment for a visit. At the visit, Mary quickly broke into tears, stating she was fearful that her daughter was suffering from the eating disorder anorexia nervosa. She described how Olivia, now fourteen years of age, had been losing weight over the last eighteen months. She refused to eat with the family, refused to discuss why she would not eat, and frequently avoided interaction with her family. Shy as a child, Olivia excelled in school and had never received a grade lower than an A. She was competitive and at times perfectionistic.

Pastor Jones had noted some of these issues with Mary during her participation in church youth activities. She frequently avoided eating in front of other youth. She seemed to be losing weight. When other youth members commented that they felt she was too "skinny," she turned red and became tearful.

Mary said her daughter's behavior was becoming a problem between herself and her husband. They argued about what to do about Olivia's weight loss and refusal to eat. Her husband wanted to be more forceful and make her eat, while Mary thought this would just escalate the situation. Mary wanted to make an appointment with a child psychiatrist for Olivia, but her husband didn't think much of psychiatrists and was adamant against the idea. Mary asked Pastor Jones, "What shall I do?"

Pastor Jones didn't know for sure what to do about this situation. In seminary, he had a class on introduction to mental disorders, but there was no discussion about eating disorders. He came up with the following plan. He prayed with Mary, asking for God's help and guidance in dealing with Olivia. He stated he had a pediatrician friend who might provide some recommendations about what to do. He asked Mary to return in three days and to bring her husband along if he would agree. *

Understanding Eating Disorders

Eating disorders are a group of mental disorders found predominantly in adolescent girls and in young women. The two primary diagnostic categories are *anorexia nervosa* and *bulimia nervosa*. Both of these disorders share a predominant fear of being fat. Although being of normal weight is an important component of a healthy lifestyle, overvaluation of being of normal weight or below normal weight is a characteristic of those with eating disorders. They often demonstrate an intense phobia of gaining weight or looking fat. This phobia or fear often predominates their life. Eating, dieting, and weight issues take up an excessive amount of mental time, making it difficult to concentrate on other issues.

Figure 6.1 demonstrates some of the dynamic features of those with eating disorders. Eating disorders are not random in the population but appear to occur in those with a variety of genetic and environmental vulnerabilities or risk factors for the disorder. Typically, individuals who develop an eating disorder may begin with psychological vulnerabilities such as low self-esteem, a sense of dissatisfaction with their weight or body, a tendency to be perfectionistic, presence of anxiety or an

---

*This case history represents not a specific case but a compilation of clinical and pastoral experiences of the authors organized to illustrate key features in individuals with eating disorders pertinent to caregiving. Names are fictitious in the account and do not represent any specific individual. The case history second visit and eventual outcome for this case will be noted later in this chapter.

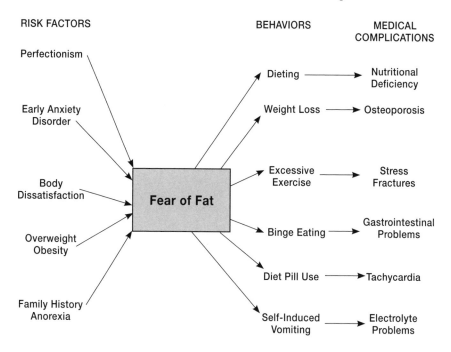

Figure 6.1. Pathways to Behaviors and Outcomes in Eating Disorders

anxiety disorder, obsessional personality features, or a history of being overweight.

These vulnerability factors contribute to an unreasonable and overwhelming fear of being fat (or becoming fat). Individuals typically respond to this fear of being fat with a variety of behaviors that attempt to reduce the fear and reduce anxiety. These behaviors can include aggressive caloric restriction including fasting behaviors. Once dieting begins, the body often responds with an increase in appetite in order to reverse the weight loss associated with dieting. This may be an evolutionary survival mechanism that reduces the potential physical consequences of insufficient calorie intake.

Increased appetite in response to weight loss can result in episodes of binge eating. Binge eating is typically described as rapid consumption of large numbers of calories in a short period of time. We have all experienced periods of strong appetite in response to skipping a meal or two. This drive stimulates consumption of large numbers of calories in an effort not only to meet our daily calorie needs but also to "catch up" on the weight that has been lost due to dieting.

Patients with eating disorders who binge eat after calorie restriction often feel guilty about "going off their diet." This distress is above and beyond what individuals without an eating disorder feel when they over-eat. Non-eating-disordered individuals will often respond to overeating by noting that this is an infrequent behavior that can be compensated for by eating a few small meals in the next few days. But eating-disordered individuals may feel panicked after a binge, with a strong urge to figure out a way to reverse the binge through purging behaviors.

Purging behaviors include self-induced vomiting, use of laxatives, use of emetics (drugs that produce vomiting), or use of enemas. Patients with bulimia nervosa often discover that they can induce vomit by sticking a finger down their throat to cause gagging and eventually vomiting. After a period of behavioral habituation, some people with bulimia nervosa can vomit spontaneously after a large meal without inducing the gagging reflex.

A variety of drug-abuse behaviors can be seen in those with eating disorders. They may use over-the-counter or prescription weight-loss drugs. Often this weight-loss drug use is above the recommended dosage level. Other drugs used in attempts to control weight include diuretic drugs, which may cause rapid weight reduction through temporary increased urination. This weight is typically quickly regained with hydration.

Excessive exercise is frequently seen in those with eating disorders. It seems to be more common among those with anorexia nervosa than among those with bulimia nervosa, who commonly are within normal limits for weight. Exercise in eating disorder patients is typically aerobic-type of exercise since this is the most efficient way to burn calories. Running is often a preferred exercise and can be combined with other intense aerobic activities, such as jumping rope or vigorous dancing workouts. Eating disorder patients frequently go significantly beyond exercise guidelines, exercising vigorously for several hours a day. This exercise frenzy and duration places them at risk for overuse injuries of the muscles, ligaments, and tendons as well as at increased risk for stress factors of bones in the lower extremities.

A medical diagnosis of anorexia nervosa or bulimia nervosa typically occurs when diagnostic criteria are met as outlined in the DSM-IV. For *anorexia nervosa* this would typically be: (1) refusing to maintain body weight within healthy range (weight 15 percent below what would be expected for height); (2) persistence of fear of fat despite being underweight; (3) failure to perceive self as underweight, excessive reliance on weight in self-assessment, or denial of the seriousness of weight on health; and (4) after onset of menses, a loss of three consecutive menstrual cycles current with low weight. For *bulimia nervosa* the diagnosis would typically be made if the following criteria were present: (1) recurrent episodes of binge eating occurring within a two-hour period accompanied by a feeling of loss of control; (2) use of unhealthy behaviors to compensate for the binge eating, such as self-induced vomiting, laxative abuse, diuretic abuse, fasting, or excessive exercise; (3) binging having occurred at least twice a week for a period of three months; and (4) evaluation of the self unduly influenced by weight or shape.

Some individuals with a clinically significant eating disorder may not meet criteria for anorexia nervosa or bulimia nervosa. These individuals may be given the diagnosis of eating disorder NOS (not otherwise specified). This allows for a description of a population with most of the criteria for a diagnosis but a somewhat atypical clinical presentation.

Binge eating alone without purging behaviors is not currently considered an eating disorder. However, binge eating appears to carry with it a significant medical and psychological burden. For the next diagnostic revision of the DSM (DSM-V, in preparation), binge-eating disorder is being proposed as a separate eating disorder diagnostic category. For the diagnosis to be present in DSM-V, binge eating will need to be accompanied by three of the following: rapid eating; eating until uncomfortably full; eating large amounts of food when not hungry; eating alone because of embarrassment about the quantity of food one is eating; feeling disgusted, depressed, or guilty after overeating. Binge eating appears to be a significant problem among obese individuals. Since DSM-V is still in draft phase, there may be changes in the binge eating disorder criteria before final publication.

Epidemiology

Epidemiology is defined as the prevalence and determinants of a disease in a population. Binge eating is a relatively common phenomenon with fewer individuals practicing the bingeing or purging behaviors required for a diagnosis of bulimia nervosa. A 2007 survey of households in the United States estimates the lifetime prevalence of anorexia nervosa as 0.9 percent for females with ten to twenty cases in women for every case diagnosed in a male. This survey estimates the lifetime prevalence rate of bulimia nervosa to be 1.5 percent in women with an estimated three cases in women for each male with the disorder (Hudson et al. 2007).

Several risk factors for anorexia nervosa and bulimia nervosa have been identified. Similar to risk factors for heart disease, these conditions indicate a higher likelihood of developing a condition. For example, high cholesterol is a risk factor for heart attacks and stroke. Having high cholesterol does not indicate an absolute risk—many with high cholesterol will die from non-heart-disease conditions. Nevertheless, identifying a risk factor in an individual can promote interventions that may reduce risk. Treatment of high cholesterol in the general population with statin drugs will lower the number of cases of heart attacks and strokes, even if many individuals may not experience a personal benefit.

In a similar way, identifying risk factors for eating disorders can provide some opportunities for interventions that may reduce risk. Risk factors can be grouped according to those factors that may be modifiable compared to those that are not modifiable. An early anxiety disorder may be a risk factor for a later eating disorder—identifying and treating this risk factor would be an example of a modifiable risk factor. Being female is a risk factor for both anorexia nervosa and bulimia nervosa, and this would in general be a nonmodifiable condition.

In addition to female gender, obsessive and perfectionist personality traits confer an increase in risk for anorexia nervosa. It is felt that this characteristic may predispose individuals to an overly valued low-weight idealization. Additionally, this type of personality may spend significant time and energy on a goal once that goal is identified. For anorexia, this could include excessive time exercising, thinking about weight and diet, and setting (and attaining) rigid goals about weight and size. Other risk factors for anorexia nervosa include passing through the period of adolescence (a high-risk time for onset of the condition), caucasian race, middle- to upper-class socioeconomic status, and family history of an eating disorder.

Early onset of an anxiety disorder commonly precedes the development of anorexia nervosa. These anxiety symptoms may emerge as part of a childhood separation anxiety that can present with difficulty separating from home and attending school. Anxiety may also be demonstrated in social situations where the child or adolescent may be hypersensitive to the evaluation and scrutiny of others.

For bulimia nervosa, female gender and perfectionist personality traits also appear to confer risk. Additionally, evidence of impulsivity appears to confer risk for impulsive bingeing and purging. Impulsivity may be demonstrated by a history of making poor choices (or acting poorly) on the spur of the moment: for instance, impulsive shoplifting, going on spending sprees, driving wrecklessly. Some of these types of behaviors indicate risk for borderline personality disorder—a disorder that is felt to increase risk for bulimia nervosa.

Being overweight or obese as a child or adolescent appears to predispose individuals to risk for bulimia nervosa. This will typically follow a pattern where being overweight is followed by very restrictive dieting. Following a period of weight loss, extreme hunger results with urges for binge eating and the initial manifestations of a diagnosis of bulimia nervosa. This pattern underscores the need to avoid crash dieting in girls and young women. Weight-loss programs in this group should be done gradually with medical supervision and monitoring.

Exposure to sports with a premium on weight control also appears to be a risk for some individuals. Gymnasts and ballerinas commonly face social pressure to maintain a low body weight. This phenomenon manifests itself among male wrestlers who have to "make [lose] weight" to compete in their weight class. For some this may be relatively easy and not a problem. For others, severe calorie restriction necessary to participate in their sport or occupation can induce an eating disorder.

Several family mental disorders appear to increase risk for bulimia nervosa. Family history of any eating disorder increases risk but also a family history of alcohol abuse or dependence or depression appears to increase risk. At least one study found that a family history of divorce was more common in young women with eating disorders, although this may have resulted from increased rates of mental disorders in the parents rather than divorce itself (Boumann et al. 1994).

Course and Outcome

Anorexia nervosa. Anorexia nervosa can become a chronic and debilitating illness (Strober et al. 1997). However, the prognosis is not universally negative. Some individuals will have a relatively mild form of the illness that may remit spontaneously or with minimal supportive interventions. One study of adolescents with anorexia undergoing comprehensive treatment resulted in a full and lasting recovery in over 70 percent of the group five years after treatment.

Individuals whose illnesses progress to a state that requires inpatient hospitalization typically have the poorest prognosis. An outcome study of hospitalized women with anorexia nervosa found 44 percent to have an outcome classified as good with 5 percent dying in the four years after hospitalization. Generally, outcomes are better for those with an adolescent age of onset and shorter duration of illness. Women presenting with the lower weights appear to have a poorer prognosis.

A study of one-year outcome for anorexia nervosa has been published using the Laureate Outcome and Genetics Initiative-Eating Disorder (LOGI-ED) data set. The study examined the effect of rate of weight restoration during hospitalization and longer-term outcome. For severely underweight women with anorexia, a primary treatment goal for hospitalization is weight restoration. The LOGI-ED study found that the rate of weight gain during hospitalization predicted outcome one year later. Women with anorexia nervosa who gained .8 kilograms (about 2 pounds) or more per week during hospitalization had a better prognosis than those gaining less than .8 kilograms per week.

Women with anorexia nervosa who stabilize with weights in the normal range may still be bothered by common psychiatric comorbidity (co-occurring disorders), such as depression, dysthymia, social phobia, obessive-compulsive symptoms, or substance-abuse problems. This makes it important to have a comprehensive assessment and treatment program that can address comorbidity factors that can influence outcome.

Some women who initially have anorexia nervosa, restricting subtype, will evolve over time and develop binge eating and/or purging behaviors. It is less common for women with bulimia nervosa at the onset to evolve to a diagnosis of anorexia nervosa.

Bulimia nervosa. Pure bulimia nervosa appears to have a somewhat better prognosis and natural history than anorexia nervosa. Short-term success for women with bulimia nervosa receiving treatment has been estimated at 50 to 70 percent, although later relapses appear to be common. Long-term remission over six years has been estimated at 60 percent for bulimia nervosa. Outpatient treatment samples typically have a better outcome than those that have required hospitalization or intensive outpatient treatment.

Factors that influence the course of bulimia nervosa include frequency and duration of binge eating, frequency of purging behaviors, and associated mental disorders. Obsessive-compulsive disorder appears to influence outcome negatively as does the presence of a personality disorder such as borderline personality disorder. Impulsive substance use can also complicate the outcome of bulimia nervosa. Follow-up studies of bulimia nervosa found higher rates of suicide attempts in those with a history of substance abuse or laxative abuse used to control weight.

Psychiatric Comorbidity

Eating disorder problems rarely occur independently. They commonly occur in the context of other mental disorders and also indicate risk for development of future other mental disorders. In the LOGI-ED study of over 250 subjects admitted for treatment of a severe eating disorder, participants met criteria for other disorders, as noted in table 6.1 below. The percent number represents the total percentage of those with an eating disorder who also met criteria for each additional disorder.

Table 6.1. LOGI-ED Sample Prevalence Rates for Psychiatric Disorders
Mood Disorders • Major depression 68% • Dysthymia 13% • Bipolar disorder 9%
Anxiety Disorders • Obsessive-compulsive disorder 44% • Social phobia 40% • Generalized anxiety disorder 26% • Post-traumatic stress disorder 24% • Panic disorder 21% • Separation anxiety 14%
Substance-Use Disorders • Alcohol abuse or dependence 28% • Cannabis abuse or dependence 12% • Stimulant abuse or dependence 5%

The LOGI-ED sample highlights the common co-occurrence of major depression, obsessive-compulsive disorder, and social phobia in those with eating disorders. The majority of those in the LOGI-ED sample met criteria for anorexia nervosa as their eating disorder diagnosis; therefore, these figures represent primarily the profile for comorbidity in anorexia nervosa.

For those with a primary diagnosis of bulimia nervosa, the comorbidity profile is somewhat different. Major depression remains a prominent additional diagnosis. Rates of substance abuse in bulimia patients tend to be somewhat higher than for those with anorexia nervosa. Patients with bulimia nervosa appear to have lower rates of obsessional and perfectionistic traits while demonstrating higher rates of impulsive behaviors and impulsive disorders.

Suicidal ideation, suicidal planning, and completed suicide are increased in those with an eating disorder. It is unclear whether this risk specifically relates to the eating disorder or to the common comorbidities.

This association requires monitoring as part of the initial assessment as well as during the treatment process.

Medical Complications

The behaviors demonstrated by those with eating disorders pose a significant risk for medical complications. If the eating disorder lasts for only a short period of time, the risk is minimal. However, with increased duration and increased frequency of disorder behaviors, the chance for a significant medical complication rises.

Although dieting and losing weight is often haled as healthy, being significantly underweight is linked to a variety of medical problems. Long-term low weight in women markedly increases the rate of osteoporosis. This is heightened by early weight loss that occurs during the key developmental time frame for lifelong bone deposition. Adolescence and early adulthood is a key time for bone mineral deposition. Impaired deposition due to low weight and low hormone levels during adolescence may not be able to be reversed at a later age.

Additional medical problems related to low body weight and malnutrition can cause medical complications. Anemia may be present in the context of iron deficiency. Vitamin B12 and folate deficiencies can emerge with restriction of protein and meat intake.

Weight-loss-related loss of menstrual cycles reflects the reduction in estrogen and progesterone levels. Reduced sex-hormone levels can impair sexual development and contribute to problems with skin and other organ development.

Binge eating stresses the gastrointestinal tract, producing bloating, cramping, and other gastrointestinal symptoms. Self-induced vomiting produces risk for electrolyte disturbances. Additionally, the acid found in vomitus can erode teeth enamel and increase risk for cavities and gum disease. Excessive use of laxatives to control weight produces a risk for hypokalemia (low serum potassium). Low potassium can trigger abnormalities in cardiac rhythm including complete cessation of the heart. This is the cause of death listed on the death certificate of the singer Karen Carpenter of the singing duo the Carpenters.

Excessive exercise poses risk for associated overuse injuries, such as tendonitis and muscle damage. Excessive exercise and low weight work together to increase risk for stress fractures as well as non-stress fractures.

Genetics

Studies of twins are a powerful clue into the genetic contribution to medical and mental disorders. In twin studies, rates of concordance (matching) for identical twins is compared to nonidentical twins. If a disorder is genetic, it should occur more frequently in the opposite twin for identical twins than for nonidentical twins. This is expected because identical twins share more genes than do nonidentical twins. Twin studies allow for an estimate of the relative contribution of genetic factors compared to environmental contributions.

Twin studies support a genetic contribution for both anorexia nervosa and bulimia nervosa. These studies suggest genetic factors account for 55 to 95 percent of risk for developing the disorder. Genetic contributions to bulimia nervosa appear somewhat lower than those for anorexia nervosa.

The search is on for more specific understanding of how genes influence risk for developing an eating disorder. Early attempts have not been successful in identifying specific genes for either anorexia nervosa or bulimia nervosa. Attention has focused on genes related to the neurotransmitters (serotonin, norepinephrine, and dopamine) and genes related to body-weight regulation (leptin and melanocortin) (Scherag et al. 2010).

Brain Imaging

Early brain-imaging studies of eating disorders looked at the effect of weight loss on brain size and structure. More recent studies have examined the correlates of eating disorder symptoms with specific brain regions. Severe weight loss results in reduction in the volume of the brain's gray matter. This atrophy may contribute to some of the cognitive and psychological features found in anorexia (McCormick et al. 2008). Many of the changes in the brain associated with starvation are reversible, but residual effects may persist.

Functional MRI is a relatively recent imaging tool that allows for study of specific brain regions tied to a cognitive or affective process. Some of the key processes in eating disorders (body-image disturbance, emotional response to food and weight, appetite and food response, reward processing, and drive for thinness) are being examined in those with an eating disorder compared to controls. Some of these early studies are intriguing. For example, women with anorexia show overactivation in the brain region known as the striatum when shown images of thin women (Vocks et al. 2010). This suggests they receive brain-reward responses to stimuli normally not rewarding to control individuals. Additional studies suggest brain deficits in regions involved in integrating body self-image (insula and anterior cingulate cortex) and increased anxiety when viewing the bodies of others (amygdala).

Brain imaging remains primarily a research tool at this time and has limited indication for clinical assessment in most eating disorder patients. Brain imaging may be indicated in cases where eating disorder symptoms occur in the context of another indication for imaging, such as cognitive impairment or a seizure disorder.

Treatment

The treatment goals for anorexia nervosa and bulimia nervosa include assessment of the medical status, normalization of eating behaviors, reduction of psychological distress, and development of a plan to reduce the risk of relapse. An initial assessment will also focus on the most appropriate setting for care. Hospital treatment may be needed for the most severely ill patients with eating disorders.

The American Psychiatric Association published guidelines for the treatment of eating disorders in 2006. This guideline addresses the most important domains of care, including care coordination and collaboration, weight restoration, nutritional rehabilitation, psychosocial interventions, medications and other somatic therapies, and relapse prevention (APA 2006).

Care coordination and collaboration. An important initial step in treatment is to identify important treatment team members and to define their roles. Given the complex nature of eating disorders, the treatment team may include a dietician, pediatrician or internist, psychiatrist, social worker, family members, and other supportive services, such as pastoral counseling and peer support. For patients treated in the hospital, it is often easier to assemble a team that has a history of working together with clearly identified roles in the therapeutic process. Additionally, a medical chart available to all team members in the hospital helps to keep everyone on the same page in the treatment process.

For outpatients, more work may need to be done in assembling and coordinating care. An identified treatment team leader should assume the role of identifying appropriate resources for individual patients. This should include a plan to share progress on treatment goals (as well as relapse issues).

Pastoral counseling can often be an important part of the process of recovery for individuals with an eating disorder. These efforts should include understanding the role of other medical and psychological professionals in the process. Pastoral counseling may be particularly important for family-member support during medical or psychiatric crises that occur in the context of an eating disorder.

Selection of site of care. Admission to a specialized hospital unit for the treatment of anorexia nervosa may be required. Bulimia nervosa is less likely to require hospitalization unless suicidality is present. Indicators of a need for hospitalization in anorexia nervosa include: (1) medical instability with low heart rate, low blood pressure, or severe drop of blood pressure on standing; (2) weight less than 75 percent of what would be expected for height; (3) rapid weight loss (several kilograms/pounds per week); (4) temperature instability or less than 97 degrees; (5) low blood glucose, sodium, or potassium; (5) severe psychiatric comorbidity; (6) active suicidal ideation and/or plan; or (7) deterioration despite aggressive outpatient treatment program.

Weight restoration. Identifying important medical complications and beginning the process of weight restoration are initial priorities in treatment. The patient's height, weight, and calculation of a body mass index (BMI) will provide a starting point in treatment planning. Weight-gain goals for inpatients are typically two to three pounds (0.5 to 1.5 kilograms) per week while weight-gain goals for outpatients are typically less, one-half to one pound (0.3 to 0.5 kilograms) per week. Weight restoration typically has two phases. The first is to stabilize weight loss and get the patient out of a medically dangerous status. The second is to restore weight to a target maintenance level. Many experts recommend a target of twenty-five for the BMI in anorexia nervosa.

Nutritional counseling. Nutritional counseling can be helpful to determine the proper daily calorie count for weight restoration. Patients with anorexia nervosa commonly have a narrow, restricted range of foods. These dietary patterns need to be identified with a goal of expansion of typical food consumed. There may be a wide range in the number of calories required for weight restoration in individual patients. For patients with large calorie requirements, supplemental formula feeding may be necessary. This may include the need for feeding via a nasogastric tube if voluntary intake is insufficient.

For patients with bulimia nervosa, a somewhat different nutritional approach can be helpful. Patients should be discouraged from skipping meals or fasting, as this can result in binge-eating episodes. Planning three or four regular meals spaced out through the day can lessen hunger and reduce binge risk. Patients may want to plan their meals for the next twenty-four hours with an effort to follow the plan as closely as possible. This reduces the need for making daily decisions on what to eat for the next meal. The dietitian can also be helpful in identifying cues for binge risk in individual patients. For example, some patients with bulimia are more likely to binge when presented with an unexpected food choice, for instance, someone bringing a cake in for all at the office. Avoiding high-risk binge situations and developing strategies to deal with them can form the basis of a nutritional counseling plan.

Psychosocial interventions. Unfortunately, little research helps to inform patients and clinicians about the best psychosocial interventions in the eating disorders. There is some evidence that for children and adolescents with anorexia nervosa, a family-based approach is the most effective intervention. This treatment uses a model based on efforts at Maudsley Hospital in London and includes the following:

- Family is actively involved in treatment.
- A blame-free environment is established.
- Families aid patients in increasing calorie intake.

- Families aid and supervise reduction in compulsive exercise and purging behaviors.
- Eating is controlled initially by family but then turned over to adolescent.

For adults with anorexia nervosa, initial psychosocial intervention commonly focuses on behavioral strategies to reestablish regular eating behaviors and caloric intake. After weight restoration, a cognitive-behavioral approach for individual patients may be helpful in reducing psychological distress and reducing the risk of relapse.

In bulimia nervosa, cognitive-behavioral interventions appear to have the most research support (Striegel-Moore et al. 2010). For those with a relatively mildly severe bulimia nervosa diagnosis, CBT (cognitive-behavioral therapy) self-help approaches have some evidence of effectiveness. For severer cases, individual or group CBT may be indicated. CBT for bulimia nervosa typically involves sixteen to twenty sessions divided into three stages:

- Stage 1: Cognitive model of bulimia explained; behavioral strategies provided to replace binge eating with stabler eating patterns.
- Stage 2: Emphasis on elimination of dieting; identification and reduction of cognitive distortions; reduce concern about size and shape; enhance problem-solving skills.
- Stage 3: Process termination of therapy and relapse prevention.

For patients who fail CBT, clinicians can consider other models, such as interpersonal psychotherapy. Additionally, failure in therapy may indicate a need for consideration of a medication trial.

Medications. Medication approaches to the treatment of anorexia nervosa and bulimia nervosa may be another key component to the treatment plan. There are no FDA-approved drugs for the treatment of anorexia nervosa and only one approved for the treatment of bulimia. However, the treatment outcome in eating disorders may be enhanced by medication trials.

As noted above, many patients with anorexia nervosa and bulimia nervosa suffer from a psychiatric disorder in which medications are approved and often effective. Selective serotonin reuptake (SSRIs) antidepressants such as fluoxetine (Prozac®) may help those with anorexia nervosa who suffer from depression or an anxiety disorder. There is some support for the effectiveness of fluoxetine in the prevention of relapse in anorexia nervosa following weight restoration. There is increased attention on the atypical antipsychotic medications in anorexia nervosa (McKnight and Park 2010). Although large randomized trials do not exist, smaller studies suggest the atypical antipsychotics can reduce depression, anxiety, and core eating disorder symptoms in anorexia nervosa.

Fluoxetine is the only FDA-approved medication for the treatment of bulimia nervosa. It appears to act by reducing carbohydrate cravings and binge eating associated with the disorder. Other antidepressants appear also to be effective, although large clinical trials have not been funded to receive federal approval. One trial using the antidepressant bupropion (Wellbutrin™) was halted due to an increased risk of seizure. Bulimia nervosa and the resulting electrolyte disturbance may increase risk of seizure for drugs that have a tendency to produce seizures.

The antiepileptic drug topiramate appears promising in both binge-eating disorder as well as bulimia nervosa. This antiepileptic drug appears also to reduce impulsivity, reduce alcohol consumption, and be associated with weight loss. These additional effects may prove beneficial in those with bulimia nervosa bothered by other impulsivity, alcohol abuse, or being overweight or obese.

Theological and Pastoral Perspectives on Eating Disorders

Mary and her husband showed up in three days. Pastor Jones said his friend the pediatrician noted that weight loss may be a sign of anorexia nervosa or a medical condition. He recommended Olivia be seen by a pediatrician he knew who had experience dealing with adolescents with eating disorders. Pastor Jones said a medical evaluation was important and asked if Mary and her husband would agree to arrange for Olivia to be medically evaluated. They both agreed to this step. Olivia had no current primary-care physician or pediatrician—someone who may also have been consulted regarding her symptoms. Pastor Jones focused on the effect of Olivia's problem on the marriage and relationship between Mary and her husband. He emphasized the importance of Mary and her husband working as a team to address this problem. He prayed with them and provided spiritual counseling on using their faith to reduce their anxiety about Olivia's problem. He scheduled another appointment in one week with the couple.

Follow-up outcome in the case: Olivia was seen by the pediatrician with expertise in treating adolescents with eating disorders. A comprehensive medical evaluation was completed, and no medical cause for the weight loss was determined. A diagnosis of anorexia nervosa was made, and the pediatrician referred Olivia and her parents to a therapist trained in family therapy for adolescents with anorexia and their families. Olivia responded well to this therapy, started to resume a more normal eating pattern. After six months her weight approached normal and her interactions with both her parents was improved. Mary and her husband thanked Pastor Jones for his assistance in providing them with the direction and support needed to help them through this difficult period.

————————————

Like many who study eating disorders, I have personally experienced the phenomenon. I trained as a professional ballet dancer until I went to college. I struggled with anorexia in my middle teens from ages fourteen to sixteen, but managed to do well without help. (Getting better without help is unusual and should not be construed as the norm.) Eating disorders are like pregnancy: you're never "just a little" eating disordered any more than "just a little" pregnant. My sibling also had issues with food. When I had children of my own, I was hypervigilant for any signs indicating that similar problems were developing. I was rather rigid about not allowing them to take extra gymnastics or dance and did not encourage sports for fear of their being around peers who might encourage anorexic behavior. The etiology or causation of such behavior was unknown, whether genetic, environmental, or a combination of both.

My family of origin was conventionally religious, but we received zero support from our parish when I was a starving teen. I was alienated from the church, and my parents would not have confided in a minister regarding the situation.

Basic Theological Issues

Probably most parents will have tried for a long time to tell themselves that their child or adolescent with an eating disorder has just been dieting or getting in shape or finally taking pains over her or his appearance. They may even have encouraged eating problems, at least during initial stages.

Many parents would rather think that the disorder is caused by faulty parenting or some past misdeed that presumably can be amended. Far more frightening is to hear that it may be genetic, biologically based, and has an uncertain prognosis. "I don't know why" is an alarming statement from a clinician. Worse are the words, "We can't guarantee anything." In the meantime, help the family access the best possible medical care and give them your ear, your prayers, and your love.

Parents often blame themselves for a child's anorexia or bulimia and will need to feel forgiven and not have others say, "It's your fault." It will be important to remind the parents that they can't "cause" an eating disorder; it is multifaceted, probably biologically based, with multiple triggers and multipliers, but there may be times when confession and forgiveness can heal in mysterious ways.

During counseling sessions, the child with an eating disorder may or may not feel guilty for the trouble her or his illness can cause the family. The expression of anger and/or "stuffing" the problem (this is common in the early stages of treatment of a family with an eating-disordered member) can result in family members under stress, periodically expressing their anger inappropriately or even abusively. Forgiveness and reconciliation will be required. A caregiver can be most useful spiritually here not by encouraging people to let it all hang out, but by helping people to manage their anger and aiding them in reflecting on mastering their less worthy emotions. Anger can be a good servant (when it motivates one to take corrective action) but a tyrannical master (when it leads one to lash out blindly).

Families experiencing treatment for this kind of a disorder will often feel like the people of Israel wandering in the wilderness for forty years (hopefully not that long!). Taking steps to follow a promising path out of a dangerous situation may nevertheless result in a far worse scenario: the child or adolescent receives treatment, improves, and then gets worse, which ignites family tempers.

Carolyn Knapp has written eloquently about appetites for love, approval, creative fulfillment, as well as food in her own struggle with anorexia. She also documents well how these disordered appetites in women's lives can contribute later or concurrently to difficulties with substance and alcohol abuse, romantic and sexual difficulties. The hungers she describes are poignant cries of emptiness and desolation for which a religious person finds some answers in faith (Knapp 1996). Of course, persons suffering these disorders (and their families) may need pastoral guidance to rediscover how God can assuage those hungers in their lives and guide them into richer, fuller lives that do not include starving and abusing their own bodies.

There will come a time in an anorexic's or bulimic's treatment when it will be necessary to remind them that their illness has social consequences and that life is not all about them. Our culture is uncomfortable with confrontation, particularly with any insistence that people who are ill be urged to behave better. One of the positive roles that faith communities play in the lives of families is in supporting the values of showing consideration for others, setting aside the self in order to be kind to others, and focusing outwardly on the needs of others.

The caregiving relationship can be a light in the darkness for a family experiencing a crisis of an eating disorder. One can do a lot to encourage constructive action if one is alert to the signs of eating disorders.

As I reflect on the case history in this chapter and the clinical observations, the images that come to mind now are of the people around me every day. These are good people and good parents. The media can easily vilify people as helicopter parents, enmeshed parents, or pushy parents. Children may be unfairly portrayed as anxious beyond measure. It is imperative to see them as people who are ill and in need of help.

What does this mean in a typical congregation, where a caregiver may be wondering about who might have an eating disorder here?

Caregiving Opportunities and Challenges

Perhaps most important in caregiving is the gift of being able to draw forth people's stories, to truly listen, understand, and respond to them with godly love, and to give spiritual direction as appropriate.

There are few things more healing for a person than telling her or his story and being understood. The Gospels are full of such stories. People are amazed and liberated when Jesus tells them the story of their lives and they are at last freed from their bondage. Jesus wasn't setting up permanent counseling relationships; rather, he was incarnating the love of God in being attentive to all people. Listening to a painful story, even once, and demonstrating that one understands, will be a great gift to a family.

Next, a caregiver is *not* a diagnostician! One must not rush to label or intervene in or lecture about even a blatantly obvious family situation. It's a rare family that consults about a stigmatizing diagnosis except in a crisis, so be glad and recognize it as a sign of health when a family does.

Virtually all people with eating disorders are still very much involved with their families of origin. If nothing else, they still need their parents to pay for their treatment. Eating disorders are often blamed on the family environment, on certain types of parenting, though today people are starting to consider biological explanations as well. Whatever the cause, the parents end up watching a beloved child starving to death, sometimes lying, manipulating, and turning the household upside down. The family may spend a fortune on care, worry constantly, get fed up that meals are a battleground, and simply want things to get back to "normal." The youngster seems to get better, relapses, stays dependent financially year after year, seems to grow up, and then relapses again. These young people are terrified; they are angry; they feel guilty, hopeless, and ashamed, resulting in isolation.

Faith communities can and should minister to families who are experiencing this ordeal. Perhaps the best thing a faith community can do for a person suffering from anorexia or bulimia is to minister to the family, keep their hopes and their spirits up, and promise to support them irrespective of the outcome. Faith communities can offer individual care, facilitate peer support groups for families, and help reconcile families broken apart by past battles over eating disorder issues.

Faith communities can have potluck suppers, coffee hours, and share pleasant meals together. These can be a welcome change from stony family suppers with a person suffering from anorexia who pushes food around and refuses to eat.

Spiritually, the community of the faithful can gently but persistently remind the family that all are loved by God and are accepted as they are. This is a welcome corrective to the obsessive efforts of a desperate person with an eating disorder to control the family environment.

Another important role of the caregiver is to remind people that they are still part of the family of God, and valued and needed irrespective of the circumstances. There are a number of ways in which belonging to a faith community can aid in healing a person who is desperately ill with an eating disorder:

- Having regular prayer (the person her/himself, the family, or prayer groups for them).
- Participating in regular worship experiences and in the life of the community to the extent that is possible.
- Being encouraged to help and contribute despite the fact that one is ill: "Will you help teach Sunday school, or help with this project?" People who are ill are often treated with kid gloves and thereby made to feel useless. Having a role that is limited but gets them in contact with others is helpful. In a healthy faith community, it is assumed that everybody helps out in some way, whether old, young, healthy, or ill.
- Having the minister establish limits for ministry and support the clinical staff treating the person with an eating disorder. At its best, an anorexic who hands food out to the hungry at a community kitchen, or who teaches a terrified child newly adopted, may be touched by another's need and reach out to them. A measure of healing is experienced in salving the wounds of another. The words of the Prayer of St. Francis may come alive for her.

Practical Advice for a Busy Caregiver

   1. *Have a plan for how to handle an eating disorder.*

- Prepare a list of local doctors and social workers.
- Find a list of inexpensive providers or pro bono agencies (money is always an issue)
- Do *not* ask someone in the faith community to see the family for free (it will be long term, demanding, with potential boundary violations).
- Talk to people on the hospitality committee about always having something "healthy" at coffee hour.
- Make sure those who work with youth go to workshops and understand eating disorders and are honest about their own experiences with them.
- Collect a good bibliography of helpful resources that can be distributed.

   2. *Cultivate your own relationship with God and model good healthy self-care.* You are a clanging cymbal unless you can share the genuine love of God and others. We love because God first loved us.

   3. *Mention eating disorders.* Make it a point with every appropriate opportunity in teaching, preaching, or caregiving to mention eating disorders matter of factly without making light of the illness with humor. Humor can be healing when it is misery shared and lightened by companionship but can be devastatingly shaming when used to judge or poke fun at people who are ill.

   As a caregiver mentioning eating disorders, don't be heavy-handed, but mention the illness as a treatable illness, just as you would allude to alcoholism and drug use as things that afflict God's people. Stress the positive, that these are illnesses that many people in faith communities have struggled with and overcome with God's help, peer and family support, and modern medical care. Introduce the topic whenever it may be appropriate without judgment or condemnation. It is important to make such subjects acceptable topics of discussion. (Treating eating disorders as a "taboo" only increases the misery, shame, and isolation of sufferers and their families.)

4. *Take care of your own family; look for the mote in your own eye.* Most caregivers, whether clergy or laypeople, take great care both to regularly retreat spiritually to restore their own prayer life and peace with God, but also to make time for fun with their families and to take care of familial needs. If someone in your own family is developing an eating disorder, take time off from your ministry to take care of her or him.

5. *Live out the core values of your faith tradition.* There are certain core values that are integral to the three major Western religious traditions of Judaism, Christianity, and Islam. The injunction to "love one another" is likely the first and most important value that these traditions hold in common. This means "love" in the deepest sense of the word, not an emotion but, rather, an "attitude" of care and concern for all of our sisters and brothers.

Give voice to the inherent worth and value of every human being irrespective of the human categories that are so often devised to exclude others. The Creator has created all creatures for relationships, fellowship, and mutual care and concern. Prejudice, discrimination, and bias are not divinely ordained; they are human constructs that have no place in faith communities.

There is a common realization that human beings are not what the divine intended them to be, therefore the acknowledgment of estrangement and alienation as realities needs to be embraced. Implementing a message, mission, and ministry that takes seriously the need for forgiveness, reconciliation, healing, and blessing, irrespective of how that is done in diverse religious traditions, is imperative.

Lifting up the reality of hope as the guiding light in life as one deals with the difficulties, pain, and all of the exigencies of life is essential. Hope springs eternal when the vision of healing, health, and wholeness is held out as a gift of the divine for humankind. This cannot be hope that is illusory or wishful thinking but, rather, realistic hope that supports, ministers to, and comforts those who are suffering with eating disorders as well as those who are negatively affected by the presence of the illness in the family or in the faith community.

6. *Get training and supervision yourself.* You will burn out fast unless you know professionals who have dedicated their lives both to studying and addressing constructively eating disorders. Secure additional

training as well as regular professional outside supervision of your work. That can involve going to workshops and establishing informal or formal relationships with local psychiatrists, psychologists, and social workers you trust to consult with when you are stymied or burned out by a series of difficult or demanding caregiving situations.

My recommendation, when all else fails, is to get therapy yourself. Only to the extent that you are grounded and self-aware will you be a better servant. Dealing with a family where the diagnosis is that of an eating disorder is demanding work and the danger of becoming a part of the problem as opposed to a part of the solution is always a concern.

It is appropriate to approach a psychiatrist, psychologist, or clinical social worker in the congregation and ask them if he or she would be willing to recommend someone who could give you supervision for difficult cases. It is, however, inappropriate for clinicians within the parish to be asked to provide therapy. Clinicians need to be able to worship and draw their own spiritual sustenance from the faith community for their own demanding vocation without having to become a pro bono resource for caregivers. Ideally, your faith community could pay for the supervision if that is feasible. The concept of the "wounded healer" is an important one to embrace, as it recognizes both the role the caregiver has in the healing process, while also being aware of her or his own wounds needing attention.

Bibliography

American Psychiatric Association (APA). 1994. *Diagnostic and Statistical Manual of Mental Disorders*. 4th ed. Washington, D.C., American Psychiatric Publishing.

———. 2006. Treatment of Patients with Eating Disorders. 3d ed. http://www.psychiatryonline.com/pracGuide/pracGuideChap Toc_12.aspx.

Boumann, Christine E., and William R. Yates. 1994. "Risk Factors for Bulimia Nervosa: A Controlled Study of Parental Psychiatric Illness and Divorce." *Addictive Behavior* 19 (6): 667–75.

Hay, Phillipa P., Josué Bacaltchuk, and Sergio Stefano, et al. 2009. "Psychological Treatments for Bulimia Nervosa and Bingeing." *Cochran Database Systems Review* 4.

Hollis, Judi. 1985. *Fat Is a Family Affair.* Center City, Minn.: Hazelden.

Hudson, James I., Eva Hirip, and Harrison G. Pope Jr., et al. 2007. "The Prevalence of Eating Disorders in the National Comorbidity Survey Replication." *Biological Psychiatry* 61 (3): 348–58.

Knapp, Carolyn. 1996. *Drinking: A Love Story.* New York: Dial.

Laureate Eating Disorders Assocation. http:/www.nationaleating disorders.com.

Maudsley Model for Treatment of Anorexia in Children/Adolescents. http://www.maudsleyparents.org/.

McCormick, Laurie M., Pamela K. Keel, Michael C. Brumm, et al. 2008. "Implications of Starvation-Induced Change in Right Dorsal Anterior Cingulate Volume in Anorexia Nervosa." *International Journal of Eating Disorders* 41 (7): 602–10.

McKnight, Rebecca F., and Rebecca J. Park. 2010. "Atypical Antipsychiotics and Anorexia Nervosa: A Review." *European Eating Disorders Review* 18 (1): 10–21.

National Eating Disorder Association. http://nationaleatingdisorders. org/.

Scherag, Susann, Johannes Hebebrand, and Anke Henny. 2010. "Eating Disorders: The Current Status of Molecular Genetic Research." *European Child Adolescent Psychiatry* 19 (3): 211–26.

Striegel-Moore, Ruth H., G. Terence Wilson, Lynn DeBar, et al. 2010. "Cognitive Behavioral Guided Self-Help for the Treatment of Recurrent Binge Eating." *Journal of Consulting and Clinical Psychology* 78 (3): 312–21.

Strober, M., R. Freeman, and W. Morrrell. 1997. "The Long-Term Course of Severe Anorexia Nervosa in Adolescents: Survival Analysis of Recovery, Relapse and Outcome Predictors over 10–15 Years in a Prospective Study." *International Journal of Eating Disorders* 22 (4): 339–60.

Vocks, Silja, Martin Busch, Dietrich Gronemeyer, et al. 2010. "Neural Correlates of Viewing Photographs of One's Own Body and Another Woman's Body in Anorexia and Bulimia Nervosa: An MRI Study." *Journal of Psychiatry Neruoscience* 35 (3): 163–76.

AUTISM

Steven D. Thurber / Hollie Holt-Woehl

7

James is a fourteen-year-old male. He was born full-term without complications. He showed early delays in motor areas, including standing, taking his first steps, and walking (he did not take his first steps until eighteen months of age). Throughout childhood he was clumsy and ill-coordinated with small-muscle difficulties (he could not tie his shoes until age ten). His language development was also delayed; he did not utter his first words until age two, with age one being the norm. He showed early problems in attending and concentration and later in impulse control, behaving aggressively toward family members. James did not seem to care when his behaviors were hurtful or painful to others. He preferred to be alone and found no pleasure in social transactions. He was observed to see other people as things or objects; he did not share possessions in his early years nor attend to activities that interested other people (mutual gaze) or imitate their actions. In early adolescence, he would talk to others but mainly for his own ends or interests; he seemed not to care or even be aware regarding the effects of his actions or communication attempts on others. He ended conversations by abruptly walking away. Correspondingly, James became increasingly distant from people, enmeshed in computer games and fantasy activities. He could be involved in computer games every waking hour unless caregivers intervened and unplugged the machine. James fantasized

*a large intricate system of interacting members of a fictitious under-
ground community with a very complicated social and organizational structure, in which he himself would act heroically in terms of
maintaining the balance among factions. As a teenager over six feet
tall and two hundred pounds, he evinced a distinctively long, rapid,
stiff-legged stride when he walked.*

*When James was tested for academic readiness and possible
emotional problems that might interfere with school performance,
he was found to have superior general intelligence but was very limited in his ability to organize or conceptualize the information he
received in the classroom. He was described as exceedingly "egocen-
tric," meaning in part that his interactions with others, increasingly limited in scope and frequency, were nonreciprocal; the only
goal was to obtain from others what he, James, wanted. He was not
impeded by concerns about distress his interactions might engender.
He was ostensibly unable to place himself mentally into the position of another, to think and feel with others in an empathic way.
When he spoke to fellow beings as an adolescent, he would discuss
his personally created imaginary world or explain how his computer
worked, totally detached from the reactions of others; he was unable
to monitor how his actions affected others and modify his behaviors
accordingly.*

Understanding Autism

James was diagnosed with "high-functioning" autism, meaning that
he had symptoms consistent with such a diagnosis but was normal in
intellectual functioning; in James's case, superior intelligence (about 70
percent of autistic children have some level of mental retardation). As
illustrated in this example, one important way of viewing autism with
individuals having normal-to-superior intellectual functioning is that it
pertains to an overwhelming interest in the physical world and a cor-
responding aloofness or disinterest in the social world. Not surprisingly,
high-functioning autistic persons are found at high rates in fields such as
computer science, mathematics, physics, and engineering (Wheelwright

and Baron-Cohen 2001). James's interests only extended to understanding computers and game software. Another point to be made is that persons with autism can be engulfed in trying to understand or involved in the construction of systems; in James's case, attempting to comprehend how computers work and constructing a fantasized, very complicated organizational structure. Such inclinations are termed "systemizing" and may be a hallmark concept in the understanding of autism; more about this later.

The Meaning of Autism

The term *autism* comes from the Greek words *autos*, meaning "self," and *ismos*, referring to "action" or "state." It originally meant (circa 1912) extreme self-absorption that prevented the individual from extending himself or herself to other people, and hence being removed from important social learning experiences (Baron-Cohen 2005). Currently, autism is viewed as *a spectrum of neurodevelopmental conditions* manifested by combinations and degrees of "impairments" in social relationships and communication, with narrow interests and repetitive behaviors. Let us analyze the core terms (in italics) of this definition.

Spectrum refers to a range or continuum and was first referenced in what is now termed "Asperger syndrome." The spectrum was a dimension from being odd but socially interacting on one end (Asperger syndrome) to complete social aloofness on the other. It should be mentioned here that there is still a debated question: Is Asperger syndrome the same as or different from high-functioning autism (i.e., individuals with symptoms of autism with normal intellectual functioning)?

Unfortunately, a confusing aspect of autism is that the spectrum is also conceptualized in other ways. To some it simply means mild to severe in degree of symptom manifestation. To others in the autism field, spectrum is understood to be related to the sheer number of symptoms being evinced, from few to several combinations. For other researchers and theoreticians in the field, the continuum relates to whether or not intellectual functioning is part of the equation. Mild autism refers to an aggregate of autistic symptoms combined with at least normal intellectual and language development, whereas severer autism involves varying degrees of subnormal intellectual functioning. Mild autism is also termed high-functioning autism and, to some, Asperger syndrome (see below). For our purposes, it is probably best to equate Asperger's with high-functioning autism.

The *neuro* part of the definition involves the notion that certain regions of the brain may be abnormal in size and function. For instance, several studies suggest that the back part of the brain (cerebellum and brain stem) is significantly smaller in size among persons with autism (Chorchesne et al. 1994); other research indicates overall brain enlargement (Bailey et al. 1993). There is also current interest in what is termed "anomalous dominance," in which the right rather than left hemisphere of the brain is ascendant among groups of autistic individuals together with a reduced size of the corpus callosum (the fibers that connect the right and left brain hemispheres (Moncrieff 2010). *Developmental* refers to age-related changes. The brains of autistic infants at birth may, for example, be normal, but both white and gray matter may increase abnormally in certain brain areas until age two or three, only to return to normal volume levels with age. Behaviorally, the types and frequency of behavioral symptoms may show a decline or modification with age. For example, the oft-cited "rocking" actions in autism are more characteristic of autistic children, not adolescents.

The aforementioned core features will be seen in varying degrees among individuals reliably classified as autistic, but there are vast individual differences in how the combinations and severity levels are manifested. In addition to the core features, there may be peripheral characteristics, such as motor difficulties (as in the case of James, above) that are consistently seen in some but not all persons with this diagnosis.

Neuroscience Findings

Weak central coherence. There are three significant findings from neuroscientists in worldwide research. The first is termed weak central coherence. It has been found consistently that individuals with autism show interest in the concrete, the particulars, and not the whole. The weak central coherence notion posits that the autistic brain processes information in a piecemeal fashion, that reasoning is from particular to particular, without fusion. The world outside the autistic individual is like a series of still photographs swirling by one by one that are never fused together into a "motion picture"; the autistic person is interested in the details but not in the whole, complete configuration.

Executive functions. These are higher mental operations that facilitate adjustment and adaptation in life. They include the rational control of impulses (response inhibition), planning and goal setting, working memory (e.g., the ability to retrieve memories that will facilitate adjustment in a given situation), and attention including the shifting of attentional focus, concentration, and vigilance. It is not surprising therefore that many childhood disorders, including Attention Deficit Hyperactivity Disorder (ADHD), may involve problems in executive functions mediated by the prefrontal (right behind the forehead) cortex. Of the executive functions listed, perhaps "working memory" is one that requires elaboration.

Theory of mind. This refers to the cognitive processes that provide the intellectual underpinning for empathy, the capacity vicariously to "feel" the emotions of another, to understand the motives and desires of a fellow human being. These processes are subserved by a special network or circuit of interconnected regions that might be termed the "social brain." It might be informative to discuss briefly those regions and their associated social functions.

The circuit comprising the social brain facilitates a "theory of mind" that enables us to predict what others are going to do based on their *desires, beliefs, and knowledge* (Frith and Frith 2010). Keep the word *predict* in mind as we proceed. This network of brain areas is located mainly in the prefrontal (behind the forehead) and temporal regions (left and right side areas) of the cerebral cortex:

- *Superior temporal sulcus (STS).* A sulcus is an indentation or groove in the cortex or outer covering of the brain. Superior refers to the more anterior part of the temporal lobes; the latter are found in front of the ears, right and left sides. This region processes changeable and movable aspects of the face, such as facial movements and eye-gaze changes.

- *Temporal-parietal junction.* This is closely adjacent to the STS and deals with object permanence. This allows us to think what an object would look like from another person's (different) position.
- *Inferior frontal gyrus.* A gyrus is an elevated convolution on the surface of the brain. Inferior means toward the back of the brain. This region is sensitive to behaviors in others that will be imitated by the observer.
- *Prefrontal cortex.* Just behind the forehead; the mid-area of the prefrontal cortex responds to subtle cues or signals from others indicating that they want to communicate (e.g., calling one by name; eye gaze).
- *Fusiform gyrus.* This is located again in the temporal lobe; it is where memories for faces are stored. It facilitates identification of individuals.
- *Amygdala.* Again, located in the temporal lobe. The word itself refers to "almond shaped." This area of the brain is activated by facial expressions of emotion, which is especially important in determining whether or not another person constitutes a threat.

Try to imagine what it would be like if this network was not operative. You could not ascertain emotions in other people, their intentions, estimates as to how the world is perceived by persons outside yourself; and you might have a difficult time identifying another person. Like James, you would be unable to monitor how your "audience" is reacting to your verbal expressions and hence could not modify your social behaviors accordingly. And, most importantly, you could not predict their reactions.

One of the best indicators that the social brain is poorly functioning stems from what is called the false belief task. Imagine a toy truck with a small figure inside representing the driver. Max is asked by an experimenter to place the driver in a desk drawer; Max then leaves the room. This is all observed by Anne, age fifteen, diagnosed with high-functioning autism. While Max is away, the experimenter takes the driver figure out of the drawer and places it under a red cup in the corner of the room. Again, this is all observed by Anne. Next, Anne is told that Max will be returning to the room. She is then asked the critical question: *Where will Max initially look for the driver of the toy truck?* The typical five-year-old child will answer consistent with the mind-set of Max. That is, Max will have the *false belief* that the figure is still in the desk drawer and will act accordingly. Even a typically developing fifteen-month-old infant will show surprise, as indicated by eye gaze, if Max does not look in the drawer first. Anne, and indeed adults with autism, will predict erroneously that Max, upon reentry to the room, will go immediately to the red cup. Why? Because that is where the figure is. Lacking a theory of mind, Anne cannot project herself into Max's thinking sufficient to understand his extant beliefs about the hiding place.

Possible Causes

The possible causes of autism are many and varied. There is certainly a genetic contribution. Twin studies indicate a 60 percent concordance rate for monozygotic (identical) twins; that is, if one twin is diagnosed with autism, there is a 60 percent chance that the identical twin will also receive the diagnosis. For dizygotic twins having 50 percent of their genes in common, the concordance rate is zero (Muhle et al. 2004). More specifically, the HOXA 1 gene, found on chromosome #7, has been implicated (Kabot et al. 2003; Stodgell et al. 2006). Nevertheless, there are a myriad of other potential causes that pertain mainly to noxious effects on fetal development in the intrauterine environment. These would include maternal rubella infections, medications taken during pregnancy, such as thalidomide, and circulating testosterone that can be a neurotoxin (Rodier 2002). Perinatal insults during and shortly after birth may possibly have a causal role; for instance, fetal distress, emergency caesarean section, and labor induction (Glasson et al. 2004).

Autistic Savants

The notion that certain autistic individuals, usually with a level of mental retardation, may paradoxically possess special skills has been the subject of newspaper and magazine articles and even motion pictures. About 10 percent of individuals with autism will display savant abilities. Most will show skills mediated by the right hemisphere of the brain, including calendar and rapid mathematical calculations, drawing, and musical skills. Some, termed prodigious savants, can perform remarkable acts. Most theories of savantism suggest that injuries or dysfunctions of the left hemisphere promote a compensatory takeover by the right hemisphere together with a predominant habit or procedural memory; this type of memory is the hallmark of savant abilities (Treffert 1994).

Systemizing

This refers to a motive to analyze or construct systems. The defining characteristic of a system is that it follows rules; systemizing is the process of discovering and identifying rules that govern the system in order to *predict* (remember the importance of the word *predict*) how the components or the system as a whole will behave (Baron-Cohen 2009a; 2009b). Simon Baron-Cohen has identified the major types of systems, for instance: *collectable systems* (e.g., distinguishing between flying and crawling insects), *mechanical, numerical* (e.g., calendar), *abstract* (musical notation), *natural* (weather patterns), *social* (patterns in a hierarchical organization), and *motoric* (step-by-step procedures for throwing a frisbee) (ibid.).

The important point here is that, unlike social interactions, a system has regularities that come from mandatory or built-in rules. They are reliable, consistent, and hence predictable. Think about a ten-year-old autistic child watching a toy electric train either in person or on film, running on a track; she or he will likely spend more time spontaneously engaging in this activity than most any other (NAS 2002). Unlike the interpersonal world, the train on track involves motion that is predictable with readily discernible rules that are invariant. The train can only move while on the track, and only forward and backward, not sideways. This is most attractive to the child with autism. If given a chance to use a control switch, he or she will repeat the back-and-forward motion over and over to ensure that the rule is never violated.

Thus the repetitive behaviors often seen in autism can be viewed as adaptive when applied to the understanding or construction of some type of system. Moreover, the emphasis in the processing of details can be better understood as adaptive when applied to systems; excellent attention details are essential to grasp the nature of the system; even a tiny detail, if lost, may impede understanding of the system as a whole. Thus the aforementioned difficulties labeled "weak central coherence" may not even exist, at least regarding systems. Attention to detail would be a strength; moreover, such an orientation to particulars occurs in the service of ultimately cognizing the system as a whole—that is, it is preparatory to conceptualizing the system. Whatever the cause of autism, it affects adversely the social network of the brain but, in the absence of mental retardation, also renders cognitive strengths regarding curiosity about the physical world together with predispositions to know and construct systems.

In sum, the message from neuroscience is that with understanding comes compassion. Indeed, any reasonable person can understand what it must be like to be in a situation that is ambiguous, unpredictable, replete with buzzing confusion, and fearful. This is the social world of autism. We can try to reach the child or adolescent with autism through the conduit of systemizing. Despite social brain inadequacies, interpersonal skills can be taught effectively, if presented in an organized, systematic manner; even the autistic child with mental retardation can benefit (Golan et al. 2010). Communication can be facilitated via modeling appropriate social behaviors while playing together with an electric train, for example, or while working together to build a machine with Legos®, or teaching the step-by-step rules for striking the tennis ball with a racket effectively.

The Faith Community and Autism

A family had been members of a certain congregation for many years. When their son with autism became a teenager and grew to be about six feet tall, some members felt threatened by his physical size and odd behavior. Conversations between the pastor, members, and family became heated and polarized. The family continued to attend worship, and the members continued to complain. Finally, the congregation took out a restraining order on the mother and her son so they would be arrested if they attended worship.

Another mother wanted her son with autism to be confirmed in the church where they were members. The priest in this large

Catholic church told the mother the child would be too much work and
they would not be able to accommodate him. She responded by imme-
diately looking for a church that would confirm her son. She found
a medium-size Lutheran congregation where she and her son felt
welcomed. This congregation had spent the last four years learning
how to welcome and accept another child with autism and his family.

———————————

Throughout history, and into the present, faith communities' responses to children and adults with autism or other developmental disabilities[1] have varied. Some faith communities have offered welcome and acceptance to people with developmental disabilities and considered them as full participants in the faith community. Others have viewed people with developmental disabilities as defective or seen their disability as the result of sin and therefore separated them from, restricted them within, or even cast them out from the community (Covey 2005; Merrick et al. 2001; Holt-Woehl 2010; Miles 1995; Morad et al. 2001). Often faith communities require intellectual belief or understanding, a notion that is challenged when a person has intellectual disabilities. Some faith communities believe that those with severe intellectual disabilities are exempt from needing God's grace in the sacraments and therefore have a special place before God. Through legislation (Americans with Disability Act, 1990), education, disability organizations (such as National Organization on Disability and The Arc of the United States), and experience, modern-day faith communities have become more accepting of people with autism and developmental disabilities.

"Autism never affects one person alone; it involves the whole family and the whole community" (Walsh et al. 2008, 12). This is also true in the faith community. Having a child with autism in the faith community not only affects parents and siblings of the child but each member and leader of the faith community. Breakdowns or successes in caring and participation may take place on any one of those levels. It is a challenge to keep all these in mind at all times in a faith community. The child with autism has different challenges or needs than the parents, siblings, and members of the faith community. The parents have different challenges or needs than the person with autism, siblings, and members of the faith community.

Research studies have reported that faith and participation in a faith community can ease the stress and provide peace of mind. A 2009 research study, "The Influence of Religiosity on Well-Being and Acceptance in Parents of Children with Autism Disorder," reports "Parents who more strongly endorsed having religious beliefs and who were more involved in religious organizations had greater well-being and were more accepting of their child's disorder" (White 2009, 111). The corollary was also reported; parents who reported little or no religious belief and little or no involvement in religious organizations had a negative impact on well-being. Therefore, faith communities may play an important role in the lives of the parents of children with autism.

Theological Issues

For the faith communities rooted in the Abrahamic tradition who use the Hebrew Scriptures as an informing document, the book of Genesis reveals God as a social, relational God. From the beginning God is in relationship with the creation. God creates and cares for all living things. In Genesis 2:4b-25, the Lord God forms a human being out of the ground (Hebrew: 'ādām, meaning "earthling" out of the 'ădāmāh, earth). God plants a garden and places 'ādām in the garden to care for it. But God says "it is not good" for 'ādām to be alone. Therefore the Lord God wants to make a helper/partner for 'ādām and begins to form animals. Of the animals there was not found a helper as 'ādām's partner, so God takes a rib out of 'ādām and forms a woman. As Old Testament scholar Terence Fretheim writes:

> The text speaks of human beings created in the image of God neither as isolated individuals nor as a generalized humanity, but as *social, relational beings*—male and female—and thereby correspondent to the sociality of God ("let us"; see Gen 1:26; 3:22; 11:7; cf. 9:6). . . . This relational understanding of image is affirmed by God's own declaration that the isolated or totally independent 'ādām is 'not good' (Gen 2:18). Generally speaking, human beings are given such gifts that they have a *communicating relationship* with one another and with God (recall that they are the product of inner-divine communication,

1:26) and can take up the God-given responsibilities specified in 1:28. (Fretheim 2005, 55)

Throughout Genesis, God is seeking a way to engage humans in relationship. Even though the actions of the humans separate them from God, God doesn't give up on them. God continues to care for them even after their disobedience; see the stories of Adam and Eve, Cain and Abel, Noah, Abraham, Isaac, and Jacob.

Since autism affects the social, relational part of human relationships, it is not only a challenge to relate to people with autism, but it is also a challenge to speak of God in relational terms to people with autism. These are individuals who struggle to be in relationship with others, and when the basic foundation of a faith community is to connect people to God and people to one another, this creates tension. Because God is relational, however, God will not give up on human beings. "O LORD, you have searched me and known me" (Ps. 139:1). God still seeks out those who are unable or unwilling to engage in relationship.

Leaders in faith communities will be called upon to engage in this question of relationship: How does God seek to engage children with autism? How does the faith community engage in a relationship with children with autism? How does the faith community teach about a relational God to children with autism?

Caregiving Challenges and Opportunities

Parents of children with autism want their child to participate in the life cycle of the congregation—birth, childhood, adolescence, young adult, and adult—and the rites that come with it—Baptism, first communion, confirmation or bar/bat mitzvah, weddings, and funerals. One family member[2] of a child with a disability states the struggle of being part of the life cycle of faith:

> There's a challenge when you're from a low church, believer's baptism tradition, as opposed to the liturgical infant baptism tradition. Because it does raise a problem if you're in a baptistic tradition there's a point at which a child will accept Jesus and they'll get baptized and at least in some measure be a part of their volition and development.

And with a clearly disabled kid it becomes problematic. . . . Jorge's teacher, who goes to our church, has a now adult 22-year-old daughter who has hardly any mental capacity. Partly at the urging of a family friend, we had a baptism service. And of course, everyone was okay with it, but the fact is she can't do the things that you normally would do. A profession of faith, an explanation, she can't do any of that. So there's a certain awkwardness and defensiveness, and it was more private too. It wasn't done in the church, it was done in the home. (Jacober 2010, 176).

The person with an intellectual disability was baptized. However, the baptism took place outside the church building and away from most of the members of the faith community. These life-cycle events/rites of faith are meaningful only within the faith community. In some traditions, Baptism is an entrance rite into the faith community; first communion is an entrance to the meal/sacrament of the faith community; confirmation or bar/bat mitzvah is an entrance into the adult membership of the faith community. A Baptism or first communion or confirmation or bar/bat mitzvah outside the community conveys the message that it is not supported by the faith community as a whole. When people with autism or intellectual disabilities take part in a life-cycle rite of the faith community, it may challenge persons' theological understanding of the rite, but it may also be an opportunity for the faith community to learn more about the rite and witness God's acceptance of all people.

A trait of autism that may be a gift for the faith community is the importance of rituals. Faith rituals and orders of worship may be comforting for a person with autism as long as too much change does not happen all at once. Liturgies and rituals do not have to become stale, but they can become a forming influence in the lives of all the faithful. If the order of worship changes totally from one week to another, it may not only be stressful to the person with autism but other members also. It is okay to have the comfort of ritual to support those who are going through tumultuous times. One congregation had a child with autism as a member, and any change in the order of worship was stressful for this child. When there was a change to the worship, someone from the congregation would contact the family a few days before worship to inform them of the change and to give them the new order of worship. This gave the family time to prepare the child for the coming worship service.

Another challenge for faith communities who have members with autism is that people may feel that only professionals who are trained in autism are able to care for and engage with the child with autism. Because the child may be a bit odd and not engage in the correct social interactions, people may think they have nothing to offer the child. However, one need not be a professional to care for another person.

How Faith Communities Might Respond to Autism

Many books and websites are available to help faith communities respond to people with autism. These resources offer techniques; outline education programs, trainings, and ministries; share personal stories; and include questionnaires and inventories[3] to be used with individuals, families, and faith communities. Seek out these resources, engage members (with and without disabilities) of the faith community in conversation, and ask questions of yourself, the tradition, and members of the faith community. A fancy program may not be needed, but welcome and acceptance are required.

The most important thing to remember is the *person* with autism. Focus on the person, not the label; this person is a child of God. The label may be helpful to know tendencies and to understand behaviors. However, get to know the child with autism by asking the child herself or her parents some of the following questions: What are her likes and dislikes? What are her favorite activities? What are the signs of stress? What is calming for her? It may take many interactions of short duration to get to know the child with autism and to engage her in conversation, but over time a relationship may develop.

It takes time and creativity to be able to reach and teach children with autism, but it will be worth it. Even if the child may not seem to learn and grow from the interaction, everyone else will learn and grow. When faith communities learn to accept one child with autism they become more accessible to all people. In welcoming, accepting, and engaging a person with autism, members of a faith community learn, in a new way, that each person is different and has something to offer the community of faith.

Bibliography

The Arc of the United States. http://www.thearc.org/page.

Bailey, Anthony, Phillip Luthert, Patrick Bolton, et al. 1993. "Autism and Megalencephaly." *The Lancet* 341 (8854): 1225–26.

Baron-Cohen, Simon. 2005. "Autism—'Autos': Literally, a Total Focus on the Self." In T. E. Feinberg and J. P. Keenan, eds., *The Lost Self: Pathologies of the Brain and Identity*, 166–80. New York: Oxford University Press.

———. 2009a. "The Empathising-Systemising Theory of Autism: Implications for Education." *Tizard Learning Disability Review* 14 (3): 4–13.

———. 2009b. "Autism: The Empathizing-Systemizing (E-S) Theory." In *The Year in Cognitive Neuroscience*, 68–80. New York: New York Academy of Sciences.

Bolduc, Kathleen Deyer. 2001. *A Place Called Acceptance: Ministry with Families of Children with Disabilities*. Louisville: Bridge Resources.

Carter, Eric W. 2007. *Including People with Disabilities in Faith Communities: A Guide for Service Providers, Families, and Congregations*. Baltimore: Paul H. Brookes.

Chorchesne, Eric, Osamu Saitoh, Rachel Yeung-Chorchesne, et al. 1994. "Abnormality of Cerebellar Vermian Lobules VI and VII in Patients with Infantile Autism." *American Journal of Roentgenology* 162 (1): 123–30.

Covey, Herbert C. 2005. "Western Christianity's Two Historical Treatments of People with Disabilities or Mental Illness." *Social Science Journal* 42 (1): 107–14.

Davie, Ann Rose, and Ginny Thornburgh. 2005. *That All May Worship: An Interfaith Welcome to Persons with Disabilities*. Updated 7th ed. Washington, D.C.: National Organization on Disability.

Frazier, Thomas W., and Antonio Y. Hardan. 2010. "A Meta-Analysis of the Corpus Callosum in Autism." *Biological Psychiatry* 66 (10): 935–41.

Fretheim, Terence E. 2005. *God and World in the Old Testament: A Relational Theology of Creation*. Nashville: Abingdon.

Frith, Uta, and Chris Frith. 2010. "The Social Brain: Allowing Humans to Boldly Go Where No Other Species Has Been." *Philosophical Transitions of the Royal Society* 365 (1537): 165–76.

Gaventa, Bill. 2009. "Dimensions of Faith and Congregational Ministries with Persons with Developmental Disabilities and Their Families: A Bibliography and Address Listing of Resources for Clergy, Laypersons, Families, and Service Providers." http://rwjms.umdnj.edu/boggscenter/products/documents/DimensionsofFaith2009.pdf.

Glasson, Emma J., Carol Bower, Beverly Petterson, et al. 2004. "Perinatal Factors and the Development of Autism: A Population Study." *Archives of General Psychiatry* 61: 618–27.

Golan, Ofer, Emma Ashwin, Yael Granader, et al. 2010. "Enhancing Emotion Recognition in Children with Autism Spectrum Conditions: An Intervention Using Animated Vehicles with Real Emotional Faces." *Journal of Autism and Developmental Disorders* 40 (3): 269–79.

Holt-Woehl, Hollie M. 2010. "Education and Inclusive Congregations: A Study of Three Congregations." *Journal of Religion, Disability, and Health* 14 (2): 143–52.

Howell, Erica J., and Melinda R. Pierson. 2010. "Parents' Perspectives on the Participation of Their Children with Autism in Sunday School." *Journal of Religion, Disability, and Health* 14 (2): 153–66.

Jacober, Amy Elizabeth. 2010. "Youth Ministry, Religious Education, and Adolescents with Disabilities: Insights from Parents and Guardians." *Journal of Religion, Disability, and Health* 14 (2): 167–81.

Kabot, Susan, Wendy Masi, and Marilyn Segal. 2003. "Advances in the Diagnosis and Treatment of Autism Spectrum Disorders." *Professional Psychology: Research and Practice* 34 (1): 26–33.

Merrick, Joav, Yehuda Gabbay, and Hefziba Lifshitz. 2001. "Judaism and the Person with Intellectual Disability." *Journal of Religion, Disability, and Health* 5 (2): 49–63.

Miles, Michael. 1995. "Disability in an Eastern Religious Context: Historical Perspectives." *Disability and Society* 10 (1): 49–70.

Moncrieff, Deborah. 2010. "Hemispheric Asymmetry in Pediatric Developmental Disorders: Autism, Attention-Deficit/Hyperactivity Disorder, and Dyslexia." In Kenneth Hugdahl and René Westerhausen, eds., *The Two Halves of the Brain: Information Processing in the Cerebral Hemispheres*, 561–601. Cambridge: MIT Press.

Morad, Mohammed, Yusuf Nasri, and Joav Merrick. 2001. "Islam and the Person with Intellectual Disability." *Journal of Religion, Disability, and Health* 5 (2): 65–71.

Muhle, Rebecca, Stephanie V. Trentacoste, and Isabelle Rapin. 2004. "The Genetics of Autism." *Pediatrics* 113 (5): 472–86.

National Autistic Society (NAS). 2002. "Do Children with Autism Spectrum Disorders Have a Special Relationship with Thomas the Tank Engine and, If So, Why." Research undertaken by Aidan Prior Communications, London.

National Organization on Disability (NOD). http://www.nod.org.

NOD Religion and Disability Program. http://www.nod.org/religion.

Newman, Barbara J. 2006. *Autism and Your Church: Nurturing the Spiritual Growth of People with Autism Spectrum Disorders*. Grand Rapids: Faith Alive Christian Resources.

Rich, Cynthia Holder, and Martha Ross-Mockaitis. 2006. *Learning Disabilities and the Church: Including All God's Kids in Your Education and Worship*. Grand Rapids: Faith Alive Christian Resources.

Rife, Janet Miller, and Ginny Thornburgh. 2001. *From Barriers to Bridges: A Community Action Guide for Congregations and People with Disabilities*. Washington, D.C.: National Organization on Disability.

Rodier, Patricia M. 2002. "Converging Evidence for Brain Stem Injury in Autism." *Development and Psychopathology* 14: 537–57.

Stodgell, Christopher J., Jennifer L. Ingram, Melanie O'Bara, et al. 2006. "Induction of the Homeotic Gene *HOXA 1* through Valproic Acid's Teratongenic Mechanism of Action." *Neurotoxicology and Teratology* 30 (5): 617–24.

Treffert, Darold A. 1994. "Pervasive Developmental Disorders." In Sandra D. Netherton, Deborah Holmes, and C. Eugene Walker, eds., *Child and Adolescent Psychological Disorders: A Comprehensive Textbook*, 76–97. New York: Oxford University Press.

Walsh, Mary Beth, Alice F. Walsh, and William C. Gaventa, eds. May 2008. "Autism and Faith: A Journey into Community." http://rwjms.umdnj.edu/boggscenter/products/documents/AutismandFaith.pdf.

Wheelwright, Sally, and Simon Baron-Cohen. 2001. "The Link between Autism and Skills Such as Engineering, Math, Physics, and Computing: A Reply to Jarrold and Routh." *Autism* 5: 223–27.

White, Stacy E. 2009. "The Influence of Religiosity on Well-Being and Acceptance in Parents of Children with Autism Spectrum Disorder." *Journal of Religion, Disability, and Health* 13 (2): 104–13.

ACQUIRED BRAIN INJURY

Steven D. Thurber / William Sheehan /
Lawrence M. Pray

8

Paul is a thirty-five-year-old man who was in an automobile accident eight months ago. He received a closed head injury and lost consciousness for over eight hours. His wife says that he currently isolates himself from her, their two young children, and the outside world. He no longer seeks contact with formerly close friends. This is in sharp contrast to the socially outgoing "life of the party" persona that characterized Paul prior to sustaining the head injury. His wife says she has tried everything in her power to help Paul return to being his old self, but every attempt has failed.

Jane is a high school teacher who was very active in athletics, including entry in several triathlon competitions. While engaged in a cross-country cycling event, she unfortunately hit a large rock on the side of a trail, became airborne, and landed in a deep culvert; the left side of her head was penetrated by a sharp rock. She lay in a hospital bed in a state of unconsciousness for three weeks; she has no recollection of her accident. Currently, Jane has difficulty preparing classroom lessons, citing problems in concentration, but having particular problems "getting started"; she now waits until the last possible moment before commencing preparation. When she finally initiates activity, she finds herself just writing aimlessly on a notepad. Writing lesson plans used to be the easiest part of her profession.

Tommy was an athletic, outgoing student in the fifth grade diagnosed with Attention Deficit Hyperactivity Disorder (ADHD) and childhood depression when he sustained traumatic brain injury (TBI) in a high-speed vehicular accident. He was unrestrained in the backseat of his parents' car when it flipped over and he was thrown through a side window, landing some forty feet away on road pavement. He was found to have a closed skull fracture (right frontal area) with other physical injuries. When he arrived at the hospital, he did not respond to questions and seemed oblivious to pain. Since his release from the hospital, his mother reports he has experienced headaches, dizziness, difficulties with attention and concentration, forgetfulness, excessive sleeping, anxiety, and impulse control problems. Tommy also seems to process information more slowly after the accident, shows a lack of mental flexibility, and has begun to have problems in academic achievement, especially in mathematics. As time goes on, he is becoming increasingly oppositional and angry.

Understanding Acquired Brain Injuries

An acquired brain injury refers to damage that occurs after birth and includes two basic types: traumatic brain injury (TBI) and cerebrovascular accident (CBA) or stroke. The emphasis of the chapter will be on presenting information relevant to the understanding and care of increasing numbers of individuals who experience TBI, including those who are victims of war-related blast injuries. The chapter concludes with poignant accounts by Larry Pray of the psychological and spiritual experiences of loss following CBA.

Traumatic Brain Injury (TBI)

Traumatic brain injury, or TBI, refers to damage to brain tissue that stems from an external force. Damage can result from falls, acts of violence, vehicle accidents, being struck by lightning, electrical shocks, sports and recreational accidents, or any other activity that results in a blow to or penetration of the head. In addition, a sudden, violent movement of the head (e.g., from explosive blasts or whiplash), not a direct blow or penetration, can also result in TBI. The latest national (yearly) information from the Centers for Disease Control and Prevention indicates 1.1 million emergency-room visits, 235,000 hospitalizations, 80,000 disabled individuals, and 50,000 deaths related to traumatic brain injuries. However, most (approximately 80 percent) instances of TBI are mild in nature (Kraus and Nourjah 1988). Nevertheless, TBI is also the most common cause of death and disability in children (Babikian and Asarnow 2009).

Basic Brain Anatomy and TBI

The two interconnected brain hemispheres literally float in cerebrospinal fluid that acts as a kind of shock absorber to protect the brain from injury. The brain is also protected by the skull. The smooth outer layer of the brain is called the "dura." If the inner area of the skull were likewise completely smooth, the brain would move or glide with even minor head movements. Instead, there are uneven, irregular, rough surfaces in the inner skull that, in effect, hold the brain in place, protecting it from injury when normal head movements occur. However, the locations of these irregular inner surfaces that encapsulate the brain are mainly at the base of the skull. This leaves the front of the brain and left and right anterior sides (i.e., frontal and temporal lobes) especially vulnerable to injury. Indeed, most cases of TBI involve damage to those areas of the brain and will be emphasized in this chapter (Bigler 2007).

Important Terminology

As indicated, TBI can result from sudden movement of the brain, causing (typically) the anterior or temporal areas to hit the inside of the skull. The result is termed *lesion*, or brain tissue damage. Sudden movement that does not involve impact between the brain and skull but is nonetheless injurious is called *shearing*, resulting in microscopic tears in nerve fibers. Subsequent bruising is termed *contusion*. Swelling of the brain is called *edema*. Penetrating wounds to the brain can result in infections called *meningitis*. Hemorrhages, leading to clots in the brain, are termed *hematomas*. Reduced blood flow to the brain is called *ischemia*.

There are *closed head* (no skull fracture), and *open head* (skull fracture) injuries. The latter can involve pieces of the skull tearing delicate brain tissue. Traumatic brain injuries are classified as *mild* (either no loss of consciousness or loss of brief duration; also called *concussion*). *Moderate* TBI involves loss of consciousness for several minutes to several hours. A *severe* TBI is based on loss of consciousness for days, months, or even years.

General Adverse Consequences of TBI

The adverse effects of TBI can be roughly divided into three classifications: *cognitive, behavioral,* and *physical. Cognitive* refers to deficiencies in reasoning abilities, concentration, memory, impulse control, planning, executing the plan, and mental flexibility (see executive functions, below). *Behavioral* is the rubric for various psychiatric disorders manifested in overt actions, including affective problems (anxiety, depression, fluctuations of emotional states), irritability, impulsivity, apathy, aggression (both verbal and physical), and substance-use disorders. The *physical* symptoms can include dizziness, nausea, fatigue, sleep disturbances, and seizures (Riggio and Wong 2009).

Factors That Influence TBI-Related Symptoms

There will be great variability between and among patients who have experienced TBI, even in patients who have sustained injuries in the same brain regions with similar levels of severity. Manifested TBI symptoms will vary according to such factors as the locality of the brain injury, whether it is in the right or left hemisphere (lateralization), the extent of damage (amount of tissue involved), preexisting psychiatric conditions, personality and behavioral characteristics, and the degree of premorbid (i.e., before TBI) adjustment; this has to do with the extent of acquired adaptation skills prior to the brain injury (Riggio and Wong 2009; Hopkins et al. 2005). Furthermore, the following require consideration for understanding the impact of traumatic brain injuries:

1. *Cognitive reserve.* This is a complicated theoretical construct related to the extent of premorbid intellectual capacity and educational level. It can involve the notion that brain pathology must

go beyond a protective reserve level before clinical manifestations are observed, or that the brain has the capacity to "borrow" from this reserve to compensate for the effects of brain insults (Stern 2009; Kesler et al. 2003).

2. *Age.* Chronological age is an indirect measure of the adverse impact of processes that affect cerebral integrity over time and make the individual more vulnerable to neurocognitive impairments involving TBI. Some experts view the developing brain as more "plastic" and capable of greater recovery after insults than the adult brain. The opposing perspective is that TBI effects on a youthful brain may disrupt and impede development and produce more adverse consequences. Data from Erik Hessen, Knut Nestvold, and Vicki Anderson suggest greater long-term adverse consequences for children when compared to adults (Hessen et al. 2007).

3. *Timing of assessment.* This has to do with how long after the brain insult a professional evaluation is made. There are data indicating that the full intensity and extensity of impairment will not be revealed until approximately ninety days following brain injury (Bigler 1996).

Thus there are numerous variables that interact to produce manifested symptoms following TBI. Therefore, it is difficult to predict for a given individual exactly what symptom constellation will be displayed. In addition to the pre- and postmorbid variables listed, we could also include the quality of family and other social and religious support systems as factors that can contribute to positive adjustment and adaptation to the specific effects of TBI. Nevertheless, there are certain characteristic cognitive and mood findings for frontal and temporal lobe injuries. Damage to the frontal lobes will likely result in impaired *executive functions*, whereas injuries specific to the temporal lobes will often result in memory difficulties and mood fluctuations.

Executive functions, subserved by the frontal part of the brain, include the capacity to establish goals and formulate plans to attain them, speed of processing information, impulse control (inhibition), self-monitoring and self-regulation, ability to conform to social rules, attention and concentration, decision making, and *working memory*. Working memory is the most sensitive and perhaps the most important of the executive function abilities because it is intertwined with many of the aforementioned frontal mental abilities. Working memory refers to an "on-line" or "in-real-time" set of mental processes involved in the various phases of problem solving. Working memory allows an individual to shift perspectives on a problem, define goals while considering several parameters of a problem simultaneously, plan a strategy while anticipating consequences, execute steps of a plan held in memory, monitor progress, detect and correct errors, and accommodate new data while filtering out interference. These abilities appear to be largely but not exclusively related to activity in the dorsolateral frontal cortex.

TBI Outcomes

The consequences of TBI for children are typically evaluated at three postinjury intervals:

1. *Post-acute period*, from zero to five months after the injury. This is where the greatest functional impairments are found.
2. *Recovery period*, from six to twenty-four months after the injury. The greatest recovery is generally observed during this time interval.
3. *Chronic period*, twenty-four months and beyond. This is the time after the greatest recovery of functions; little if any improvement occurs thereafter, though it is always important to remember that every case is unique, and embracing realistic hope facilitates healing.

Talin Babikian and Robert Asarnow have conducted a comprehensive "meta-analysis" (combining the results of independent scientific investigations) on outcomes for children and adolescents (Babikian and Asarnow 2009). Data across the best TBI outcome studies with children indicate that for individuals who experienced mild brain injuries, few, if any, impairments were found at any of the above time periods, including the post-acute phase. For children with moderate TBI, impairments were noted at all time periods in general intelligence and the executive function of processing speed, with only modest improvements in the recovery period. Children with severe TBI displayed large impairments in general intelligence and the executive functions of processing speed, attention, memory, and problem solving with little recovery noted. It should be emphasized that defects in executive functions after moderate to severe TBI is a frequent finding in the literature (ibid.).

Unfortunately, TBI outcomes for adults have not been addressed as rigorously or systematically as they have with children. It is likely that there have been greater concerns of the future adjustment of young people after TBI than for adults. It is fair to say that findings related to mild brain injuries are much the same for children and adults. For adults experiencing moderate to severe TBI, research has focused on occupational adjustment. Rachel Devitt and her colleagues found that preinjury behavioral problems and postinjury cognitive (executive functions, again) and physical deficits predicted poor occupational performance (Devitt et al. 2006). Research by Aase Engberg and Thomas Teasdale evaluated TBI survivors (moderate to severe levels of severity) five, ten, and fifteen years postinjury (Engberg and Teasdale 2004). The main reported concerns were an inability to maintain work and learning at preinjury levels together with problems in emotional control (executive function, again).

Treatment Considerations

The case materials, presented above, involve TBI at the three levels of severity. In the matter of thirty-five-year-old Paul with moderate severity, there is a prototypical outcome of TBI, symptoms of *depression* manifested by a change from preinjury gregariousness to postinjury social isolation. He is eight months postinjury and may show symptom reduction over time as a function of the adjustment and compensatory processes indigenous to the brain itself. Jane experienced severe TBI and has a common symptom of depression, that of lowered motivation (difficulty "getting started"), combined with difficulty in sustained attention and concentration, and problems in organization and planning (probably related to working memory), all executive functions. Tommy did not respond to questions for a time after his injury, but there was no indication of unconsciousness. He had premorbid ADHD, so it may be that the symptoms of poor concentration and impulse control dysfunctions are a carryover from his past or are perhaps more pronounced postinjury. Additionally, he is still showing the accident-related physical symptoms (headaches, dizziness, excessive sleep), negative emotional conditions (anxiety, anger), and executive-function problems (mental inflexibility, perhaps working-memory difficulties). The accident may also have affected adversely his general intelligence (slower information processing). The aggregate result seems to be reduced academic competence. Given his age and premorbid conditions, he is less likely than the adults to show spontaneous reductions of symptom severity.

In our comprehensive literature search, no articles were found specific to pastoral response to individuals who evince emotional and behavioral symptoms related to brain insults. What we did find is that persons who deliver pastoral care tend to perceive themselves to be competent in dealing with grief, death and dying issues, anxiety, and marital difficulties but tend to be challenged in relation to effective interventions for persons with depression, alcohol/drug problems, domestic violence, and severe mental health difficulties (Moran et al. 2005). The mental health sequelae of TBI can involve instances of behavioral and emotional symptoms for which pastoral counselors may think of themselves as least prepared. Fundamentally, pastoral counselors will likely be dealing with depressive symptoms and executive-function deficits (e.g., impulse-control problems such as aggression) among individuals experiencing moderate to severe TBI.

Depression

Depression is the most frequent mood disorder following TBI. Symptoms such as low self-esteem, inability to initiate activities, sadness, hopelessness, and sleep and eating problems are likely to occur. It may be that the brain injury directly affected emotionality; it is more likely that stress encountered in the adjustment process is the major cause of depression. The remedy for the adverse effects of brain insults requires adjustments and change. Tasks that were deemed easy prior to the injury are now difficult; for example, changes in how one selects different tasks to accomplish or tries to recover preinjury functions is now mandated. When the individual's capacity to make the necessary changes is severely taxed, the immune and endocrine systems of the body may become dysregulated causing the person to become more vulnerable to stress-related disturbances, with depression being the common outgrowth of this type of stress. Inability to function at premorbid levels, chronic pain from the brain insult, and TBI-related litigation are potential stressors faced by individuals with moderate to severe TBI (see Bay and Donders 2008 for further discussion). In addition, if, as supported in the research literature, stress is the major component of depression, there is probably a continuity between preinjury stressors (e.g., economic and unemployment hardships) that predispose the individual with TBI toward depressive symptomatology.

For TBI depressive symptoms, stress-management procedures would likely be one treatment of choice. These techniques emphasize the development of relaxation skills that in turn reduce the biochemical components of the body's stress reaction (for details, see Walker 2000).

Executive Functions

A metacognitive teaching strategy has been used successfully with survivors of TBI. Metacognition refers to "thinking about thinking." The step-by-step procedures involve setting goals, self-monitoring of progress toward the goal or actual goal attainment, decision making regarding subgoals and strategies, selection among possible alternative solutions (also called rational self-control), and, finally, implementation of the selected potential solution, or what amounts to executing a change in one's behavior. Mary R. Kennedy and her colleagues report improved, rationally controlled behaviors among TBI patients when the therapeutic goal is to enhance skills related to problem solving, planning, and organizing behaviors by adults with TBI-related executive problems (Kennedy et al. 2008).

Recent attempts to improve working memory are encouraging. Torkel Klingberg, Hans Forssberg, and Helena Westerberg worked with children having impaired frontal lobe functioning (Klingberg et al. 2002). They attempted to improve working memory through various forms of practice. They placed in front of the children, one at a time, printed circles varying in size. After a delay, the task was to reproduce a particular sequence. The number of circles in a sequence was gradually increased. A digit-span task involved presenting increasing numbers of digits in a sequence, both visually and orally, while gradually increasing the number of digits that had to be reproduced backwards. In a letter-span procedure, letters were read aloud, one at a time; the child then was asked to remember the identity of each letter and the appropriate sequence. These techniques were used daily for about twenty-five minutes across a five-to-six-week period. The result of this training was significant improvement as well as generalization to working memory tasks that were not part of the specific daily practice.

Behavioral Interventions

Mark Ylvisaker and his colleagues provide a review of behavioral interventions with children and adults following TBI (Ylvisaker et al. 2007). Behavioral problems relate to the fact that the rational control of behavior (one of the executive functions) may attenuate as the result of brain injury. Difficulties involving failure to control impulses (especially aggression) and emotional expressions can occur frequently with TBI. Behavioral procedures include the following:

1. Contingency management, using techniques that involve rewards and other consequences to increase positive behaviors and decrease or extinguish disturbing or undesirable behavioral acts.

2. Promoting desirable behaviors through direct instruction (step-by-step procedures) or modeling, especially in natural settings (home, school, on the job).

3. Facilitation of social behaviors via actual interactions in natural environments coupled with direct communication and feedback.

In the review of worldwide investigations by these authors, studies using such interventions resulted in significantly improved behavioral functioning following TBI.

Blast-Related TBI

As in all wars, the conflicts in Afghanistan and Iraq have brought a unique set of horrors. World War I brought horrendous pulmonary injury from mustard gas. World War II brought massive civilian casualties from aerial bombardment and the first cases of radiation injury. Korea brought frostbite and freezing to soldiers unprepared for the climate. And Vietnam brought, among other issues, drug addiction and exposure to defoliants. All brought the insidious disease of post-traumatic stress, termed "shell shock" in World War I and "battle fatigue" in World War II. All left permanent scars.

Given the improvement in defensive armament, including body armor and highly efficient Kevlar helmets, today's soldiers are often surviving previously fatal attacks. Kevlar helmets have reduced the number of piercing open-skull brain injuries and decreased mortality, yet this war is being fought with improvised explosive devises (IEDs), and soldiers are now faced with "blast injuries." Our clergy are now facing the prospect of veterans returning with a combination of post-traumatic stress (PTSD) and TBI. PTSD can involve "reliving" the traumatic event(s) as well as having intrusive and recurrent memories and dreams about the experience(s). Additionally, the emotional and behavioral impact of blast-related brain insults occurs in the context of combat veterans being in constant threatening situations, having prolonged periods of nervous system "hyperarousal," while often witnessing violence and death (Wrobel and Stewart 2008).

Blast injury is caused by "super-excited" air molecules passing through the helmet, skull, and brain structures, shearing neurons as they pass. Resulting brain damage can range from mild to severe, with unique symptoms developing in each victim depending on the variables mentioned above. Clergy need to be alert for returning veterans with TBI as well as PTSD. It is important for the clergy to remember that the entire family is victimized by blast injury. All will need education, counsel, and spiritual support. Further, stress reduction though the development of relaxation skills can be helpful.

Stroke

Cerebrovascular accidents (strokes) stem from a disruption of blood supply to the brain due to blockage or the bursting of a blood vessel. As mentioned, individuals with TBI are most likely to experience executive function and emotional disturbances. Victims of stroke can evince several classes of difficulties depending on where in the brain the disturbance is located. These include paralysis, problems controlling movement, sensory disturbances (e.g., a limited visual field), disruptions of the use or understanding of language, and problems in thinking and memory.[1] Although recovery from strokes may occur over a prolonged period, most significant changes occur during the first six months following the brain insult (Skilbeck et al. 1983). Again, from the standpoint of emotional functioning, depression is a common response. Key elements in adjustment to cerebrovascular accidents are the degree of mobility within a year after the insult and the ability to perform routine activities of daily living (King et al. 2002).

Pastoral Care for TBI and Stroke Survivors

One moment, he is fine. One moment, she sings in choir.

Suddenly, to our surprise, the language of loss makes its unexpected appearance. A billion or so neurons have disappeared. Vessels that once brought life-giving oxygen to the brain have hemorrhaged or clogged. Cells suffocate. Sometimes the damage comes from inside the brain. Sometimes it comes from a fall, a blow to the head, or an explosive device. There are ways in which the two are different. Each has its own ancillary issues. Post-traumatic stress, for example, may well have to be addressed for soldiers returning with TBI. And each has its own gradations. The trauma of TBI occurs but once. Stroke patients, on the other hand, may well have another stroke. The effect of a stroke tends to be local, such as the loss of movement on one side of the body, or speech, whereas the effect of a traumatic brain injury tends to be more global. Dr. David Gumm, the neuropsychologist with whom I wrote my book *Over My Head*, notes that "when it comes to helping people with difficulties with the brain, one size does not fit all. Everyone's injury or illness is unique, and we need to know them in their uniqueness and meet their individual needs."

Either way, an acquired brain injury (ABI) changes life and the perceptions of life. And either way it is authenticity that leads the road to healing. We can only write what we know and what we have learned when one life has been swept away and another has yet to emerge. Not surprisingly, after the injury the language of loss emerges.

"Can you feel that?" the doctor asked as she pricked my left hand with a needle.

"No," I said.

"Your right brain is swollen, and that's not good," the neurologist said after he reviewed the CAT scan that verified I'd had a right-brain stroke of massive proportions.

"The woman we worked with in Paraguay, what country did she live in?" my doctor asked me.

"Spitzerland," I said. "No, that's not how you say it," but that's the way I said it in a voice suddenly without lilt, without inflection, without a hint of personality.

"What time is it?" the nurse asked me. "Look at the clock and tell me what time it is."

What could be simpler than that? I thought. On the wall, over the foot of my bed, there was a hospital clock. The kind of clocks kept in schoolrooms. It was big enough to be easily seen. No-nonsense numbers made no attempt to disguise the time. Neither did the hands.

"What time is it?" she asked.

I looked again, thinking I could answer her question in a heartbeat. But nothing happened. I, who knew how to tell time, could not tell time. I stared at it and waited. Nothing happened. A wave of disbelief passed through me, ran over me. Still no traction.

I couldn't tell the time.

I didn't know then that the right brain is responsible for relational thinking. To tell the time is actually a complex process. One must discern the numbers and the relation of not just one hand, but two hands, to those numbers. Only when the big hand is three-quarters of the way around the dial, pointing at the number nine, a quarter turn away from the number one, little hand is three-quarters of the way between twelve and itself once again, only then does the clock read 12:45.

This language of loss.

It is easy to describe. Death always is. It doesn't move. Finding what's wrong, performing an autopsy, is never as challenging as finding life that has a way of never standing still.

This language of loss.

He's not able to understand, the nurses said, and they were right. I would read the paper, and, like the clock, the words had no traction, no meaning. "Who would write a sentence as terrible as that?" I'd say to myself. But it wasn't the reporter, it was my capacity to decipher meaning that had been lost.

I didn't know at the time that the brain's primary function is not coming up with a thought, but filtering a million and one perceptions until only a few are left. With brain injury, be it from an external or an internal cause, the filter is lost. On the way home from the hospital, we stopped in a store. I went in with my wife, only to realize within a minute or two that I could not handle it. All those beeps, all those shelves, all those people, all those sounds, all that commotion. I quickly headed back to the car and fell immediately asleep.

Once upon a time, sleep meant rest.

Not now. Now it meant recovery. Sleep was a return to the deep darkness of Genesis before the world formed.

All these losses, each one attributable to an injury.

It's odd that although we think with the brain, we don't think much about it. We don't realize it is through the brain that we perceive all there is to perceive about life. Without the brain, meaning loses coherence. Without the brain, we cannot order our perceptions. It is interesting that "brain dead" is our way of saying, "Really dead." I hasten to point out that being in a coma may or may not be akin to being brain dead. Many of the patients in my rehabilitation "class" had endured a long coma but came out intact. Changed, to be sure, but intact.

This language of loss.

"Let's pray," my minister said to me.

"Okay, but you'll have to do it," I said. The language, the feel, the understanding of prayer had all departed. A word I'd loved, cared about, preached about, and thought about was suddenly empty. What is prayer? It is relational. God says something I say something there is a dialogue between us. "Oh Master let me walk with thee," we sing. "What a friend we have in Jesus," we sing.

Relating to another, understanding of the other, was as indecipherable as the telling of time.

"How are you, Dad?" my children would ask.

"Fine," I said. "But it's not me."

Loss. And the language of loss.

"You will not be able to work."

"Ever?"

"Probably not."

"What about working on Christmas Eve? It's a month away."

"No. It's too dangerous," said my doctor.

Finally, after a month, we went to a neurologist. Surely a specialist would hold the key to recovery. Surely something could be fixed. Surely the losses could be stemmed.

"What do I do?" I asked as she showed me the MRI of my brain. The entire right side looked like Antarctica, an entire continent of white. The area was not small but was easily the size of my hand.

"But what do I do?" I asked again.

"You don't understand," she said. "Those cells are dead. They cannot grow back."

Pastoral care is aware of loss. But it has a far deeper calling. It is the calling of creation itself.

We look into the eyes of someone who has been touched by a stroke; we struggle to understand what they are saying; we wonder what we can say. We wonder if there is any way to transcend the reality of loss. To which I answer: there is, but we must turn from the language of loss to the language of life. Something is happening in there, in that brain that is in the midst of reordering the world, struggling to accept a new set of bearings. In this new beginning, there is something going on. We find ourselves taking to heart and living through the first lines of Genesis.

In the beginning God created the heavens and the earth. Now the earth was formless and empty, darkness was over the surface of the deep, and the Spirit of God was hovering over the waters. *And God said, "Let there be light," and there was light.*

In such waters we with brain injury find ourselves.

The language of creation replaces, and transcends, the language of loss, just as it does in life. Our question is not, "What have you lost?" but "What's it like?" and "What's happening?"

It saddens me that in my experience this most theological of all questions is rarely asked by clergy. They want to be sympathetic and supportive, but they tend not to be very curious. Many are afraid. In my case, when I most needed my denomination to be present, those responsible for pastoral care were missing. Perhaps it is because they take the words of the neurologist too seriously: "Those cells are dead." The diagnosis of death is sad but safe. No miracle is expected. No prayer will turn back the clock. And so we're tempted to put in an appearance rather than trying to discern what God is doing.

It is, of course, a pitfall not only for those who care for us, but for ABI patients themselves.

"What are your goals?" the director of rehabilitation asked me when I entered a cognitive treatment facility.

"I want my life back," I said with passion, and even a flash of anger that had suddenly appeared without the calm-down filters that once kept me on an even keel. I loved ministry. I loved my church. I loved my calling. I wanted my life back.

I knew, even as I spoke the words, that they were denying creation itself. It wasn't "my life." Nobody can return to the exact person they were. Rehabilitation is not about returning to what was. I often wish the syllable *re* could be taken from the word *rehabilitate*. "Re" takes us into the past. If we go there, comparison becomes an enemy, and the long list of losses gains an edge that traps us in the past and views the present as a deficit.

Instead, something else had to happen. Figuring out what it is, and what it is like, may be the hardest work of a person's life. We are virtually starting life all over again. And, as Phyllis Trible said in her first Old Testament lecture at Union Theological Seminary, "Beginnings are difficult." They are by necessity uncertain. They can be anything but safe. There are setbacks. Most of all, progress is invariably slow. Here, too, the creation story frames our experience. Creation did not happen in one day. It took seven. Not many years ago, neurologists thought that the progress made in the first few months after a stroke or a TBI reflected all the progress one could make. It is now understood that it takes five or six years to "recover" from a serious brain injury. Which is to say, it takes five or six years to find a sense of self, an appreciation of relationships, and a new understanding of life that makes emotional, physical, and spiritual sense.

Five words full of hope were the single most important words of pastoral care I ever received. "Time is on your side," a therapist said. With time, remaining neurons that were once responsible for only a certain function find they can take up some of the slack. The brain, it turns out, is plastic. It is always changing. Always mending. Always healing. Always perceiving. Time is a blessing.

So, of course, are relationships. Healing, not only should not be, but is not a lonely experience. Family, colleagues, friends, and faith community are all essential. I had the extraordinary blessing of a loving, compassionate, and caring church. Their kindness, their patience, their sheer goodness surrounded us with love that made up for the emptiness we so deeply felt. This all happens *over time*. I want to emphasize those last two words. Healing happens over time. Hospitals or clinics give us a diagnosis, but healing happens somewhere else—somewhere "out there." It is, of course, the calling of churches to travel with us through our lives over time. I will never forget a couple I shared rehab with. When she awoke from her coma after a car accident, she could not recognize her husband. Ten years later, they were still together, and she was still in therapy.

"What's life like?" I asked them.

"It's us," he said. That summed it up. I hasten to mention that although it is often said that TBI/stroke vastly increases the chances of a divorce, statistics do not bear this out.

Pastoral care for one in a congregation involves caring about a person over time. The stroke/TBI patient may have lost a job, may have even lost a calling, but we trust that something will emerge, and, more importantly, that something is emerging. We stroke survivors live in an emergent world. We are no longer of the same substance. Or, as the

Greeks put it, we are no longer *homousian*. But spiritually we are of the same essence. We are *homoiousian*. A list of our losses is of no help in proclaiming a new world. A simple question, "What's happening?," ever so rarely asked, helps us find a way. It is, of course, the same as asking, "What is God doing?" It is the essence of pastoral care.

Although it would be "best" if stroke patients and TBI patients could have separate groups in a treatment facility, the truth is this is beyond the reach of most, if not all, churches. But no matter. When ABI survivors meet together, we have these stories. The rope that broke, the truck that didn't stop, the accident, the day strength left, and the way we've learned to encourage each other. In such groups, no translation is necessary. We "get it." There is no reason in the world a church cannot organize such groups, led by a pastor, a social worker, and a nurse.

There are two other takes on pastoral care that are equally crucial and ever so difficult for ABI survivors. We all know that it is easier to marshall one's strength for a battle than it is for a war. I would do whatever they asked of me in cognitive therapy. I could do that, exhausting as it was. I would fight the good fight. But after the battle, I didn't expect a continuing war on not just one but two fronts.

The first front is depression. It comes with the territory. It often disguises itself as "truth." The truth seems to be a seemingly unending string of losses. In such a time, the presence of friends makes all the difference in the world. It is especially important for a former boss, or perhaps a denominational executive, to say, "There's a table set for you, somewhere." W. E. B. Du Bois began his famous book, *The Souls of Black Folks*, with the line, "What does it feel like to be a problem?" Not good, is the answer. With a fully functioning brain we might be able to slough off the feeling. With a brain that has "lost" its capacity to moderate perception, believing one is a "problem" is heartbreaking. In such a place, the giver of pastoral care simply must find a way to affirm, to ask about purpose, and to discern what God is doing. This does not mean, "God had a plan for you and it included an IED or a stroke." Such rationalizations can be detected a mile away. But the wounded healer has something to say, however halting it may be.

The second is related to the first but is perhaps more difficult. For insurance companies, TBI/stroke patients are a "problem." When we are at our most vulnerable, they are adamant in doing what they can to throw us overboard. It is essential to have some competent and perceptive help in figuring out the ins and outs of insurance claims. We will, of course, have more bills than ever. And we will, not unexpectedly, have fewer ways to pay our bills. Battles with insurance companies almost broke my spirit. Pastoral care for TBI/stroke patients involves not just their spiritual welfare, but also their very economic survival. Problems with insurance are to be expected, and they are part of the healing process. Navigating these waters calls for a calm but firm hand that calls for hope, trust, and courage.

Change the brain and you change the way life is perceived. Change the brain and you change faith. It is as simple as that. Yes, there are losses. But something is happening. A new way of perceiving self, others, and God can't help but emerge. One language is lost. Another takes its place, whether or not we are able to speak it.

I end these writings with two stories.

The speech therapist asked me to take one minute and say every word I could that began with the letter *S*.

What could be simpler? I was a pastor. A writer. A lover of words. And lots of words begin with the letter *S*.

"Okay," I said.

"Begin," she said.

I waited for the first word to appear. Nothing happened. Not a single word beginning with the letter *S* appeared. Five seconds. No word. Fifteen seconds. No word. Finally, one made its way into sound. I almost fell out of my chair.

"What happened?"

"Well," she said. "Your brain is like a file cabinet full of files. The stroke pushed the cabinet over and threw the files all over the room. None of them were lost, but you don't know where to find them. Everything is out of order. So when you search for a word beginning with *S*, or *T* or any other letter, it is chaos."

Now the earth was formless and empty.

A year after cognitive therapy, I attended worship in Red Lodge, Montana, a city we moved to after my second stroke—this one on the left side of the brain. I could not keep up with the pace of the service and felt fatigue creep through me three-quarters of the way through the service. I knew I had to leave, go home, and crash.

I quietly stood up and walked to the door. Then I walked to the outside door and pushed it open, glad to be away from trying to "keep up" with all that was going on. There is a sumac tree just beside the church door. In it there were perhaps fifty cedar waxwings in the shimmering sunlight. They did not take flight. I took one step forward, moving a bit closer. Still they did not take flight. Another step. Another person came out. Still the waxwings stayed in the tree. And then, in one astonishing moment, they took wing.

For a year my prayers had nowhere to go. But in that moment, I knew with inner certainty, my words finally found their way home. One day, Jeremiah saw a flowering almond branch. One day, Moses saw a burning bush. One day, Amos saw a plumb line. One day, in each of our spiritual lives, something happens. For me, one day, I knew for sure what Jacob had spoken:

Surely God is in this place and I did not know it.

I wish you well in your call to care.

Bibliography

Babikian, Talin, and Robert Asarnow. 2009. "Neurocognitive Outcomes and Recovery after Pediatric TBI: Meta-Analytic Review of the Literature." *Neuropsychology* 23 (3): 238–96.

Bay, Esther, and Jacobus Donders. 2008. "Risk Factors for Depressive Symptoms after Mild-to-Moderate Traumatic Brain Injury." *Brain Injury* 22 (3): 233–41.

Bigler, Erin D. 1996. "Brain Imaging and Behavioral Outcome in Traumatic Brain Injury." *Journal of Learning Disabilities* 29 (5): 515–30.

———. 2007. "Anterior and Middle Cranial Fossa in Traumatic Brain Injury: Relevant Neuroanatomy and Neuropathology in the Study of Neuropsychological Outcome." *Neuropsychology* 21 (5): 515–31.

Devitt, Rachel, Deirdre Dawson, Angela Coantonio, et al. 2006. "Prediction of Long-Term Occupational Performance Outcomes for Adults after Moderate to Severe Traumatic Brain Injury." *Disability and Rehabilitation* 28 (9): 547–59.

Engberg, Aase W., and Thomas W. Teasdale. 2004. "Psychosocial Out-come Following Traumatic Brain Injury in Adults: A Long-Term Population-Based Follow-Up." *Brain Injury* 18 (6): 533–45.

Hessen, Erik, Knut Nestvold, and Vicki Anderson. 2007. "Neuro-psychological Function 23 Years after Mild Traumatic Brain Injury: A Comparison of Outcome after Paediatric and Adult Head Injuries." *Brain Injury* 21 (9): 963–79.

Hopkins, Ramona O., David F. Tate, and Erin D. Bigler. 2005. "Anoxic versus Traumatic Brain Injury: Amount of Tissue Loss, not Etiology, Alters Cognitive and Emotional Function." *Neuropsychology* 19 (2): 233–42.

Kennedy, Mary R., Carl Coelho, Lyn Turkstra, et al. 2008. " Interven-tion for Executive Functions after Traumatic Brain Injury: A Sys-tematic Review, Meta-Analysis and Clinical Recommendations." *Neuropsychological Rehabilitation* 18 (3): 257–99.

Kesler, Shelli R., Heather F. Adams, Christine M. Blasey, et al. 2003. "Premorbid Intellectual Functioning, Education, and Brain Size in Traumatic Brain Injury: An Investigation of the Cognitive Reserve Hypothesis." *Applied Neuropsychology* 10 (3): 153–62.

King, Rosemary B., Yvonne Shade-Zeldow, Carolyn E. Carlson, et al. 2002. "Adaptation to Stroke: A Longitudinal Study of Depressive Symptoms, Physical Health, and Coping Process." *Topics in Stroke Rehabilitation* 9 (1): 46–66.

Klingberg, Torkel, Hans Forssberg, and Helena Westerberg. 2002. "Training of Working Memory in Children with ADHD. *Journal of Clinical and Experimental Neuropsychology* 24 (6): 781–91.

Kraus, Jess F., and Parivash Nourjah. 1988. "The Epidemiology of Mild Uncomplicated Brain Injury." *Journal of Trauma* 28 (12): 1637–43.

Moran, Michael, Kevin J. Flannelly, Andrew J. Weaver, et al. 2005. "A Study of Pastoral Care, Referral, and Consultation Practices among Clergy in Four Settings in the New York City Area." *Pastoral Psychol-ogy* 53 (3): 255–66.

Riggio, Silvano, and Meredith Wong. 2009. "Neurobehavioral Sequelae of Traumatic Brain Injury." *Mount Sinai Journal of Medicine* 76: 163–72.

Skilbeck, Clive E., Derick T. Wade, R. Langton Hewer, et al. 1983. "Recovery after Stroke." *Journal of Neurology, Neurosurgery, and Psychiatry* 46 (1): 5–8.

Stern, Yaakov. 2009. "Cognitive Reserve." *Neuropsychologia* 47: 2015–28.

Walker, C. E. 2000. *Learn to Relax*. New York: Wiley.

Wrobel, Thomas A., and Cheryl L. Stewart. 2008 (unpublished). "PTSD Treatment Outcomes in Military Samples: A Meta-Analysis." Paper presented at the annual meeting of the American Psychological Association.

Ylvisaker, Mark, Lyn Turkstra, Carl Coehlo, et al. 2007. "Behavioural Interventions for Children and Adults with Behaviour Disorders after TBI: A Systematic Review of the Evidence." *Brain Injury* 21 (8): 769–805.

Dementia

Ruth Marie Thomson / Elayne Lipp

9

"Maria Rodriguez" was celebrating her eightieth birthday, but her family was distraught because as of late Maria's personality had changed. She was forgetful, often repeating herself, and she was fearful of going outside because she could so easily get lost. She seemed moody and not her "old self," became irritated with her grandchildren whom she dearly loved, and sometimes could not remember their names. Her physician suspected that some form of dementia could be the issue. The family was devastated, knowing the implications of such a diagnosis. They were concerned about her life of faith as well, since she refused to attend Mass and had withdrawn from all of her usual social activities.

Understanding Dementia

Dementia is arguably one of our society's most significant challenges of the future. When the baby boomers reach retirement age, our population demographics will be skewed more heavily toward the elderly than ever before. This demographic change will result in many challenges to provide a myriad of services for an aging population. The medical community is currently poorly equipped to provide for the needs of these individuals, and the exponential increase in the level of need is sure to outstrip available resources. The faith community will also be challenged by these population-based changes, and it will be imperative that faith-community leaders have a solid understanding of the disease state labeled dementia in order to meet the needs of their communities. Faith-community leaders who are well aware of what constitutes dementia and the issues surrounding dementia will be best equipped to provide guidance and support for the increased numbers of individuals and families who will be affected by this class of diseases. The first part of this chapter addresses the basic facets of what constitutes dementia, including the definition of the disease and relevant epidemiologic aspects. Issues and concerns that are pertinent to this diagnosis, such as treatment and management, including long-term-care placement, will also be addressed. The second part of this chapter is written from the perspective of an individual who is personally aware of what a diagnosis of dementia intimates as she is a pastor who cared for her husband as he developed and eventually succumbed to this disease state. This chapter provides basic information regarding the dementias. Those who desire more detailed knowledge are encouraged to utilize the references found at the end of this chapter.

Personal Impact of the Diagnosis of Dementia

Few medical terms provoke more fear or anxiety in the hearts and minds of mature adults than dementia. The term *dementia* is loaded with meaning for those concerned for their own cognitive functioning or that of a loved one. It represents the destruction of all of our hopes for our "golden years" and a loss of all that we spend our youth working for: independence, financial well-being, and a carefree, happy, and fulfilling retirement. A diagnosis of dementia means a loss of the opportunity for aging with dignity, and the loss of potential years of pleasure after a lifetime of delay of gratification. The diagnosis of dementia means that everything that was worked for in life is slowly and painfully stripped away from us at a time when we should be enjoying the fruits of our labors. The word brings to mind images of lonely old people sitting in wheelchairs in nursing homes with strangers providing for their most intimate needs. The thought of a diagnosis of other terminal illnesses such as cancer is also devastating but generally doesn't invoke the same response as that of dementia. When diagnosed with cancer, a person is able to "fight" the disease with a number of treatments and isn't relegated to passively allowing the disease to strip him or her of the very essence of what makes a person uniquely human. There are presently no "cures" for dementia; no opportunity for remission, only a steady decline toward incapacity and eventual death. The purpose of this chapter is not to dwell on the bleak reality of this disease state but, rather, to acknowledge the gravity of the diagnosis and then focus on aspects pertinent to the proper diagnosis, optimal management, and research of dementia. Hope truly can be found in the rapidly growing field of knowledge regarding diagnosis, treatment, and management of dementia. We may not currently have a "cure" for dementia, but we are fastidiously working toward the development of medical treatments to help manage the symptoms and to further knowledge of the epidemiologic aspects of the disease and of basic scientific information regarding the complex etiology of this group of diseases. This vast expanse of knowledge is constantly expanding because of the tremendous focus of research conducted by industry and governmental bodies. All of this research is critical. The hope of a future replete with greater understanding, treatment, and management options lies in this research. We all have the opportunity to keep this research moving forward through our active support and participation.

Impact of the Dementias on Society: The Tip of the Iceberg

Dementia can be regarded as one of societies' most significant future challenges based on the basic characteristics of the disease and sheer projected numbers of elderly people in the population. Quite simply, dementia is a common affliction of the elderly, and the world's population is aging. The baby-boomer generation, a group of an estimated 70 million Americans, is just beginning to reach their golden years. The first of the baby boomers reached the milestone of age sixty-five in 2011. The number of people aged eighty-five and older in the United States was estimated to be 5.5 million in 2010. This number is estimated to be 19 million in 2050 (AlA 2011). The impact of an aged population is just beginning to be recognized, and our entire society will feel that impact in a variety of ways as the baby-boomer generation begins to age. Concern for the great increase in numbers of elderly and how to provide for them goes beyond the shores of America. Many countries have been experiencing an aging of their populations, and there is worldwide concern for the capacity to provide resources to match the increased level of need (Larson 2010).

People generally do not look forward to aging. The media portrays the elderly as incapable, obstinate, ineffective, feeble, and plagued with somatic concerns despite the fact that history is rife with examples of scholars and artists contributing significant works in their elderly years. Examples of individuals producing such work are numerous: Giuseppe Verdi, Johann Wolfgang von Goethe, Galileo Galilei, Pierre-Simon Laplace, Charles Sherrington, and Pablo Picasso, to name but a few. The general public holds many misconceptions regarding aging, but changes such as diminished vision, hearing, sense of smell, speed, agility, and muscular power certainly do occur. The general public often thinks of loss of memory and cognitive prowess as an expected part of aging; however, dementia is not part of the normal aging process. Age-associated changes in cognitive functioning do occur, but the steady decline in cognitive functioning does not begin in old age. Rather, its onset is at approximately age thirty!

The cognitive decline observed in dementia goes well beyond any age-associated cognitive decline. Aging, or senescence, has been studied rather extensively, and individuals are known to experience structural and functional decline with maturation. Biologists have studied these changes and have established "norms" of structural and functional change between the ages of thirty and eighty (Ropper and Brown 2005). The entire organism is known to be affected by the process of senescence. Functions as varied as hand grip to cellular water content have been measured and are known to diminish by the age of eighty (ibid.). When comparing elderly people, it becomes obvious that individuals vary greatly in their ability to function as they age. Some individuals remain remarkably independent well into their late nineties, while others begin having functional challenges as early as their sixth or seventh decade of life. Nasiya Ahmed and associates established use of the term *frailty* to describe the presence of three components; physical frailty, impaired neuropsychiatric functioning, and disability that are cornerstones of global decline in the elderly (Ahmed et al. 2007). Dementia is part of the neuropsychiatric-functioning aspect of frailty. It is important to be aware of the concept of frailty, because individuals who are identified as frail are at risk of suffering adverse outcomes. Those who experience a functional decline that interferes with their capacity to thrive independently will require others to provide for their needs. Care of ill or dependent family members was once provided by the family or clan; however, changes in the structure of our society have created obstacles and challenges in the delivery of this care.

The amazing medical innovations of the twentieth century have provided for an increase in the typical life span. People are living longer than they ever have lived, and as a result these individuals develop and live with more chronic health problems than previous generations. With these illnesses, individuals can experience an erosion of their quality of life. Dementia may not be a normal process of aging, but it becomes very common as age advances; dementia is known to afflict people at increasing rates as age advances. The statistical-term incidence describes the number of new cases of a disease state in a given time. The incidence of dementia doubles every five years after the age of sixty-five (AlA 2011). Another important statistical term for describing the frequency of a disease is prevalence, which is the rate of a disease state. This statistical measure is calculated by the total number of people with a disease divided by the total number of people in the entire population in a specific time frame. The prevalence of dementia in populations of greater than eighty-five years of age in the United States is over 30 percent (ibid.). Clearly, dementia is a common disorder that will become even more common as our population ages. We have only begun to see the tip of the iceberg.

Dementia is generally a disease of old age, and as the U.S. population becomes generally more elderly, the rates of dementia are certain to increase at rates never seen before. It is estimated that 5.3 million Americans were living with Alzheimer's disease in the year 2010. A large majority of these individuals are elderly; 5.1 million over the age of sixty-five and only 200,000 less than sixty-five years of age. The number of people diagnosed with Alzheimer's disease is expected to increase significantly by the year 2025. Areas that are expected to experience 30 to 50 percent increases in the number of individuals with Alzheimer's include the South, Midwest, and Western states. States such as Alaska, Colorado, Idaho, Nevada, Oregon, Utah, and Wyoming are expecting increases of 93 to 127 percent by 2025. The number of people over the age of sixty-five and diagnosed with Alzheimer's disease is estimated to reach 7.7 million by the year 2030, an increase of more than 50 percent. This number is expected to increase at an even greater rate to between 11 and 16 million by the year 2050. This will mean more than 60 percent of those greater than age eighty-five will be diagnosed with Alzheimer's disease (ibid.). Dementia affects individuals not only in America, but all over the world. It is thought that more than 37 million people are currently afflicted with dementia throughout the world.

Dementia is a disease with a long course; individuals may live for more than twenty years after they are diagnosed with this disease. This long duration of disease course makes the monetary costs of caring for those with dementia extremely high. This high cost of care for people with dementia is demonstrated by the vast discrepancy in Medicare costs for individuals with dementia when compared to those who do not carry this diagnosis. People aged sixty-five or older who have dementia have Medicare payments that are nine times higher than those in the same age group who do not have dementia. The total projected Medicare and Medicaid costs for services caring for people with dementia for the year 2010 was $123 billion. This does not take into account the costs that are covered by private insurances, health-maintenance organizations, and out-of-pocket expenses to individuals. It has been estimated that American businesses pay an additional $24.6 billion dollars for long-term care and hospice services for individuals with dementia. The out-of-pocket expenditures of nonspousal, unpaid family members and unpaid nonrelated caregivers was an average of $219 per month (ibid.). The cost of providing care for those afflicted with dementia is already high and is expected to increase exponentially in the future (Larson 2010).

The Dementias Defined

Dementia is a term that encompasses a wide variety of disorders with unique diagnostic characteristics; however, all of these disorders result in a final common pathway of loss of independence and the great potential of normal aging. Individuals with dementia experience their disease in unique ways, but all individuals with a progressive neurodegenerative disease such as dementia will have memory loss that affects their ability to carry out their usual tasks at work, home, and play. People without memory problems often misplace items or have difficulty with finding words, but an individual afflicted with dementia is not able to take the necessary cognitive steps required to retrace and relocate items or identify words that have escaped their memory. The hallmark of the dementias is the progression. The brain begins to have neuropathic changes that follow a characteristic pattern. This pattern of neuropathologic deterioration was first described in the brains of individuals with Alzheimer's disease by Drs. Heiko and Eva Braak in the early 1990s. Since that time a specific neuropathic progression has been demonstrated in other neurodegenerative diseases, including Parkinson's disease (Dickson et al. 2010). The critical point is that a specific dementia follows a characteristic pattern of neurodegeneration in the brain of the afflicted individual. The specific location of the brain that is affected will result in a given symptom, as the human brain has specific locations that are responsible for given functions.

As dementia progresses and becomes severer it becomes increasingly difficult for the individual to compensate for these mounting deficits. The earliest symptoms reported are generally episodic memory problems including difficulty with naming objects and finding words especially names of people (AAN 2010). Patients with dementia will often find orientation to time and place challenging and will also find communicating with others difficult due to language deficits. Difficulty with visuospatial skills will often appear as the disease course progresses. These symptoms often are first recognized when patients become easily disoriented and lost in once familiar surroundings. Families will often relate tales of their loved one venturing out in the car to run an errand in their neighborhood only to end up several hundred miles away.

Judgment becomes an issue as well. Patients will have poor judgment with regard to general rules of safety and will have difficulty with tasks such as cooking and driving. Family members may be shocked when a patient starts a fire in the kitchen while preparing food or comes to a stop while driving on a freeway in order to pick up aluminum soda cans for recycling. People with dementia may often experience neuro-psychiatric symptoms, including depression, anxiety, agitation, apathy, paranoia, and delusions (ibid.). Later stages of the disease are hallmarked by further deterioration of language and cognitive skills. Patients will eventually reach a state of reduced speech production and social inter-action. The end stage of dementia is characterized by profound loss of language skills and memory. Patients in the late stages of dementia often do not recognize their families and may not be oriented to self or recog-nize themselves in a mirror. There are often behavioral disruptions and disordered sleep-wake cycles.

Each of the disorders that fits into the classification of a dementia has hallmarks and characteristics that are important in understanding and treatment of the disease. These disorders have typical symptoms experi-enced by individuals due to the specific neuropathologic process that is at work. Alzheimer's disease is the most common type of dementia, and these two terms are often used interchangeably by the general public. People with Alzheimer's dementia often first notice that they have dif-ficulty remembering names or recent events. Patients and their families find that they often keep very detailed lists to assist with their function-ing. As the disease progresses, patients will begin to exhibit difficulty with functional and spatial tasks, such as the use of household appliances. Patients will then experience impairment of judgment, confusion, and disorientation. Alzheimer's dementia makes up the vast majority of the dementias; roughly 60 to 80 percent of total cases are of this classifica-tion. The areas of the brain that are affected by Alzheimer's disease fol-low a very specific and predictable pattern relating to the cortical areas (areas of higher cognitive functioning) and the hippocampus (memory centers) (Braak and Braak 1991). *Vascular dementia* is the next most com-mon type of dementia and accounts for nearly 18 percent of all dementia cases (Battistin and Cagnin 2010). The symptoms do not vary signifi-cantly from those of the Alzheimer's dementia but are caused by vascular problems that cause injury to the brain, such as strokes (Orgogozo et al. 2002).

The other dementias make up the minority of cases of dementia, roughly 5 percent. Individuals afflicted with the frontotemporal degeneration (once referred to as Pick's disease or frontotemporal dementia) will often experience personality changes and behavioral disturbances in addition to language disturbances. Loved ones will often comment that these individuals have bothersome behaviors that are out of character for them and may include odd or inappropriate sexual or impulse control problems. The areas of the brain that are affected by the frontotemporal dementias are the frontal lobes and the temporal lobes that are found in the front and the sides of the brain, respectively. Patients who have *Lewy body dementia* will often have problems with tremors, visual hallucinations, and muscle rigidity along with the usual cognitive decline seen in Alzheimer's dementia. Lewy bodies are abnormal protein deposits of a specific protein called alpha-synuclein that forms in the nerve cells in brains of people with Lewy body dementia. Individuals with Parkinson's disease often experience dementia in the later stages of their disease course. These patients will also have Lewy bodies in their brain tissue. The rapidly progressing dementias are a special form of dementia that results in death within weeks to months of symptom onset. This form of dementia is caused by varied etiologies including infections with proteins called prions. Prions cause rapid neurologic deterioration in animals, the best known being "mad cow disease." The human variant of mad cow disease is Creutzfeldt-Jacob disease, a type of dementia with a very rapid course that results in death in a matter of months. Cruetzfeldt-Jacob disease is not always caused by a known infectious source but does occur sporadically. This disorder is associated with memory and behavior problems, along with difficulty in coordination.

The last type of dementia to be touched upon in this chapter is *normal pressure hydrocephalus*. Patients with normal pressure hydrocephalus experience difficulty with memory and urinary incontinence and have problems walking. The problem is caused by abnormalities in the flow of cerebral spinal fluid, the fluid that normally bathes the brain and spinal cord. Surgical intervention with placement of shunts can sometimes correct the problem and result in improvement in symptoms, but the incontinence and difficulty walking are often more amenable to treatment than the cognitive problems.

Dementia is clearly a complex diagnostic category. The dementias are a heterogeneous group of diseases with distinct characteristics that superficially appear to be easy to distinguish from each other, but in practice a great deal of overlap exists. The differentiation between disorders in the group is not always straightforward in practice and it is thought that patients may often be concurrently affected by more than one process. This is especially true with the concurrent presence of a vascular dementia and another neurodegenerative process (Battistin and Cagnin 2010). It is critical for families and communities generally to be aware of the heterogeneity that exists in the diagnostic class of dementias and recognize that their loved one or community member will experience their illness in unique ways based on the specific diagnosis.

All faith-community leaders will be faced with individuals who are requesting advice and support regarding perceived cognitive problems in themselves or a loved one. At some point every leader will receive a call or service request from an individual who thinks they personally or their spouse or aging parent is "losing it." Many people experience increased forgetfulness, word-finding difficulties, and planning problems as they age. Doctors are frequently visited by people who are worried about their memory, or that of a loved one who has been dragged to the doctor's office for evaluation. Not every visit results in the diagnosis of a dementia, but there are at times findings that are of concern but not diagnostic of dementia. This cognitive problem has recently been labeled as *mild cognitive impairment*. Mild cognitive impairment is a disorder of cognitive functioning including judgment, memory, and language that does not meet criteria for a dementia because a person's ability to function in daily life is not significantly impaired. The term *mild* is perhaps a poor choice in labeling and may lead to misunderstandings of the significance of this problem. It does not mean that the patient and his or her family are not experiencing symptoms that warrant concern; the symptoms experienced do represent a real change in cognition. There has been a great deal of research conducted on mild cognitive impairment, and this disorder does not appear simply to be a prodrome to dementia. Some patients do progress to dementia, but others do not experience a decline in cognition, and still others may experience an improvement or resolution in symptoms. Research examining the area of mild cognitive impairment is beginning to blossom. Clinical trials examining medications that are used for dementia have generally not been found to be helpful; in fact, some studies have indicated that the risks of taking these medications is not warranted as there appears to be little benefit (Birks 2006; O'Brien and Burns 2010; Orgogozo et al. 2002). Individuals who are beginning to become concerned for their cognitive function should always be referred to the medical community for proper assessment.

Assessment and Diagnosis of Cognitive Decline

Some patients and family members feel that they would rather not be seen by a doctor for assessment of their cognitive problems because they feel that they would rather remain uninformed than be faced with the bad news of a dementia diagnosis. These individuals will often state that there is little that can be done, so they would rather not know the truth. Although one can relate to this sort of thinking, it generally is best for individuals to be assessed early for cognitive decline. Memory loss and difficulty with cognitive functioning may have etiologies other than a progressive neurodegenerative disease such as dementia. Early assessment and diagnosis of cognitive decline is critical because early detection allows for identification and treatment of potentially reversible conditions, such as thyroid disease, alcoholism, depression, and other psychiatric disorders, infectious diseases such as syphilis, cancers, and vitamin B12 deficiency (AAN 2010). When these diseases are left unchecked, they may result in development of permanent problems that could have been reversed given proper identification and treatment. Proper assessment also allows for better planning and management as needs change and safety concerns arise. A complete assessment for dementia includes a thorough history and physical examination including a neurologic examination and neuropsychological assessment. Laboratory evaluations should be obtained to ensure that medical disorders that often mimic dementia are ruled out (ibid.). Neuroimaging including MRI brain imaging or a noncontrast CT of the head is part of the American Academy of Neurology's recommended routine dementia evaluation.

A patient's primary care provider is an appropriate place to start the process of assessment for cognitive decline, and subsequent referral to a neurologist, geriatric psychiatrist, neuropsychologist, or geriatrician may be indicated.

Treatment

The treatment options for the dementias are quite limited despite the growing body of knowledge that has been constructed through millions of dollars dedicated to development of treatments and years of extensive research. Because Alzheimer's disease is the most common dementia, most of the research has been focused on this disease state. There are currently five medications that have Food and Drug Administration (FDA) approval for the treatment of Alzheimer's disease in the United States. These medications fall into one of two classes of drugs; cholinesterase inhibitors or NMDA-receptor antagonists. The cholinesterase inhibitor medications currently approved are tacrine, donepezil, galantamine, and rivastigmine. These medications appear to function by inhibiting the breakdown of acetylcholine, a chemical that acts as a chemical messenger in the brain and is associated with memory function (Birks 2006). These four medications seem to be most useful early in the course of dementia and are approved for standard use in mild to moderate dementia by the American Academy of Neurology. These medications are compared to placebos, or sugar pills, in research studies. Placebo-controlled studies have shown that they have modest effects on cognition and global function. These medications do not reverse dementia or improve symptoms but appear to delay nursing-home placement by a few months. These medications are generally quite well tolerated; patients may experience nausea, diarrhea, insomnia, vivid dreams, leg cramps, and slowed heart rate. Tacrine is rarely used today due to side effects, including liver problems.

The second drug class has a different biochemical effect than the cholinesterase inhibitors, but there is only one FDA-approved medication in this class. The medication memantine is an N-methyl-D-aspartate (NMDA) receptor antagonist that is thought to protect nerve cells in the brain from abnormalities in neurotransmitters that are thought to cause accumulation of amyloid-beta and tau proteins. Investigational trials have demonstrated improved cognition, behavior, and functioning in patients with moderate to severe Alzheimer's disease. Memantine has proven to be well tolerated and did not have a side-effect profile that was significantly different from the sugar pill used for comparison. The two classes of medications are sometimes used concurrently in practice and do seem to have additive effects. It must be recognized that even when these medications are used in conjunction, the effects are modest. Much room for improvement in treatment efficacy remains.

The five medications noted above generally result in a slowing of the progression of disease that delays nursing-home placement by a few months. There are active clinical trials ongoing that will hopefully provide more effective therapies for dementia. The Alzheimer's association and the Centers for Disease Control are both good resources for finding out more information about ongoing research, including information regarding clinical trials that are open for participation. The other dementias have also been studied, but larger studies including more patients are required before any real conclusions may be reached. There has been some preliminary research indicating that memantine may be helpful for patients with vascular dementia (Orgogozo et al. 2002) and patients with Lewy Body Dementia (Emre et al. 2010). Research has not been as promising with this medication in the frontotemporal dementias and Parkinson's disease dementia (ibid.). The need for additional research in the non-Alzheimer's-type dementias is even greater than that of Alzheimer's dementia. Other medications, including the anti-inflammatory medications, the statin anticholesterol medications, vitamin E, and gingko biloba, have been purported to be effective in preventing and treating Alzheimer's dementia. None of these medications has been proven to be efficacious to date (O'Brien and Burns 2010). Research investigating nonpharmacologic treatments for the cognitive symptoms of the dementias has not resulted in a great deal of evidence favoring efficacy. The idea of cognitive rehabilitation is under active investigation. Yamaguchi and associates in Japan have been studying brain-activating rehabilitation and feel that positive results can be seen through motivation of the patient to use remaining function and prevent disuse of brain function. They feel that patients and caregivers benefit from improvements in cognitive function and have improved behavioral and psychological symptoms with brain-activating rehabilitation (Yamaguchi et al. 2010). Prevention remains the best treatment for all of the illnesses of modern life, and the dementias are likely no exception. Research seems to indicate that the dementias may be delayed or perhaps even prevented through the control of vascular risk factors such as hypertension and heart disease, physical exercise, and mental exercise (Larson 2010).

Individuals afflicted with dementia commonly experience challenging behaviors, such as delusions, hallucinations, aggression, and agitation. Rates of these symptoms are thought to be as high as 60 percent in individuals cared for by their families in the community and 80 percent of those receiving institutionalized care. The development of these symptoms often results in the end of home care, as these behaviors provide challenges that outstrip a family's capacity to provide care at home. These behaviors had historically been managed with neuroleptic medications, including olanzapine, quetiapine, resperidone, ziprasidone, and aripiprazole. Research conducted early in the new century demonstrated that these medications were not only associated with deleterious side effects, including low blood pressure, high cholesterol, weight gain, and diabetes, but even more serious effects, including stroke and death. Few alternatives to these medications exist at this time, and their use remains common, if not necessary.

Interest in the nonpharmacological management of the symptoms of dementia is an area that has begun to be studied extensively as a need for alternatives to the major tranquilizers has been established. There are several nonpharmacologic therapies aimed at the management of challenging behaviors, such as agitation, wandering, incontinence, and "sundowning" (a form of agitation and increased confusion that often occurs in the evening) (Yamaguchi et al. 2010). Alternative treatment modalities, including art therapy, music therapy, activity therapy, complementary therapy, aromatherapy, bright-light therapy, and multisensory approaches, can do much to improve the quality of life of those afflicted with dementia. Psychological therapies, such as behavioral therapy, reality orientation, validation therapy, and reminiscence therapy can be efficacious in managing deleterious behaviors (ibid.). Brief cognitive therapies, such as cognitive-behavioral therapy and interpersonal therapy, have been found to be useful in individuals suffering from dementia, especially those in the early stages of the disease (ibid.). These therapies focus on the issues that are critical to those afflicted with a terminal illness, including interpersonal disputes, interpersonal and personality difficulties, bereavement, life transitions, and life events (ibid.). Additional research is needed to determine the efficacy of these modalities, but much excitement surrounds their potential usefulness in this population.

Providing Care for Those Afflicted with a Dementia

Americans provide a great deal of care to their loved ones at home. The types of care provided include but are not limited to shopping, meal preparation, arranging for and transportation to appointments such as medical appointments, general hygiene, management of medications and other health-care treatments, bathing, dressing, feeding, and toileting, ensuring safety through supervision, providing for entertainment and social needs, providing for administrative and financial management such as bills and taxes, and household duties such as housework, home maintenance, and car and lawn care. Obviously, this list is merely the tip of the iceberg. We all know there are innumerable tasks that are completed without notice and only become obvious when the individual who is responsible for the task is no longer able to do so. Patients with dementias often have a long duration of disease course and therefore require many years of care. It is estimated that roughly 11 million people provide unpaid care for an individual with dementia (AlA 2010). This estimate includes both family members and non-kin caregivers, including family friends. A total of 12.5 billion hours of unpaid care was provided in the year 2009, an amount of care that is valued at nearly $144 billion (ibid.). This already impressive amount of financial contribution does not take into account the impact of hours of employment and income lost by these caregivers. Out-of-pocket expenses associated with providing care to an individual with dementia are also substantial and include insurance premiums, deductibles, and service co-payments for private insurance and governmental plans. There are also innumerable nonmonetary costs associated with providing care to an individual with dementia. These include the psychosocial impact on families who are providing care for a dementia patient, especially those who are simultaneously providing care for children in their homes. This so-called sandwich generation makes up an estimated 30 percent of the unpaid caregivers providing care for individuals with a dementia. Another unique group of caregivers are those providing care from a distance; roughly 10 percent of caregivers live more than two hours from their loved one (ibid.). It is quite an understatement to say that the stress and strain placed on all of these individuals providing care can be extremely high.

Those who provide for the spiritual needs of others are well aware of the fact that all kinds of illnesses affect the entire family. When a person is afflicted with dementia, the effects are substantial, and social support is critical. People with dementia are generally cared for by their loved ones in the home in the early stages of the disease. Care may be provided by a spouse, son or daughter, grandchild, sibling, family friend, and in rare cases even a parent. The level of care provided increases as the disease progresses, and care in the home becomes increasingly difficult and potentially unsafe as the individual's neurological status deteriorates. These families will need additional resources from the community as their capacity to cope is challenged. It is common for those afflicted with dementia to become disoriented to time and place, resulting in wandering and sundowning. Caregivers may find when these behaviors begin to appear they are no longer able to manage care for their loved ones in the home. Placement of a loved one in institutional care is never an easy decision. Placement in institutional care is a significant hallmark that reflects progression of dementia to a level that the patient requires twenty-four-hour care. Most households are not able to provide around-the-clock care for a family member who is ill without significant stress to the caregivers. Placement in institutional care does not mean an endpoint of caregiving. Family members generally remain highly involved in their loved one's care, providing visits at the nursing home, supervision of caregivers to ensure appropriate care is being provided, and even direct care in some cases. Providing care for a loved one with dementia at home or in an institutional setting is a highly stressful endeavor regardless of whether care is provided in the home or in an institutional setting.

Individuals who experience a functional decline that interferes with their capacity to thrive independently will require others to provide for their needs. The care of ill or dependent family members was once provided by the family or clan; however, changes in the structure of our society have created obstacles and challenges in the delivery of care to those who are unable to be independent. Care of individuals with dementia is often provided in the home in modern times, but our nuclear families have constructed households that are poorly equipped to provide care for the individual afflicted with a dementia. The younger members of the family who are better physically equipped and able to meet the challenges of providing care are often in separate households or are out of the home during working hours. Caregiving is often left to spouses who may have health concerns of their own. These elderly caregivers will often experience detrimental effects on their own health. Even the most robust caregiver will experience difficulties juggling the demands of employment, exhaustion, loss of income, and financial strain. Adult-child family caregivers may have great difficulty fulfilling the great demands of both full-time employment and caregiving and are at risk of experiencing depression and strain from these incompatible obligations (Wang et al. 2011). Research seems to demonstrate that providing care in the home for an elderly person may cause health problems for the caregiver. Unpaid caregivers have been found to have higher levels of stress hormones, poor immune function, poor wound healing (Lutgendorf et al. 1999), development of hypertension (Shaw et al. 1999), and heart disease. There are also deleterious psychological effects resulting in caregiver depression, anxiety, and other psychiatric perturbations (Zarit et al. 1989). Caregivers of all kinds suffer from a sense of guilt related to their caregiving; this is no doubt related to the contradictory obligations of maintaining a healthy lifestyle for themselves and completing the never-ending tasks associated with caregiving. These feelings are especially poignant at the time of placement into institutional care; however, placement of the demented family member into an institutional-care setting may provide some relief of the psychological and physical strain of caregiving. Some studies suggest that caregivers' quality of life and health improves when they are assisted with institutional care for their loved one. Joseph Gaugler and his associates conducted research that demonstrates that caregivers report a significant reduction in depressive symptoms once their loved one suffering from dementia was placed in institutional care (Gaugler et al. 2010).

Spiritual Care with Alzheimer's Patients and Their Caregivers

It happened during the time when my husband realized that he was having problems with his memory, and he worried about what was happening to him. But this was before he entered a place of oblivion and then was unaware that he had problems with his memory. As a result of his memory loss, he no longer worried. He had a particularly frustrating experience that both embarrassed and annoyed him, and he finally turned to me with a pleading look in his eyes and said, "Don't throw me away!" It was one of those phrases that cuts to the heart of every caregiver, and of course I reassured him that I would never do that. It is also the theme of this portion of the chapter about caring for people with Alzheimer's disease and their caregivers.

My experience with Alzheimer's disease is both as a pastor and as a caregiver. During my years of professional ministry, I visited many people who suffered from this devastating disease. I also learned about this disease in a personal way when my husband, of blessed memory, was diagnosed with it. My remarks will deal with both aspects of spiritual care. First I will address the needs of the patient as I have perceived them, then the needs of caregivers as I experienced them and learned about them from others in my support groups. These observations may or may not all apply to the people you encounter in your ministry.

A social worker in an Alzheimer's unit once told me, "If you have seen one person with Alzheimer's, you have seen one person with Alzheimer's." Her words emphasize the reality that while there are many similarities among people with Alzheimer's disease, there are also many differences. The differences are due to each person's unique personality, his or her personality before the disease and the one that continues or changes as the disease progresses. The only certainty is that the disease will progress and continue to destroy more and more of the cognitive abilities of its victims.

The first and perhaps the most important task in ministry with people who have Alzheimer's disease is to maintain a relationship and a regular schedule of contact. When someone's world is coming apart and is full of uncertainty and confusion, it is reassuring to have a few people and events in it that are familiar and dependable. You may feel uncomfortable or even afraid at the prospect of going to visit someone with Alzheimer's disease, but it may ease your anxiety to remember that one of the greatest losses suffered by these people is loss of companionship and even social isolation. Often, even longtime friends stay away because they don't know what to say or how to act or because they worry about how the person with Alzheimer's will act. And often, being with someone who has this disease is a reminder that they, too, could be afflicted in the same way.

The most important thing is to be there as a caring person for as long as you are needed, in your place of worship, in their home, or in a long-term care setting. Since leaders of a faith community are often among the first to encounter signs of memory loss in others, learn to recognize some of these signs so that if you notice changes, you can talk about them with a family member. Some of these early signs are changes in cleanliness or neatness of appearance, uncharacteristic rudeness, inappropriate anger or poor judgment, neglect of regular responsibilities, struggle to find words or use of inappropriate words, inability to use familiar equipment or tools.

Family members may not notice these changes, as they may occur gradually, or family members may be in denial about what is taking place. If you notice significant behavior changes, speak to a family member. Be honest and respectful about what you see and hear. You may be met with denial or with great relief that someone else has noticed the things they have been worried about. Ask if they have had a medical evaluation, and if not, encourage them to do so. If the person lives alone, try to contact a family member or a trusted friend and share your observations with them.

Create a faith community that is Alzheimer's friendly by raising awareness of dementia in adult forums, sermons, and newsletter articles and by modeling acceptance of unkempt appearances or unexpected behaviors.

About Visiting

For people with Alzheimer's disease, the world can become a confusing and unfamiliar place filled with strange people and unsettling situations. In the early stages of the disease, when the person is still aware of her or his memory loss, people suffering from the illness may feel anxious about what is happening, or they may feel ashamed that they can no longer remember names and places and words. If this is the case, be honest and acknowledge that they are in a difficult situation. At this stage of the disease, people often need reassurance that they will not have to face these worries and fears alone.

As with other diseases, some people may be concerned that God is punishing them by afflicting them with this illness. This can be a painful thing to hear, and it will be important to help them process these feelings and to draw upon the resources of your faith story to help them discover a different experience of God.

When you go to visit, remember that people with Alzheimer's can be easily startled, so approach them slowly, from the front. Say your name and your connection with them, even if they have known you for many years. When you speak, look directly at them and maintain eye contact. Speak slowly and in a calm, low-pitched voice. If other people are present in the visit, be sure to include people with memory loss in the conversation, because they can become agitated if they feel left out. And of course, never speak about them as if they aren't there. If touch is appropriate to your relationship, offer a handshake or a hug.

If you are seeing the person on a regular basis, you will be able to discern the level of interaction that is appropriate each time. The quality of your interaction will change as the disease progresses. If there is such a thing as a "typical" spiritual-care visit, this will not be it. Indeed, the situation may change from visit to visit, or it may change during your visit. The key is to stay present and be flexible and be prepared to go with whatever the person is able to offer in terms of a connection.

In the early stages of the disease, a simple conversation is still possible. Be open to experimenting gently with conversation starters and change your strategy when necessary. It is okay to offer help when she or he is searching for words. When you can't make sense of what he is saying, focus on the feelings behind the words and offer back words of reassurance or understanding. If she is worried that people are stealing things, or she wants to go home or is searching for a loved one who is long dead, respond with your feelings, not your thoughts. For example, "I am sorry that is happening to you," or "We'll go soon," or "You miss your sister very much." Don't quiz, confront, correct, explain, or rationalize. These responses will only frustrate the person and may cause unnecessary agitation.

Look around the room for items that will show you what is important to the person—family photos, evidence of interests or hobbies, souvenirs from trips, or other mementos from the person's life. Bring a magazine or a book about something of interest to the person. These items provide good topics for conversation or simply the enjoyment of looking at them together. Some people enjoy seeing or reading the daily newspaper. People with memory loss can often read words long after they have forgotten what they mean. Some families have photo albums available, and these are an immediate and easy way to interact with a person.

Be prepared to take the lead in the conversation, and allow plenty of time for a response. Then go with whatever she says. Think of the conversation as an exploration into her new reality, and go with the flow. Enter her world and explore it with her. The most important thing is that the person feels acknowledged and engaged. People with memory loss are still sensitive to the emotional content of their interactions, and their feelings can be hurt if they feel ignored or patronized. Laughter is okay, especially if they make a joke about not remembering something. Just be sure that you laugh with people and not at them.

Questions may or may not be appropriate, certainly not if people are unable to answer them as they may feel embarrassed or angry that they cannot hold up their end of the conversation. Questions that can be answered with a yes or no are often best. It is very important to present only one question or idea at a time. Remember, people with Alzheimer's disease are working very hard to stay connected and to follow the conversation. One of the things these people lose early on is the ability to make choices when several things are presented at once. Too much stimulation can be exhausting.

Reminisce about former interests, shared experiences, mutual friends, family, or the person's career. Play simple games. Some of these kinds of things, especially longtime hobbies or careers, are stored in what is sometimes called "overlearned memory" and will remain intact and retrievable for quite a while.

Some people retain long-term memory well into the disease and will talk about people they knew and events that happened years ago as if they were occurring today. Others seem to lose both short-term and long-term memory quite early in the disease and live very much in the present moment. One thing I can guarantee is that in your contact with a person with Alzheimer's disease, you will have the opportunity to learn the ability to be in the present moment, for as the disease progresses, that is where the person lives.

As the disease progresses, the person may become more anxious, and it may sometimes become necessary to use the "therapeutic lie." For example, if she cannot find her mother, don't try to convince her that her mother has been dead for many years; simply acknowledge that you know she is missing her and that she will be back later. Then, change the subject or redirect her to another topic or activity. People with Alzheimer's disease can often be easily redirected, which is a very useful strategy if someone is anxious or acting out in other ways. Remain calm, use a gentle voice, and remember that sometimes a warm smile can work wonders. Hugs can work, too, but be sure that the person is comfortable with that kind of touch.

If you are visiting a member of your faith community, wear clerical attire. This will help him to identify you. Bring familiar symbols of your faith, a holy book, images or pictures, something that he can touch or hold while you visit. Holding something can help him feel grounded and connected. On the other hand, don't be surprised if he gets up and walks away in the middle of a ritual, a prayer, or a reading. Invite him to read along with you if he is able. Many folks can read words long after they remember what they mean and will remember prayers, songs, Scripture verses, and rituals long after they can carry on a conversation. Some faith communities have members who knit prayer shawls. One of these can be a comforting gift for a person with memory loss.

Learn to be comfortable with silence. Resist the need to talk all the time, and especially avoid talking at the person. Simply sitting next to someone, maybe holding her hand, can be comforting and reassuring to someone whose world is a mass of confusion. Often, your presence says everything that needs to be said.

As difficult as it may be for you as a caregiver, it is critical to continue to visit the person, even when she no longer knows who you are or appears not to respond to the rituals of your faith. Leave a card or a note so that the family members will know that you have visited. When the time of death draws near, offer a blessing of the dying if it is part of your tradition. The person will hear your voice and feel your touch, and the family will appreciate deeply both your comforting support and presence.

Remember that even as the disease progresses and people with Alzheimer's lose more and more of their cognitive abilities, they never lose their emotional awareness. People who have ceased to speak at all will look up for some sign of recognition when someone enters the room. Even in the last stages of the disease, they are aware of and attuned to facial expressions, tone of voice, and how they are touched or handled.

While it true that what makes us human and different from the other animals of creation is our minds and our ability to reason and to speak, my experience with people with Alzheimer's disease has shown me that perhaps an even more significant part of being human is our ability to feel and express our emotions, because even when cognitive abilities are gone, emotions, and their expressions remain intact.

Spiritual Care with the Caregiver

I begin this section of the chapter with the same words I used to begin the section on spiritual care of the person with Alzheimer's disease. Maintain the relationship and a regular schedule of contact, whether this is by telephone, e-mail, thinking-of-you cards, or face-to-face contact. As with the patient, the most important thing is to be there, as a caring person, wherever "there" is, for as long as you are needed.

Loss of companionship and social isolation are also two of the biggest losses faced by caregivers as outings become increasingly difficult and finally impossible. As even longtime friends drop away, the caregiver is often deprived of any kind of meaningful conversation. When spending time with caregivers, listen to their concerns, take them seriously,

and do not minimize or rationalize by saying things like "everyone for-
gets things from time to time." Listen for veiled complaints about their
lives and their relationships with their loved ones. You may hear things
like, "It's no use to go anywhere anymore, because he just wants to go
home right away," or "I get so tired of having to say the same thing over
and over and over again." The caregivers' complaints and concerns may
be their first small cry for help.

Every caregiver faces what I call "arrow-through-the-heart moments."
These are the moments when the tragic reality of the disease is unmistak-
able and the loss of the life that was shared is painfully exposed. From the
time we first met, my husband and I played regular, lively, and competitive games of double solitaire. One evening, not long after his diagnosis,
he sat beside me playing solitaire. Suddenly he looked at me and asked,
"Did you ever play double solitaire?" Every caregiver who has one of
these moments will remember the exact time and place when it occurred.

Resist the temptation to interpret the caregivers' experiences
with comments like, "It's good that you had so many wonderful years
together." Instead, allow the caregivers to discover meaning in the situation for themselves by listening carefully and commenting gently on
their words in a way that invites further conversation.

Create a faith community that is caregiver friendly by hosting a
support group in your house of worship. Arrange for someone to sit
with caregivers and their loved ones so that caregivers can occasionally worship without distraction. Bring a worship experience to the family if it becomes impossible for them to come to the house of worship
and engage other members in providing caregiver support according to
their gifts and talents. Many congregations are fortunate to have a parish nurse on staff. A parish nurse can be a regular visitor, a supportive,
caring presence, and a listening ear. She can also be aware of the many
resources available to assist caregivers.

Listen for signs of spiritual struggles and for signs of spiritual
growth. Signs of struggles may be heard in words about feeling abandoned, guilty, or being punished by God. Signs of spiritual growth may
be heard in words about seeing the presence of God in people who come
to help or in the staff at long-term care settings. They may be in words
about learning what it means to fully enter into the suffering of another

person or learning how to love another person without expectation of that love being returned. Again, acknowledge and accept what is being said, and respond in ways that encourage further conversation.

Don't assume that every family or caregiver is feeling burdened or resentful. People adjust differently to the crises of life, and in some situations this disease is more easily accepted as one of the many possibilities of the elder years. Listen and learn from the caregivers as they talk about their experiences.

Be aware that family members will often respond differently. Adult children are often in denial, unable to accept that a once strong and intelligent parent is losing his or her cognitive abilities. Sometimes the spouse who has grown used to the slowly increasing changes is in denial, and the children who see their parent less frequently notice the changes and are keenly aware of a problem. Some family members are readily present, and others cannot get past their own feelings and may not even be able to come and visit the person with memory loss.

Encourage everyone to join a support group and take advantage of educational programs sponsored by the Alzheimer's Association. The more the caregivers know about the disease and its progression, the easier it will be for them to adjust and to accept the changes when they occur. This was proven in a study designed by the department of nursing at the University of Minnesota called Partners in Care Giving. In this study, groups of caregivers were provided with the same information that was given to nurses caring for patients with dementia. The outcomes showed lower stress levels and better coping skills in the group that got the information than in the control group that did not.

Even when caregivers have respite care, it is often difficult for them to continue their own activities and involvements, because they may feel guilty about going out and doing things when their loved ones cannot. Therefore, it is important to affirm and encourage the decisions they make for their own self-care. Be aware of the home-care providers that are available in your area. Be ready to support and even encourage a decision to place their loved one in a long-term care facility. Familiarize yourself with assisted living and long-term care facilities that have respected memory-care units. Offer to visit these facilities with caregivers as they make their decisions about placement.

Spiritual leaders can be resource people for caregivers and family members by learning which resources are available to help them. These include among others the Alzheimer's Association with a twenty-four-hour help line, educational programs, support groups, resources for respite care, Safe Return (Medic Alert® and Alzheimer's Association Safe Return® bracelets) or even more current locator systems, names of elder law attorneys for long-term-care advance planning, powers of attorney, and health-care directives. You may even be asked to help convince someone to stop driving the family car.

One thing caregivers need most when their loved one is still living at home is respite care. At first people with Alzheimer's can be left alone; however, as the disease progresses, they often become very attached to their caregivers and become anxious if those people are out of sight. They don't know if the caregivers have been gone five minutes or five hours; they only know they feel abandoned and alone and afraid. Eventually, it becomes dangerous to leave people with dementia alone, as they may wander away or do something to harm themselves, like leaving a pan unattended on a stove or trying to use power tools. This possibility is complicated by the fact that it is difficult, if not impossible, to predict when these kinds of dangers will occur.

At this point, caregivers are on duty 24/7 and desperately need to get away once in a while. Unfortunately, most caregivers don't know where to start when they realize they need respite care. As mentioned earlier, sources of respite care and/or adult day programs can be part of a spiritual leader's resource file and offered when caregivers are in need. Sometimes a spiritual leader or a parish nurse can find people in the faith community who are willing to provide occasional respite care. Often caregivers have a variety of different sources of respite that work together to give them much-needed time away, such as friends, volunteers from community organizations, activities at senior centers, and day programs.

Be aware that caregiving is exhausting in many ways. Caring for a person with increasing dementia is like caring for a small child, except that the child continues to learn new things and becomes more and more independent while the person with Alzheimer's disease continues to forget what he has learned and becomes more and more dependent.

Caregivers are exhausted *mentally* due to the strain of feeling verbally connected one minute and then suddenly losing that connection; because they are always thinking and planning for another person, continually repeating the answer to the same question, continually adjusting the environment for safety and to lessen their own stress; because they never know for sure how their loved ones will react to a given situation and never know what new and often strange behavior will appear. These may include sudden loud clapping, putting things in strange places, wanting to go somewhere all the time, or following the caregiver around all day. One support-group leader cautioned a group of caregivers not to be eager to change any of these behaviors, because the next one might be even more troubling.

Caregivers are exhausted *emotionally* due to the ambiguous loss of a relationship with a person who is physically present but relationally absent, the loss of remembering their shared history together, the loss of hopes and dreams for the future, uncertainty about what will happen next, giving love when a loved one can no longer give it back in familiar and expected ways, and being in a constant state of unresolved grief as the losses occur and multiply one after another.

Caregivers are exhausted *physically* due to the difficulty of bathing, toileting, or dressing an adult and cleaning up after toileting accidents, and to sleep deprivation due to night wandering or worry about night wandering. Sometimes the simple act of buckling an adult into a car seat belt can seem like an overwhelming task.

All of this is to say caregivers are often and sometimes always tired in some way. Caregivers need people who will listen to them, cry with them, and give them hugs. They need reassurance that someone will walk beside them on this difficult and painful journey for as long as it lasts.

Spiritual leaders can watch for signs of caregiver burnout. Caregivers are like the frog in the pot of water who doesn't know he is about to die until the water begins to boil. They keep adapting to the changes in their loved ones and in their lives because they happen one at a time. They think they can handle each new thing in addition to all of the other new things in their lives, until suddenly they discover that they are in way over their heads and if not being boiled alive, drowning in a sea of responsibilities.

Some signs to watch for are difficulty with organizing and managing the tasks of daily life, having frequent colds or other illnesses and expressing feelings of hopelessness and despair. Some caregivers give up most or all outside activities; have difficulty making decisions; show impatience with coworkers, family members, or the person with Alzheimer's disease; cry easily and often; and feel overwhelmed by the little irritations of life.

Caregivers often carry a heavy load of guilt:

- guilt about losing patience with their loved ones and raising their voices and seeing the hurt in their eyes;
- guilt about not knowing what to do when behaviors are difficult;
- guilt about having their own feelings of loss when their loved one is struggling with a terrible disease;
- guilt about going out and doing things without their loved one;
- guilt about having to place their loved one in long-term care.

Caregivers need someone to hear their confessions and to remind them that all of these feelings and actions are normal in their situation. They need to be reassured that God gathers all of these things up with infinite wisdom and compassion and then gently lets them drift away into a sea of understanding and forgiveness.

And when their loved one nears the end of life, caregivers appreciate the presence and support of their spiritual leaders, perhaps to conduct the rituals that bless the dying or perhaps to simply sit with them as they keep vigil during those last few days as their loved one is making the transition from this life to the next. Ask how you can help and then follow their lead.

Through this entire process from diagnosis to end of life, caregivers have need of spiritual care as well:

- Sometimes they need to pray.
- Sometimes they need to be angry about what is happening in their lives.
- Sometimes they need to be angry with God.
- Sometimes they need the rituals of their faith community.
- Sometimes they need comfort food or a soothing beverage.

- Sometimes they need someone to cry with them.
- Sometimes they need someone to laugh with them about the strange things that are happening at home, because if they don't laugh sometimes, they will be crying all the time.
- Sometimes they need to say that they just want it all to end.

Always, always, they need to know that someone will continue to care about what is happening to them and to their loved one. And they need to be reassured that they will never have to deal with the ravages of this disease alone.

Alzheimer's disease often arouses our deepest fears about forgetting and being forgotten. A faith tradition that teaches us about a God who will know our name even when we have forgotten every name we have ever known, including our own, can be a comforting reminder to both people with this disease and their caregivers. We can embody the presence of that remembering God in their lives and remind them that the God who created them will never forget or forsake them in this life or the next.

Bibliography

Ahmed, Nasiya, Richard Mandel, and Mindy J. Fain. 2007. "Frailty: An Emerging Geriatric Syndrome." *American Journal of Medicine* 120 (9): 748–53.

Alzheimer's Association (AlA). National Office: 225 N. Michigan Ave., Floor 17, Chicago, IL 60601. 1-800-232-0851. http://www.alz.org.

———. 2009. *2009 Alzheimer's Disease Facts and Figures, Special Report: Mild Cognitive Impairment and Early-Stage Alzheimer's Disease*. 61–64. www.alz.org/national/documents/report_alzfactsfigures2009.pdf.

———. 2010. *Alzheimer's Disease: Facts and Figures*. http://www.alz .org/alzheimers_disease_facts_and_figures.asp. http://www.alz.org/ national/documents/report_alzfactsfigures2010.pdf.

American Academy of Neurology (AAN). 2010. "Dementia." *Continuum* 16 (2): 15–31.

Battistin, Leontino, and Annachiara Cagnin. 2010. "Vascular Cognitive Disorder: A Biologic and Clinical Overview." *Neurochemical Research* 35 (12): 1932–38.

Birks, Jacqueline. January 25, 2006. "Cholinesterase Inhibitors for Alzheimer's Disease." *Cochrane Database of Systematic Reviews*, no. 1, article no. CD00593.

Boss, Pauline. 2000. *Ambiguous Loss: Learning to Live with Unresolved Grief.* Cambridge: Harvard University Press.

Braak, Heiko, and Eva Braak. 1991. "Neuropathological Staging of Alzheimer-Related Changes." *Acta Neuropathologica* 82 (4): 239–59.

Dickson, Dennis W., Hirotake Ulchikado, Hiroshige Fujishiro, et al. 2010. "Evidence in Favor of Braak Staging of Parkinson's Disease." *Movement Disorders* 25 (supp. 1): S78–S82.

Emre, Murat, Magda Tsolaki, Ubaldo Bonuccelli, et al. 2010. "Memantine for Patients with Parkinson's Disease Dementia or Dementia with Lewy Bodies: A Randomised, Double-Blind Placebo-Controlled Trial." *The Lancet Neurology* 9 (10): 969–77.

Gaugler, Joseph E., Mary S. Mittelman, Kenneth Hepburn, et al. 2010. "Clinically Significant Changes in Burden and Depression among Dementia Caregivers Following Nursing Home Admission." *BMC Medicine* 8 (1a): 85.

Genova, Lisa. 2007. *Still Alice.* New York: Universe.

Jeste, Dilip V., Dan Blazer, Daniel Casey, et al. 2008. "ACNP White Paper: Update on Use of Antipsychotic Drugs in Elderly Persons with Dementia." *Neuropsychopharmacology* 33 (5): 957–70.

Kessler, Lauren. 2008. *Finding Life in the Land of Alzheimer's: One Daughter's Hopeful Story.* New York: Penguin.

Kimble, Melvin A., and Susan H. McFadden, eds. 2003. *Aging, Spirituality, and Religion: A Handbook.* Vol. 2. Minneapolis: Fortress Press.

Koenig, Harold G., and Andrew J. Weaver. 1998. *Pastoral Care of Older Adults.* Creative Pastoral Care and Counseling. Minneapolis: Fortress Press.

Larson, Eric B. 2010. "Prospects for Delaying the Rising Tide of Worldwide, Late-Life Dementias." *International Psychogeriatrics* 22 (8): 1196–1202.

Lutgendorf, Susan, Linda Garand, Kathleen C. Buckwalter, et al. 1999. "Life Stress, Mood Disturbance and Elevated Interleukin-6 in Healthy Older Women." *Journal of Gerontology Series A: Biological Sciences and Medical Sciences* 54 (9): M434–439.

Lyketsos, Constantine G., Martin Steinberg, JoAnn T. Tschanz, et al. 2000. "Mental and Behavioral Disturbances in Dementia: Findings from the Cache County Study on Memory in Aging." *American Journal of Psychiatry* 157: 708–14.

Mace, N., and P. Rabins. 1999. *The 36-Hour Day: A Family Guide to Caring for Persons with Alzheimer Diseasse, Related Dementing Illnesses, and Memory Loss in Later Life.* Baltimore: Johns Hopkins University Press.

MacKinlay, Elizabeth, ed. 2006. *Aging, Spirituality and Palliative Care.* Binghamton, N.Y.: Haworth.

O'Brien, John T., and Alistair Burns. 2010. "Clinical Practice with Anti-Dementia Drugs: A Revised Consensus Statement from the British Association for Psychopharmacology." *Journal of Psychopharmacology*, online article (November 18). http://jop.sagepub.com/content/early/2010/11/17/0269881110387547.

Orgogozo, Jean-Marc, Anne-Sophie Rigaud, Albrecht Stöffler, et al. 2002. "Efficacy and Safety of Memantine in Patients with Mild to Moderate Vascular Dementia: A Randomized, Placebo Controlled Trial." *Stroke* 33 (7): 1834–39.

Ropper, Allan H., and Robert H. Brown. 2005. *Adams and Victor's Principles of Neurology.* 8th ed. New York: McGraw-Hill.

Shaw, William S., Thomas L. Patterson, Michael G. Ziegler, et al. 1999. "Accelerated Risk of Hypertensive Blood Pressure Recordings among Alzheimer Caregivers." *Journal of Psychosomatic Research* 46 (3): 215–27.

Testad Ingelin, Aina Marie Aasland, and Dag Aarsland, 2007. "Prevalence and Correlates of Disruptive Behavior in Patients in Norwegian Nursing Homes." *International Journal of Geriatric Psychiatry* 22 (9): 916–21.

Wang, Yu-Nu, Yea-Ing Lotus Shyu, Min-Chi Chen, et al. 2011. "Reconciling Work and Family Caregiving among Adult-Child Family Caregivers of Older People with Dementia: Effects on Role Strain and Depressive Symptoms." *Journal of Advanced Nursing* 67 (4): 829–40.

Watkins, Derrel, ed. 2003. *Practical Theology for Aging.* Binghamton, N.Y.: Haworth.

Yamaguichi, Haruyasu, Yohku Maki, and Tetsuya Yamagami. 2010. "Overview of Non-Pharmacological Intervention for Dementia and Principles of Brain-Activating Rehabilitation." *Psychogeriatrics* 10 (4): 206–13.

Zarit, Steven H., Richard C. Birkel, and Eileen Malone Beach. 1989. "Spouses as Caregivers: Stresses and Interventions in Family Involvement in the Treatment of the Frail Elderly." In Marion Zucker Goldstein, ed., *Family Involvement in the Treatment of the Frail Elderly*, 345–60. Washington, D.C.: American Psychiatric Publishing.

CONCLUSION
PSYCHOPHARMACOLOGY

William H. Meller / Sarah J. Meller

꿰ᐸ This chapter is not intended to turn caregivers into psychophar-mocologists; nor will it describe the mechanism of action for hundreds of psychoactive drugs. It is, rather, an attempt to briefly describe how various families of psychiatric drugs came to be, with the hope that this knowledge will increase understanding and acceptance. In truth, we know very little of the workings of the human mind. Although we do know what some individual medications do to a specific receptor in the brain, the huge jump from molecular interaction to improvement in mood, cognition, and reality testing remains a mystery. When the church father Origen was asked, "Who wrote the epistle to the Hebrews?" he responded, "On truth only God knows" (Fuller 1995, 3). This response remains appropriate for the question, "How can this pill make patients quit wanting to kill themselves?"

History

Psychopharmocology has been with us for thousands of years. Opium was available in the second millennium BCE (Lyons and Petrucelli 1978, 97). Coca leaves, which contain cocaine, were used to treat mental illness as early as the Incan civilization (ibid., 50). Ancient practitioners had hundreds of herbs and potions. However, many were probably more dangerous than helpful.

Barbiturates were developed in the late 1800s by Adolph Von Baeyer, founder of Baeyer chemical company. The name *barbituric acid* was inspired by the day on which it was invented, St. Barbara's Day. In 1912, Phenobarbital was invented, and the search for sleeping medication and anti-anxiety agents took off (Boudinot 2010). In the beginning of the nineteenth century, "bromides" were still in vogue and available in a wide variety of pharmaceutical mixtures, including "triple bromide," available in an effervescent tablet (Modell 1995, 155). Unfortunately, this led to bromide poisoning, allowing barbiturates to become the drug of choice.

There was increasing concern about the addictive properties of barbiturates and their frequent use in suicides. In the 1950s meprobamates were developed. The assumptions that these are safer and less addicting than barbiturates proved to be false. Despite these failings, the remarkable financial success of the early use of meprobamotes led pharmaceutical companies to begin examining substances with similar effects (Kaplan and Sadock 1985, 1548–49). In 1950 Leo Stennbach was cleaning out his laboratory, mostly throwing out old chemicals, when he decided to investigate two final compounds before completely closing his lab. One was chlordizepoxide, the first benzodiazepine. Stennbach went on to discover Valium, which by the early 1970s became the most prescribed drug in the world (Callahan and German 2005, 107).

Valium, which came to be called "Mother's little helper," due to its reported use and abuse among stay-at-home housewives, soon inspired great concern over the perceived overmedication of society. We now know that these medications also have severe addictive potential and other troubling side effects. This illustrates a common experience with psychotropic medications, in which the beneficial effects are often embraced before the unintended side effects are known. This phenomenon is also demonstrated by Sigmund Freud's initial obsession with cocaine. It is unclear why Freud eventually turned away from cocaine, but likely it was because he felt it inferior to psychoanalysis (Freud 1974). The letter he wrote to his young fiancé is quite illustrative of Freud's earlier enthusiasm: "Woe to you, my Princess, when I come. I will kiss you quite red and feed you till you are plump. And if you are forward you shall see who is the strongest, a gentle little girl who doesn't eat enough or a big wild man who has cocaine in his body" (ibid., 10).

These early psychotropic medications were often used with little specificity to measured diagnosis or specific symptomology. It was not until the "modern era" of psychopharmocology, starting with the discovery of chlorpromazine, that psychiatric medications began saving lives and improving the tremendous suffering of individuals afflicted with the severest major psychiatric conditions.

Chlorpromazine and the Modern Era of Psychopharmacology

Consider a close friend or family member, restrained and terrified, perhaps chained to a wall. Imagine the individual experiencing horrific hallucinations and delusions, which are perceived as completely real. Even in the best asylums, these patients were in miserable shape, and in the poorest asylums life would have been unbearable. Then consider how these individuals and their loved ones must have felt when restraints were no longer necessary, horrible symptoms improved, and patients could begin to make sense out of reality. This was the miracle of chlorpromazine and the beginning of modern psychopharmacology.

While not everyone responds to chlorpromazine, and psychosis continues to be terrifying, chlorpromazine did usher in a new era of hope and in real terms allowed for the unlocking of restraints and deinstitutionalization of hundreds of thousands of psychotic patients throughout the world. Psychiatrists in the United States actually accepted these medications belatedly, but once employed, they enabled President Kennedy's community mental health center movement and massive deinstitutionalization throughout the country. "Chlorpromazine initiated a revolution in psychiatry, comparable to the introduction of penicillin in general medicine" (López-Muñoz et al. 2005). Chlorpromazine (trade name Thorazine®) was the first of a variety of antipsychotic medications, and the chlorpromazine molecule was later even altered to produce our first antidepressants. The full story of the discovery of the molecule fills books, but a brief history is appropriate here.

Chlorpromazine is derived from a family of chemicals known as phenothyazines, first developed by the German textile industry in 1883 (ibid.). These chemicals were later modified as substitutes for quinine in the fight against malaria during both world wars. In 1949 a French Army surgeon, Henri Marie Luborit, began studying the antihistamine effects of phenothiazines for use in anesthesia to prevent postsurgical shock, and in 1950 the actual chlorpromazine molecule was synthesized and provided to him. Laborit noticed its calming effects and convinced some army psychiatrists to try it on their patients while eating at the hospital canteen in 1952. The results were remarkable, validating the use of a postsurgical shock medication as the first antipsychotic.

Tricyclic Antidepressants

By 1955 the serious side effects of chlorpromazine began to be understood, and by 1960 the first reports of tardive dyskinesia, a permanent movement disorder, appeared (ibid.). Very shortly after the development of chlorpromazine, pharmaceutical companies began altering the original molecules in an attempt to develop an active antipsychotic agent with fewer side effects. A Swiss company made some very minor changes to the molecule and named it imipramine. This drug was given to a Swiss psychiatrist, Roland Kuhn, to test on psychotic patients. Dr. Kuhn noticed few antipsychotic effects but was surprised to discover that imipramine was a remarkable antidepressant. Thus a drug developed to be an antihistamine became our first antipsychotic, and a drug developed to be an antipsychotic became our first antidepressant (Callahan and German 2005, 100). Like chlorpromazine, imipramine was a tricyclic compound and was the first of tricyclic antidepressants, a family of antidepressants still widely used throughout the world.

MAOIs

At roughly the same time in history, post–World War II, chemists were looking for peacetime uses of wartime chemicals. Hydrazine had been used as a rocket propellant in German V2 rockets and was inexpensive and easily obtained after the war. Chemists began looking at hydrazine derivatives as antibiotics to fight the tuberculosis epidemic (ibid., 97). Nurses working in the tuberculosis sanitariums began to notice that some very dysphoric tuberculosis patients became euphoric, even hypersexual when given the drug. By the late 1950s iproniazid was found to be a monoamine oxidase inhibitor and became available as an antidepressant. However, soon it also produced unique and life-threatening side effects (ibid., 98) and severe reactions from interactions with many other drugs. When these effects were understood and could be prevented, MAOIs became popular for certain depressive states and are still among the most potent antidepressants for some people. Thus a drug developed for tuberculosis began a family of antidepressants, the MAOIs.

Lithium

In many ways the story of lithium for the treatment of mania is similar. Lithium was likely first used in psychiatric patients by the Danish psychiatrist Carl Lange. It was "rediscovered" by Dr. John Cade, an Australian military physician, again by serendipity. Cade was using lithium as a solvent in experiments on guinea pigs and noticed that the guinea pigs became very calm. Applying this observation, he began to use lithium on manic psychiatric patients (ibid., 95). Lithium is now widely used in the treatment of bipolar disorder.

As we can see, none of these medications were initially produced to treat the illness they are now treating. Smart, observant doctors and nurses simply noticed the effects of medications and thought of alternative applications. However, no one had a clue as to why medications work as they do.

How Do They Work?

Over the years since the discovery of these medications, many scientists began trying to figure out what these drugs do inside the brain. Through a wide array of scientific techniques and careful observation, it is now clear that many of our medications work by enhancing or blocking intercellular communication. They are thought to work at the neural synapse, a space between neurons where chemical transmitters interact with their receptors, very much like a key interacts with a lock.

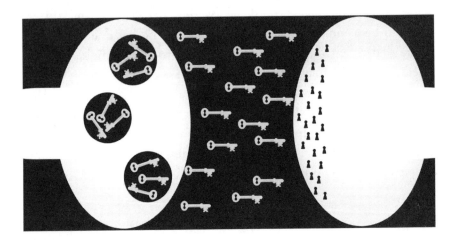

Figure 10.1

Antipsychotic drugs tend to block dopamine receptors while antidepressant drugs tend to block serotonin or norepinephrine receptors that regulate transmission. Antipsychotics decrease dopamine activity, whereas antidepressants increase serotonin and norepinephrine activity. Although tremendously simplified, it is this knowledge that has allowed second- and even third-generation medications to be synthesized in laboratories specifically looking for improved psychiatric medications.

Our newer medications are synthesized to be much more specific in their receptor interactions, affect fewer receptors, and have fewer side effects. They are much safer, better tolerated, and have relieved suffering and enhanced countless lives. Yet psychopharmacology remains in its infancy. We still need much better medicines with greater therapeutic effects and fewer side effects.

The human brain is the most complex entity in known creation and may never be fully understood. We have come a very long way in sixty years, but the current answer to our most perplexing question, "How does it work?" remains "only" God knows.

Bibliography

Boudinot, Sally. *History of Barbiturates*. 2010. http//www.chemcases.com /phenol/pheno01.htm.

Callahan, Christopher M., and German E. Berrios. *Reinventing Depression: A History of the Treatment of Depression in Primary Care, 1949–2004*. New York: Oxford University Press, 2005.

Freud, Sigmund. *Cocaine Papers*. Ed. Robert Byck. London: Stonehill, 1974.

Fuller, Reginald H. "Hebrews." In Gerhard Krodel, ed., *The General Letters: Hebrews, James, 1-2 Peter, Jude, 1-2-3 John*. Proclamation Commentaries, Minneapolis: Fortress Press, 1995.

Kaplan, Harold I., and Benjamin J. Sadock, eds. *Comprehensive Textbook of Psychiatry*. 4th ed. Baltimore: Williams and Wilkins, 1985.

López-Muñoz, Francisco, Cecelio Alano, and Eduardo Cuenca, et al. 2005. "History of the Discovery and Clinical Introduction of Chlorpromazine." *Annals of Clinical Psychiatry* 17 (3): 113–35.

Lyons, Albert S., and R. Joseph Petrocelli, R.J. *Medicine: An Illustrated History*. New York: Abrams, 1978.

Modell, Walter. *The Relief of Symptoms*. Philadelphia: Saunders, 1955.

NOTES

Chapter 1: Depression

1. British Broadcasting Corporation News, *Depression Looms as a Global Crisis*, September 3, 2009.

2. Centers for Disease Control (CDC), *Web-Based Injury Statistics Query and Reporting System*, 2007.

3. My spiritual director, the Rev. William A. Smith, in a session following the tragic death of our son, listened quietly and intently to my despair and in response uttered these profound words.

4. This is a story told by a friend of mine who was ministering to a teenage male dying of Hodgkins disease.

5. Nikolai F. S. Gruntvig, "Built on a Rock," trans. Carl Döving, in *The Pilgrim Hymnal* (Cleveland: Pilgrim, 1986), 270.

Chapter 2: Anxiety Disorders

1. OED Online, October 23, 2010, http://oxforddictionaries.com/definition/anxiety?region=us.

2. National Health and Nutrition Examination Survey, "National Institute of Mental Health Diagnostic Interview Schedule for Children (DISC): Questionaire, Survey Years: 1999 to 2004," 14, http://www.cdc.gov/nchs/data/nhanes/limited_access/ydq.pdf.

3. The phrase "not otherwise specified" means that there is no question that a disorder is present, but that the signs, symptoms, and time course do not meet criteria for another anxiety disorder.

4. The names used in this case study and throughout the chapter are pseudonyms to protect the identity of the participants.

Chapter 3: Psychotic Disorders

1. Joretta is deeply indebted to her sister, Dana, for teaching her much about what it means to live meaningfully. Dana has read this chapter, offering advice and help along the way. Joretta and Dana live together with their mom and Joretta's partner, and they represent an alternative model of "family" at multiple levels.

2. Various authors who draw upon postmodern and social-construction theory offer a critical lens to the development of the concept of mental illness. For example, Allen Horwitz suggests that "contemporary psychiatry and psychiatric epidemiology considerably overestimate the amount of mental disorder" (Horwitz 2002, 37). Such critique does not deny the presence of hallucinations but does raise questions about the historical nature of the interpretation of symptoms.

3. Church libraries need to include some of the books listed in the bibliography of this chapter, including theological, socio-psychological resources, and the biographies of persons who have written about their experiences.

4. Historian and theologian Rosemary Radford Ruether's discussion of the various ways in which the culture has understood the causes related to schizophrenia is a helpful summary. Her family's experience with David, their son, offers an exceptional discussion of the illness and its effects on their family (Reuther 2010, ch. 3).

5. Just as there is debate about the role of "diagnosis" and the use of the DSM-IV, there is concern over the relationship between psychiatrists and the pharmaceutical industry (Ruether 2010, 119–35). The exaggerated claims of great superiority of the "atypical" antipsychotics have been exposed as wishful thinking combined with savvy and sometimes underhanded marketing. While medication does not help every patient, and there is much research to be done to develop innovative drug and nondrug therapies, the scientific evidence is overwhelming that judiciously prescribed antipsychotic medication is beneficial to most persons living with schizophrenia but also leaves the majority with residual dysfunction that is only partially addressed with the best community support and rehabilitative care.

6. Ruether talks poignantly about this as she notes that she and her husband are in retirement and trying to make plans for their son. She notes the struggle to provide housing, meaningful work, and a safe environment. This perspective is shared by many of the biographies that illustrate the complexity of living with schizophrenia; see, for example, Earley 2006; Saks 2006.

Chapter 5: Substance-Use Disorders

1. This was spoken by a man whose mother asked me to call on him in the hospital prior to his death.

2. Among the earliest and most fundamental works are Black 1982; Beattie 1987; and Woititz 1990.

Chapter 7: Autism

1. Although there is some literature that is specific to autism and faith communities (see Howell and Pierson 2010; Newman 2006; Walsh et al. 2008; White 2009), there is a greater portion of the literature available on the topic of developmental disabilities (an umbrella under which autism is often classified) and faith communities (see Bolduc 2001; Carter, 2007; Covey 2004; Davie and Thornburgh 2005; Gaventa 2009; Merrick et al. 2001; Miles 1995; Morad et al. 2001; Rich and Ross-Mockaitis 2006; Rife and Thornburgh 2001). For this essay, both will be used.

2. The following quote comes from an exploratory study of families with adolescents with disabilities and their experiences and interactions with a variety of churches, church programs, or youth ministries; see Jacober 2009.

3. See the following in the bibliography. *Autism specific*: Newman 2006; Walsh et al. 2008. *Developmental disabilities and education*: Carter, 2007; Rich and Ross-Mockaitis 2006. *Developmental disabilities and ministry*: Bolduc 2001. *Disabilities and community life*: Davie and Thornburgh 2005; Rife and Thornburgh 2001. Web sites: The Arc of the United States, NOD Religion and Disability Program. For an extensive bibliography of developmental disability resources, see Carter 2007 and Gaventa 2009.

Chapter 8: Acquired Brain Injury

1. National Institute of Neurological Disorders and Stroke, 2009, http://www.ninds.nih.gov/disorders/stroke/stroke.htm.

INDEX